URBAN AND PERI-URBAN AGRICULTURE IN AFRICA

Urban and Peri-Urban Agriculture in Africa

Proceedings of a workshop: Netanya, Israel,
23-27 June 1996

Edited by
DAVID GROSSMAN
Bar-Ilan University, Ramat-Gan, Israel
LEO M. VAN DEN BERG
Staring Centrum, Wageningen, The Netherlands
HYACINTH I. AJAEGBU
Population, Environment and Development Agency,
Jos, Nigeria

Ashgate

Aldershot • Brookfield USA • Singapore • Sydney

Published by
Ashgate Publishing Ltd
Gower House
Croft Road
Aldershot
Hants GU11 3HR
England

Ashgate Publishing Company
Old Post Road
Brookfield
Vermont 05036
USA

Ashgate website: http://www.ashgate.com

British Library Cataloguing in Publication Data
Urban and peri-urban agriculture in Africa : proceedings of
    a workshop, Netanya, Israel, 23-27 June 1996
    1.Urban agriculture - Africa 2.Food supply - Developing
    countries 3.Land use, Urban - Africa 4.Subsistence economy
    - Africa 5.Africa - Economic conditions
    I.Grossman, David II.Berg, Leo van den, 1948- III.Ajaegbu,
    H. I. (Hyacinth Iheanyichuku), 1937-
    338.1'4'096

Library of Congress Catalog Card Number: 98-74842

ISBN 1 84014 910 8

Printed and bound by Athenaeum Press, Ltd.,
Gateshead, Tyne & Wear.

Contents

Part II: THE JOS (NIGERIA) PERI-URBAN STUDIES

Part III: ACCESS TO RESOURCES AND INPUTS: CAPITAL, TECHNOLOGY AND INFRASTRUCTURE

PART IV: THEORETICAL ISSUES, APPROACHES TO DEVELOPMENT AND POLICY CONSIDERATIONS

List of Tables

List of Figures

List of Contributors

Dr. Edwin Aguigwo

Department of Geography, University of Jos, Jos, Nigeria

Prof. Hyacinth I. Ajaegbu

Population, Environment and Development Agency (PEDA), 7 Murtala Mohammed Way, P.O. Box 6115, Jos, Nigeria

Mr. Michael Atzmon

Director, Africa-Asia Desk, Center for International Agricultural Development (CINADCO), P.O. Box 7011, Tel-Aviv, Israel

Mr. Menakhem Ben-Yami

Fisheries Development and Management Adviser, 2 Dekel Street, Kiryat Tiv'on, 36056, Israel

Dr. Hendrick J. Bruins

Ben-Gurion University in the Negev Negev Center for Regional Development & J. Blaustein Institute for Desert Research, Social Studies Center Sede Boker Campus, 84990, Israel

Dr. Tjalling Dijkstra

African Studies Centre, P. O. Box 9555, 2300 RB Leiden, The Netherlands

Prof. Richard Ford

Center for Community-Based Development International Development Program, Clark University, Worcester MA, 01610, U.S.A.

Ms. Rahila P. Gowon

Population, Environment and Development Agency (PEDA), 7 Murtala Mohammed Way, P.O. Box 6115, Jos, Nigeria

Prof. David Grossman   Department of Geography, Bar-Ilan University Ramat-Gan, 52900, Israel

Dr. Dieter Martin Hörmann   Institute for Horticultural Economics University of Hannover Herrenhäuser Strasse 2, 30419 Hannover, Germany

Prof. Obiora Ike   Catholic Institute for Development, Justice, Peace and Caritas (CIDJAP), Enugu, Nigeria

Mr. Raanan Katzir   Center for International Agricultural Development (CINADCO), P.O. Box 7011, Tel-Aviv, 61070, Israel

Mr. Henk Kramer   The Winand Staring Centre for Integrated Land, Soil and Water Research, Marijkeweg 11/22, 6700 AC Wageningen, The Netherlands

Dr George G.D. Lulandala   STOAS Agriprojects Foundations Sub-Saharan Africa, P.O.Box 33536, Dar Es-Salaam, Tanzania

Mr. Shaul Manor   Consultant, IrrigationManagement and Agricultural Extension, 47 Hersehnzon Street, Rehovot, 76484, Israel

Dr. Beacon Mbiba   Department of Rural & Urban Planning University of Zimbabwe, Mt. Pleasant, Harare, Zimbabwe

Dr. Malongo R.S. Mlozi   Sokoine University of Agriculture, Department of Agricultural Education and Extension, P.O. Box 3002, Morogoro Tanzania

Mr. Sunny O.S. Okwudire

Population, Environment and Development Agency (PEDA), 7 Murtala Mohammed Way, P.O. Box 6115, Jos, Nigeria

Mr. Emmanuel O. Omomoh

Population, Environment and Development Agency (PEDA), 7 Murtala Mohammed Way, P.O. Box 6115, Jos, Nigeria

Dr. Uri Or

Netafim, Kibbutz Magal, M.P. Hefer, 8845, Israel

Prof. Poul Ove Pedersen

Centre for Development Research, Gammel Kongevej 5, DK-1610 Copenhagen V, Denmark

Dr. Hopolang Phororo

UNDP, P.O. BOX 301, UN House, UN Road, Maseru, Lesotho

Dr. Dan Rymon

Department of R & D Economic Agricultural Research Organization, The Volcani Center, Bet Dagan, Israel

Prof. Krystof Schoeneich

Department of Geography, University of Jos, Jos, Nigeria

Prof. David Smith

Department of Geography, University of Liverpool, Liverpool, L69 3BX , U.K.

Dr. Leo M. van den Berg

The Winand Staring Centre for Integrated Land, Soil and Water Research, Marijkeweg 11/22, 6700 AC Wageningen, The Netherlands

Preface

This volume is the outcome of a workshop, which was conducted in Netanya, Israel, between June 23 and June 27, 1997. The participants came from a wide variety of countries. Seven of the paper presenters were from Africa, and the rest mostly from Europe and the USA.

The workshop consisted of three parts. The first was devoted to paper presentations, while the second was made up of discussion sessions, in which the main issues raised by a paper session were identified and opened for comments and a free exchange by all participants. The third part consisted of field trips, devoted to a demonstration of some of the existing Israeli systems, which were relevant to the workshop's themes. They included visits to various places which represent stages of production and marketing of a vertically integrated cooperative, a kibbutz factory which produces drip-irrigation equipment, and an Arab village engaging in modern horticulture.

The chapters of this book consist of the edited papers that were presented in the first part of the workshop. However, the book's last section contains a summary of the discussions of the second part. It reveals the scale and complexity of the issues and ideas which came up in the discussion. We consider this chapter to be an appropriate way to conclude the book.

Unfortunately, not all of the 24 paper presenters, submitted a written manuscript for inclusion in this volume. We decided, nevertheless, to include in the proceedings also the abstracts of three orally presented papers. All three deal with the Israeli experience in methods to promote agricultural planning and with various suggestions for improving urban or peri-urban development in Third World countries. We presented these abstracts in a single chapter.

We are deeply indebted to numerous persons and institutions for assisting us in organizing the workshop and publishing this compendium. Significant financial help was provided by NIRP (Netherlands-Israel Development Research Program). The officials of NIRP, especially Ms. Miriam Bar-Lev and Mr. Henk Mastebroek, have been very supportive and encouraging. We also benefited from a grant by MASHAV (The International Cooperation Agency of the Israeli Foreign Ministry) and of CINADCO (Center for International Agricultural Development and

Cooperation). We are grateful for the assistance of Bar-Ilan University. Its former Rector, Dean, and the Chairperson of the Geography Department, Professors Zvi Arad, Ben-Zion Zilberfarb, and Gabriel Lipshitz, respectively, who provided highly needed material help as well as moral support. The present Dean, Professor Lavee, and the Geography Department's Chairperson, Dr. Maxim Shoshany, were also very helpful and encouraging. Of the other Department's staff we must single out mainly Ms. Orly Haimy, who used her skills to do the computer-drafting of several figures.

Special thanks are due to Mr. Zvi Herman of CINADCO. He was deeply involved in the planning of the workshop, and in organizing the excursions, and found the time to take an active part in the workshop's sessions and discussions, despite his many duties. The excursions were guided by Mr. Ozer Dafna (first day) and by Mr. Uri Or (second day). Both are worthy of our gratitude for their highly professional work.

We are also indebted to Mr. Itzhak Abt, then the Head of CINADCO, whose sympathy was a prime factor in our ability to solicit assistance from other Israeli offices.

A key role in the publication of this volume was played by Professor Eliezer Ben-Rafael. His encouragement and constructive suggestions were important for us throughout our Jos-Bukuru research. The present form of publication is, to a great extent, the outcome of his specific advice.

Dutch Institutions and colleagues have also contributed substantially to the progess of our work. We cannot name all of them. However, we must express our gratitude to the Agricultural Research Department (DLO-NL) in Wageningen for allocating precious researchers' time to our project.

Dr. Ahmadu Adepetu, of the University of Jos, deserves special credit. Although he has not contributed directly to this volume, his teaching and research accounts for much of the research findings reported by the four Nigerian chapters included here.

Finally, we must pay special tribute to Michal (Marcia) Grossman. She has never refused to do the language editing or provide other help for her husband. She has not written any chapter for this book, but her share in its scientific standard is nevertheless significant.

There are many other persons who helped us to produce this book, but it is impossible to list all of them here. We hope that there is no major omission here, and that those not personally mentioned will forgive us.

Introduction
The Main Themes of the Book: Significance and Implications

THE EDITORS

The Purpose and the Main Themes of the Book

The collection of articles presented in this book is based on papers presented in a workshop which took place in Netanya, Israel, in June, 1996. It deals with the subject of urban and peri-urban agriculture in Africa.

The eighteen articles included in this collection demonstrate how widespread urban agriculture is, but they also reveal that it is highly varied in nature. Despite its significance, the role played by urban farming in feeding numerous urban people in many parts of the world, is relatively unknown. However, the phenomenon has recentl;y generated much interest and has stimulated research which is supported by the United Nations as well as by research institutions. Some of these institutions are represented in this book, as can be seen from a short glance at the list of contributors. As an opening discussion of this short review we would like to quote Catherine Waser, who has recently devoted an issue of the Arid Lands Newsletter to this subject. In the Editorial to this issue she points out that urban agriculture is not a new phenomenon. In China, the urban cultivators have political support. In inner-city neighborhoods, urban agriculture plays an important role in a family's survival.. 'It is perhaps this role -- the ability of urban agriculture to enhance household food security -- that is currently drawing the most attention. Urban agriculture can also play a very important role in the absorption of labor -- particularly women and youth -- so that urban households are better able to take full advantage of their own human resources' (Waser, 1997).

The points mentioned in this short quotation are the core themes of our book. However, the book is not limited solely to the study of intra-urban agriculture. It is also concerned with intensive gardening, devoted mostly to vegetable growing, which is carried out in the peri-urban space rather than in the urban area proper. There are a number of similarities between this form of farming and the intra-urban ones. For example, both types tend to use irrigation water, though rainfed farming is dominant during the rainy season. However, the peri-urban gardeners have access to greater amounts of water than the urban ones, because the latter have to be satisfied with leftovers.

The difference between the two types is even more pronounced where availability of land resources is concerned. Urban gardeners have to be satisfied with small patches of land, but competing land uses may threaten their existence, and cause harsh legal conflicts and even crop destruction. They are often confronted by negative governmental policies, especially when they use open public spaces. But where agriculture takes place in backyards, tenure tends to be more secure than that of the peri-urban farmers who often rent land on a short term basis. Evictions by builders and local governments are widespread, however, in both areas. Commercial activity is also prevalent among both groups, but inner city agriculturalists benefit from better access to market and can do their own trading, while peri-urban ones have the benefit of scale economies, even though they have a relative disadvantage of distance and have to resort to indirect marketing. Many of the problems and prospects are, thus, shared in some degree or another by all gardeners. Other comparisons between the two types relate to use of inputs, such as organic manure and other refuse, relative exposure to sanitation, industrial or residential pollution hazards, access to information, capital, labour and other resources. In most of these categories, the differences between intra-urban and peri-urban agriculture are a matter of scale or extent rather than of nature. (The term *peri-urban agriculture* applies, in this context, to intensive farming whose main advantage is accessibility to nearby urban market. It is usually market-oriented, and differs from 'normal' African agriculture (i.e., conventional rainfed farming practiced in most rural locations) by focussing on holticultural production. It also differs from the typical urban agriculture, which is mostly devoted to meeting household food needs.

The Book's Structure and a Short Summary of its Articles

The book consists of 18 articles (excluding the introduction and the conclusion) which are presented in 4 parts. The first two parts are devoted to regional studies, while the other two deal with more general economic or methodological issues (Part 3), or to theoretical and policy issues (Part 4). However, this classification is somewhat artificial. It is, in fact, a matter of relative emphasis, because practically all articles cross the regional-general 'border'. The following short summary does not fully observe, therefore, the order of the book's table of contents.

The practice of farming as a survival strategy in urban areas by growing rain-fed crops and raising animals in the urban space is more dominant than market gardening, as can be learned from the studies of (Drakakis) Smith in Harare, Zimbabwe, Mlozi and Lulandala in Tanzania, and Phororo in Malawi. Each of these studies emphasizes some other aspect of the benefits and difficulties associated with urban agriculture. It is generally agreed, however, that the large extent of the agricultural activity in the cities is an expression of poverty and the inadequacy of food supply in Africa. The studies also suggest, on the other hand, that intra-urban land holds an as yet underused potential for solving this problem, at least partly. This is why favorable government policies are so strongly needed. Even though growing crops in the city may expose urban dwellers to aesthetic and sanitary difficulties, it is argued, in Bruin's words, that 'legislation for the use of land, in or near the cities, for farming purposes should be made as flexible as possible'. This point is the main message of Mbiba's contribution, which is based on his comprehensive research of Harare's urban agriculture.

A recurrent theme in this book is the need to promote self-help and participatory development rather than rely on official 'top-down' projects. A strong case for this approach is taken by Ford, but Bruins believes that participatory development of urban and peri-urban farming can be used even for reducing health hazards, by enabling 'proper integration between central planning of wastewater treatment and its use by private farmers'. The potentially important role which can be played by intermediate bodies, such as research and development foundations or church-sponsored institutions and other NGOs, is illustrated by Lulandala and by Ike who report on experiences from Tanzania and Nigeria. Lulandala's words, concerning the evaluation of a project undertaken in Tanzania are of particular relevance: 'Sustainability is the single most important factor if the project is to survive on a long-term basis. Commitment, responsibility, action, tangible outcome, and a sense of local ownership are essential for a sustainable development of the project'.

A similar approach is presented in the five papers which refer to the study conducted among the gardeners of the peri-urban zone of the Jos-Bukuru area of Nigeria. The Korot village sub-project reported by

Okwudire, is an example. One of its purposes was to promote self-help among the villagers. They were taught the use of a local plant material for producing insecticides, how to prepare and apply manure and how to use water more efficiently. Ajaegbu's paper puts this work in a wider perspective. It reveals several additional aspects of the Korot sub-project which was part of an extensive study conducted under his supervision through the NGO managed by him and supported by NIRP (Netherland-Israel Research and Development Programme). A third article under the same umbrella is that by van den Berg and his colleagues in Jos and The Netherlands. They demonstrate that modern remote sensing techniques hold great promise in helping field studies and land use improvement in Africa. They also show, however, that the techniques are still imperfect and that the peri-urban gardens (even more so, urban ones) cannot alway be identified with certainty. The other two Jos-Bukuru works are those of Gowon and Omomoh. The latter provides an economic analysis of the Jos peri-urban market gardening. Gowon's study is quite unique. It is the only contribution in this volume which focuses on female cultivators. It reveals that, at least on the Jos Plateau of Nigeria, gender inequality is still a major issue. Women are good workers, but very few of them are given a chance to become garden owners or managers.

Another study which emphasizes self-help and participatory development is that of Benyami. His main message is that even capital inputs can be provided by the grass-root approach. Indigenous institutions, such as the *esussu clubs* should be preferred over commercial banks or any government-sponsored project, to solve the difficult problem of capital provision. He convincingly demonstrates that the interest level of loans obtained by these community institutions is far lower than that of the banks. There are other advantages, but also disadvantages. The latter are associated with the small scale of the operation.

The problem of funds and small scale is another recurrent issue. It emerges, naturally, in the articles which focus on marketing and on the distribution sectors. Dijkstra, based on Kenya's experience, is the traders' advocate. He illustrates and explains the vital role played by the middlemen, who are commonly believed to exploit the farmer and pocket too much of the sales proceeds. He believes that much of their income is fully earned because of the risks and uncertainties which the small-scale traders and transporters have to undertake. He argues that,

> being a middleman is not easy. The rewards a middleman receives for taking the risks are, however, substantial, and farmers might be able to

get a larger share of the cake when transporting their produce to Nairobi themselves. However, very few horticultural farmers travel to large urban markets to sell their commodities, even if such markets are located within their district.

Pedersen, whose study deals with small Zimbabwe towns, reaches similar conclusions, but adds an interesting perspective, which stresses the vital, indispensible roles of African traders. This positive role is closely related, paradoxically, to the negative characteristics of the trading business:

> Contrary to the traditional view of African rural trade, which has tended to see rural trade as overdeveloped and rural traders and middlemen as superfluous, we shall argue that it is precisely because trade plays such an important role in the development process that profiteering and corruptive practices have become associated with it.

Another paper which is largely devoted to the analysis of trading is that of Hɜrmann, whose data is based on the Tanzanian experience. Hɜrmann's contribution adds an important theoretical dimension which stresses the need for scope and comprehensiveness. His study encompasses, therefore, the whole range of the activities, e.g., vertical and horizonal integration, as well as the relative merit of cooperation. He considers and analyzes diverse issues such as access to capital, to land, especially irrigible land, and to other resources, as also to information and transport.

A useful demonstration of the potential impact of the accessibility to information is provided by Rymon and Or. Their contribution refers to irrigated agriculture practiced by Arab tribesmen near the Jordan Basin. The farmers were very successful in adopting modern irrigation and soil management techniques. The authors name several factors contributing to the success: suitable techniques, adequate access to credit and infrastructure, good extension service, and backing by the government. Practically all these ingredients are in 'short supply' in Africa. The most difficult problem may be associated with access to proper public assistance and information. Accessible markets which cater to consumers with relatively high purchasing power, are also scarce in most African countries. These deficiencies may account for the difficulty of applying the technology transfer methods, which were successfully implemented in the Jordan Basin, in other traditional farming communities.

Who are the Potential Readers of this Book?

The variety of the approaches outlined here can provide rich material for researchers and will hopefully stimulate additional research on urban and peri-urban farming on related subjects. This book is, indeed, research oriented, and its readers will come mainly from the academic sector. This does not mean that it should be exclusively aimed at the academic community and research libraries. There is much good information here for policy makers, who should, in fact, be its main customers. We can only express our hope that they will look at it, or at least, that it will be brought to the their attention. The topic of the book is, after all, well within the category of applied science. We call for applying its findings to the benefit of African farmers and gardeners.

Reference

Waser, Katherine (1997), 'The newly recognized importance of urban agriculture' *Aridlands,* No. 42 (Internet Version).

PART I
FIELD STUDIES FROM EASTERN AND SOUTHERN AFRICA

1 Urban Agriculture in Harare: Socio-Economic Dimensions of a Survival Strategy

DAVID SMITH

The Growing Interest in Urban Agriculture

As many writers have pointed out (Mougeot 1994), urban agriculture is not a new phenomenon. Until the industrial revolution led to much more intensive forms of development, urban morphologies often contained active agricultural and/or animal husbandry sectors. In recent years the debate within industrial societies on the nature of the urbanization process has shown concern over the sprawl of urban activities, values and culture into the countryside. Until very recently, however, much less interest has been shown in the retention and expansion of rural activities within and around the city (Tinker 1994).

In developing countries, however, the situation has always been different with urban agriculture persisting throughout the colonial and post-colonial periods on a widespread basis. But it is the massive and sustained increase in urban populations during the final quarter of this century that has re-focused our attention on this phenomenon. This growth has been accompanied by an apparent expansion of urban agriculture in spite of competition from other urban land uses. Frequently, this expansion faced strong opposition from urban planners and administrators. The fact that urban agriculture has increased, has been reflected in the number of studies undertaken of its dimension and characteristics. To be sure, agronomists and other agricultural scientists have been investigating the production process for many years, whilst nutritionists have often highlighted the dietary problems evident in Third World Cities. But it is only relatively recently that physical, natural and social scientists have begun to work together to investigate a major aspect of the urbanization process as a whole, one which is increasingly blurring the traditional dichotomous distinctions of what is urban or rural. As yet, however, little distinction is made between the growth of small-scale commercial agriculture, which responds to new market opportunities in growing cities, and the growth of urban subsistence agriculture as a survival strategy. This paper is focused on the second of these situations.

This neglect of what is for many the most important basic need in the city living is brought into sharper focus by the extensive literature, increasingly interdisciplinary, on essential needs such as education, health care and housing. The last of these, in particular, indicates the very positive impact that interactive research and discussions can have on planning for, and provision of, policies to meet the basic needs of the urban poor; Zimbabwe's aided self-help programme of the 1980s being a particularly positive example of such policies.

At present, much of the work on urban food systems is geographically and intellectually fragmented and has still to generate the conceptual, empirical and policy momentum of housing studies. Moreover, as with much of the early work on shelter, a good deal of our discussion of urban agriculture seems to take place in isolation of the totality of urban life and urban economics. In any city there is an overall urban food supply system of which urban agriculture is only one component whose importance varies in terms of household food satisfaction. Our discussions of urban agriculture in Harare and elsewhere need to bear this in mind, particularly with regard to the policy implications of such research. We need to know more about the totality of the system before we start tinkering with the production, distribution, marketing and consumption of any one component of it. This brief introduction will, therefore, attempt to set out some of the characteristics of urban food systems in general, and for Harare in particular, before moving on to discuss the situation relating to urban agriculture itself (see also Drakakis-Smith et al. 1995). Finally, it will present a brief overview of recent studies undertaken on urban agriculture and food systems in Harare.

Urban Food Systems in Developing Countries

There are clearly two distinct dimensions to any urban food system, viz supply and demand. For most investigations these have been simplified to food production (including urban agriculture) and consumption. Very few have adequately considered the role played by distributive and marketing systems or the nature of the links between these and both production and consumption. The resulting matrix can, indeed, be complex (Figure 1.1) but it does emphasize the need for a thorough understanding of the system as a whole before policy decisions for any one section can be taken. Certainly the consumption aspects of this system have changed tremendously in many developing countries over the last 20 years.

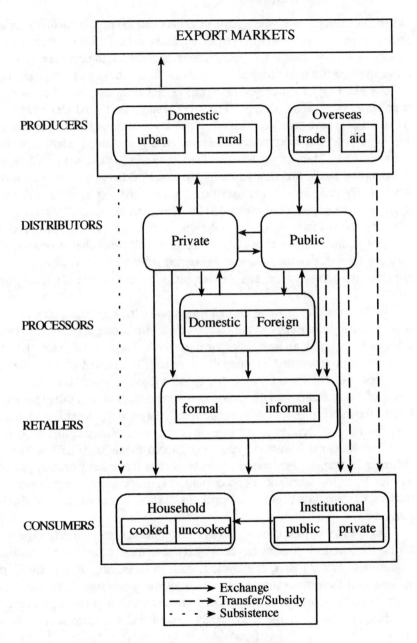

Figure 1.1   The Marketing System and Its Components

Urban populations everywhere have increased enormously, particularly in the poorest countries, as a result of both in-migration and continuingly high rates of fertility. The consequence for many countries has been almost unprecedented pressures on urban resources and the ability of the urban poor to meet their most basic needs. Despite the alleged development bias towards cities, there are still huge numbers in urban poverty. The World Bank (1991) and United Nations (UNDP 1991) have both identified urban poverty as their highest priority for the 1990s and produced major policy statements on how to manage urban expansion in this context. Many of the new urbanites, particularly those who have moved in from rural areas, find themselves for the first time living in a cash economy where traditional support and exchange systems may not operate. Earning money in order to purchase basic needs, therefore, becomes essential, particularly when the state cannot, or will not, intervene in order to subsidize this process. Here, of course, structural adjustment programmes have often worsened the situation through their emphasis on market-led development and cuts in public spending on bureaucracies and welfare programmes (Gibbon 1992; Moser, 1994).

In the context of growing unemployment and retreating public services, the poor have had increasingly to fall back on their own coping mechanisms, often collectively referred to as the informal sector. These small-scale, labour-intensive family-orientated, or often illegal or semi-legal activities have always been present in Third World cities, but appear to have expanded considerably in recent years in parallel with the growth of urban populations and urban poverty. Indeed, the informal sector has been specifically targeted and identified by many governments and agencies as a means whereby the harsh social and economic effects of structural adjustment can be cushioned through self-help schemes. Urban agriculture is often considered to be part of this informalization process but this is far too simplistic a conceptualization as there are diverse modes of production, some formal, others informal. In addition, consumption must also be considered.

So, in terms of food consumption the urban market has definitely expanded but the food security of many has decreased due to their reduced access to basic entitlements, such as land, employment, cash incomes etc. But it would be misleading if the deteriorating food security of the urban poor were attributed solely to entitlement deprivation. Other factors are also important, particularly the changing nature of the food supply system and changing socio-cultural factors.

In almost all aspects of life in the Third World city there has been an intensification of capitalistic activities that have increasingly thickened the ties between the local and global economies, albeit within fluctuating circumstances.

As far as food systems are concerned this has involved what Macleod and McGee (1990) have termed the industrialization of food supply, which is largely coincident with the so-called 'second food regime' (Le Heron and Roche 1995), in which the durable foods and grain-fed livestock production of the developed countries came to dominate world markets.

Whilst there has undoubtedly been an economic imperative behind this 'industrialization' of food supply, it has also been underpinned by both political and cultural factors. For example, the United States in the 1960s deliberately exported very cheap wheat to the developing world in order to bring about increased dependency (Andrae and Beckmann 1985), a process which also reinforced the growing westernization of diets brought about both by aggressive marketing by food multinational companies and by the erosion of indigenous cultural values.

The impact on food supply systems has been rapid and extensive. The changes outlined above, together with the introduction of new technologies and retail organizations, have led to the rapid spread of supermarket style selling which had come to dominate food retailing across social classes and geopolitical boundaries. The power of the supermarket as a medium of retailing and market control is encapsulated in the struggle between Proctor and Gamble and Unilever for dominance in the massive Indonesian food market. The associated shift within this process to packaged food in standardized units has raised the cost of food purchases for many at the same time as their incomes have become less reliable.

Two aspects of the food supply system illustrate these changes well. First, there is the shift from indigenous basic carbohydrates, such as taro or millet, to imported produce. The growth in consumption of bread is particularly noticeable in this respect, occurring in countries that do not and cannot grow durum wheat. Moreover, much of this change is urban-based. In Dakar, for example, the average annual per capita consumption of maize, rice and wheat is 10kg, 77kg and 33kg respectively; the rural equivalent is 158kg, 20kg, and 2kg (Charvet in Goodman and Redclift, 1991). The rapid growth of franchised fast-food outlets provides a second illustration of the kind of change that has occurred over the last few years. In Singapore, for example, the annual turnover of DeliFrance, a relatively minor international food organization, was, by the early 1990s, over US$10 million. Even the remaining bastions of socialism are crumbling under the onslaught of fast food chains, with the traditional political and cultural icons (Marx and Mao) being replaced by a new big M (=McDonalds) in both Moscow and Beijing.

In almost all of these changes the state has played a fundamental role in facilitating the penetration of modern, often western, capital, commodities and values. Sometimes this involvement is direct, for example, through the operation of state food stores, but more often it is indirect, for example through the introduction of new hygiene or health standards which the state chooses when and how firmly to enforce. Certainly, such legislation has been extensively employed to suppress competition from the informal food retailing sector. Often this sector is accused of selling food which is relatively costly per unit, unhygienic and of poor nutritional value. But as Tinker (1997) and Atkinson (1991) reveal, street foods often add variety and value to otherwise monotonous diets and are no more unhygienic than many domestic cooking arrangements for poor households. Moreover, they are usually sold in smaller quantities which lie within the spending capacity of the poor.

Notwithstanding these important functions, the informal food sector remains an easy and often pursued target for the urban authorities. However, there have also been very few studies which have investigated the role of the informal sector within the broader context of the urban food system. Not since Jackson (1978, 1979) has there been a comprehensive study of the links between production and consumption, particularly those that operate across the modes from formal through to subsistence. In Asian cities (Yeung 1988) these links are well established and complex, with surplus urban production from both legal and illegal gardens being efficiently collected and redistributed throughout the urban marketing network, bringing benefits to the poor in terms of providing both income and cheaper food. It is this integrational dimension which is missing in many urban African contexts, resulting in an inefficient system which disadvantages both low-income sellers and buyers.

Urban agriculture, although part of the overall urban food system with all of its national and global linkages, tends to operate in a somewhat different context. It usually refers to the cultivation of crops at both the subsistence and commercial levels, as well as to the keeping of small livestock in open spaces in urban areas. The activity is widespread throughout Africa and has become a permanent feature of the urban landscape (Rogerson 1992). Although much activity occurs within house-gardens (where these exist), it has also been fostered by the availability of unused open spaces (Mosha 1991, Maxwell and Zziwa 1992) and utilises resources in urban ecosystems which would otherwise be initialized (Smith and Nasr 1992). The importance of urban agriculture within the context of city development can be best demonstrated by linking the activity with three purposes: 1. the mitigation of hunger and malnutrition and the attainment of food security at the household level; 2. poverty alleviation especially during periods of economic restructuring; and 3. improvement of the urban environment through greening and pollution reduction.

Rapid urban growth rates, and a diminishing ability of many countries to feed these increasing populations, are issues which require immediate attention by African policy makers. Two possible solutions for attaining greater food security are to stimulate the production of food crops in the rural areas or to promote food production within urban settlements (Gutman 1986). However, we need to establish the extent to which urban agriculture can be a potential, albeit partial, solution to the problem of food insecurity at the household level. To date, most research findings have not provided that kind of data for they have been largely of a baseline nature, outlining the incidence of urban agriculture, and informing policy makers of its positive features. They have highlighted the importance of urban agriculture as a socioeconomic survival and livelihood-enhancing strategy for the urban poor, but only a few studies have attempted to measure the yields from the cultivated plots. Some have nevertheless given production figures and examined the special role of capital-intensive horticulture and dairying in urban areas. Also, there is need to contextualize the phenomenon of urban agriculture within the broader urban economy and within the structure of urban management, and to plan for the activity by making it one of the main land uses within space abundant African cities (Wekwete 1993). There is, moreover, a need to highlight the linkages between urban agriculture, waste management and health. The factors constraining the development of urban agriculture too ought to be identified, as a pre-requisite to more sweeping and positive changes.

Research on Urban Agriculture and Urban Food Distribution in Harare

In Zimbabwe agriculture within urban and peri-urban areas is a widespread activity but in most cases it is subsistence agriculture that involves limited capital inputs. In Harare, the capital, urban agriculture is extensive in private gardens (especially in the high-income low-density areas) and in public open spaces, such as undeveloped industrial and residential areas and road or railway reserves. The earliest comprehensive research was undertaken by David Mazambabi (1982a, 1982b) who examined the activity in the city of Harare in between 1950s and 1980s. However, he was less concerned with urban agriculture within the urban economy and more concerned with the fact that it seemed to be transforming an urban environment into a rural landscape (Wekwete 1993). Academic research on urban agriculture *per se* in Harare resurfaced in the early 1990s with the works of Mbiba (1994, 1995) and Drakakis-Smith et al., (1995). The research by Mbiba, who classified urban agriculture by type of product (arable or non-arable), by spaces used (on-plot or off-plot) and by institutional settings (legal or illegal), addressed the issue of the role of urban agriculture in Harare and the legislative and policy issues. Drakakis-Smith et al. (1995) attempted to establish if there are linkages between urban poverty (including that induced by the structural adjustment programme) and the increasing incidence of urban agriculture in Harare. The studies are important because they attempt to place urban agriculture within a much broader contextual framework. However, it still remains to be seen whether the studies have provided policy makers and planners with implementable policy prescriptions.

Prior to this, broader research on the nature of urban food systems had been undertaken by Drakakis-Smith and Kivell (1990), Drakakis-Smith (1992), and Drakakis-Smith and Tevera (1993), whose major objectives were to investigate the nature and origin of food production activities within Harare and its periphery. These studies revealed a number of things. First, that household members who engaged in urban food production undertook several other roles in relation both to production and reproduction. Second, that in the three highly differentiated sub-urban areas in Harare, i.e. Glen View (high density area), Mabelreign (middle income area) and Epworth (upgraded former squatter settlement) about 80% of those interviewed grew crops in their gardens primarily for household consumption (Drakakis-Smith and Kivell 1990). The studies noted that in Epworth there was a greater tendency for families to keep small livestock, such as chickens and goats, than in the other residential suburbs. There is ample documentation of the various foods that farmers grow and the kind of animals they rear in the places they live within the urban and periurban areas. Third, that undernutrition characterises the lives of many urban poor, despite the fact that most low-income households in Harare spend over half of their income on food (Drakakis-Smith and Tevera 1993). Fourth, that extensive illegal cultivation regularly covers public open spaces during the rainy season from November to March and that growers tend to cultivate open spaces close to their homes, with vegetables and maize being most commonly grown. Fifth, that urban farmers receive minimum support, if any, from central government or the local authority. Generally, there are no urban extension services for crop production and livestock rearing, and credit facilities for urban farming are almost non-existent hence the current low investment in urban agriculture. Sixth, that recently officials have been more accommodative of urban agriculture, as is reflected by the general moratorium on maize slashing.

These recent studies reflect the growth in recognition of the importance of urban agriculture in Harare and also a recognition of the need for more information on the subject. The three independent research projects launched in the early 1990s by geographers from the University of Zimbabwe, Keele University and the School of Oriental and African Studies, by planners from the

UZ, and by ENDA are important because they have succeeded in placing urban agriculture within a much broader contextual framework and are producing very important results for the benefit of local authorities and central government. For academic investigation to be truly valuable, it must have a pragmatic, useful outcome to the benefit of those under scrutiny - the urban poor. The link between these two groups, academics and the poor, is the state and it is for this reason that we must present to the planners and policy-makers the results of these investigations. That there is a need for detailed information cannot be doubted for many policy makers are as yet unaware of the extent to which urban agriculture lies beyond the influence of the planning and administrative process. A recent survey of approximately one third of Harare's councillors revealed that only a small proportion believed that most of the urban agriculture in their wards was illegal. The remainder assumed that it was occurring within cooperatives after official permission had been obtained. This contrasts markedly with the findings presented below. Notwithstanding this situation most councillors were unsympathetic to illegal urban agriculture because of suspected environmental damage or misuse of land designated for other purpose. However, the environmental situation has been very poorly documented to date and, as Bowyer-Bower and Tengbeh (1995) have revealed, the impact of urban agriculture needs to be carefully reassessed before making too many assumptions as to the nature of the policy response. It is with such planning and policy vacuums in mind that the research reported below was undertaken and it is hoped that the information presented will enable a realistic and fruitful appraisal of the situation in Harare.

Research Background

The growing interest in urban agriculture in developing countries is, in many ways, expanding at a rate which rapidly exceeds hard information on this important phenomenon. Whilst it is true that a research literature is beginning to accumulate, as noted earlier, much of this is fragmentary and not only lacks context but also appreciation of related social, economic and environmental processes. To give an example of this, in 1995 two publications appeared which relate closely to the subject matter of this volume. In the first, Gibbon et al. (1995) reviewed the impact of economic and social adjustment on Zimbabwe and in the second, Beacon Mbiba (1995) investigated the subject of urban agriculture directly. Although these two excellent volumes addressed components in a continuum of cause and effect, neither contained any real discussion of the subject matter of the other. Gibbon et al. (1995) barely mentioned one of the most fundamental consequences of the food and health problems discussed in the volume, whilst Mbiba (1995) felt it unnecessary to engage in an extensive discussion of the political economy background to increasing urban agriculture. It was in response to this growing but fragmented research background that the survey on which this chapter is based was undertaken. This report, in particular, seeks to characterize the producers themselves and to find out why they are involved in urban agriculture and what they wish to get out of their engagement in this activity. It also seeks to identify the differences, if any, between garden and off-plot (illegal) production and, in particular, to investigate the use to which the products are put or may be put, in the context of the household economy itself. It is vitally important that all these social and economic aspects of urban agriculture are fully understood if policy responses, either by national or city authorities, are to be effective not only in improving the quality of life for the urban poor in the context of tough economic times, but also in ensuring the sustainability of urban development in Harare.

The Survey Population

The investigation of household food production in Harare encompassed 390 interviews in nine different locations of the city (Figure 1.2). The districts were chosen on the basis of their environmental characteristics (geology, soil type and slope) and their socio-economic attributes, ranging from high-density, low-income areas (both squatters and government assisted) to low-density, high-income areas.

Although ENDA allege that almost 90 % of urban agriculture occurs in high-density districts, there is also substantial cultivation in open spaces in low density areas, but the cultivators are not necessarily residents of those areas. Within these parameters, interviewers were directed to areas of illegal or off-plot cultivation with instructions to interview on-site cultivators, if possible. Many of the respondents were of course, not representative of the status of the district itself, although they were resident there, usually as domestic workers or gardeners.

The profile of the respondents is, therefore, of a predominantly, but not exclusively, low-income population. About half were home-owners, living largely in self-built housing, with most of the remainder either being employees living in accommodation (usually room) provided by their employer (mostly in low-density areas) or renting rooms in high-density zones and in garden shacks. Two-thirds of the respondents were aged between 30 and 50 years. The majority were males, as were heads of household in general (85%). About the same proportion were married. Most of the single heads of household were female.

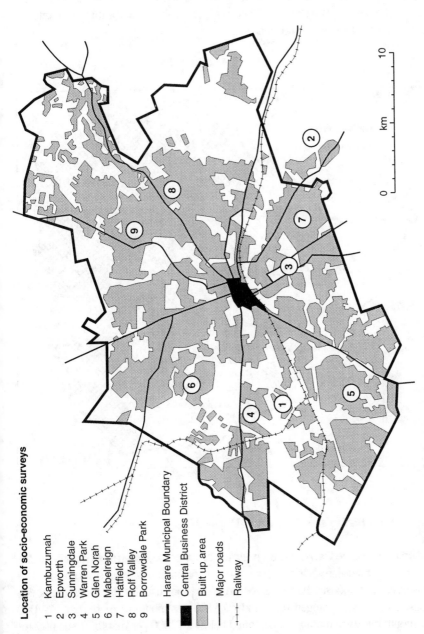

Location of socio-economic surveys

1 Kambuzumah
2 Epworth
3 Sunningdale
4 Warren Park
5 Glen Norah
6 Mabelreign
7 Hatfield
8 Rolf Valley
9 Borrowdale Park

	Harare Municipal Boundary
	Central Business District
	Built up area
	Major roads
+++	Railway

Figure 1.2 Location of the Socio-Economic Surveys

Rather surprisingly only 22% of heads of household were born in Harare or Chitungwiza, the remainder originating from a wide range of areas within and outside the country (Figure 1.3). This confirms the high rate of migration into the capital, particularly since independence.

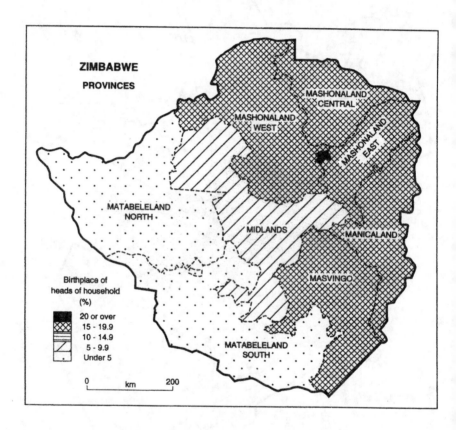

Figure 1.3   Birthplace of Heads of Households

Occupations ranged across the spectrum but were concentrated mainly in the blue-collar or service sector (Figure 1.4). Approximately 17% of both heads of household and spouses had received no education, usually the older members. Household incomes ranged from under Z$500 per month to more than Z$7000 per month but were mainly concentrated below Z$2000 per month. Some 60% of the household could be found in this class (Figure 1.5). These income levels compared reasonably well with the overall profile for Harare presented in the 1992 census, although the upper-end of the income spectrum was under-represented, as might be expected. Interestingly over half the respondents classified themselves as poor or very poor. Most of the remainder claimed to be middle or lower-middle class. There was not always a close correlation with income in this context (Table 1.1), probably due to the impact of family size.

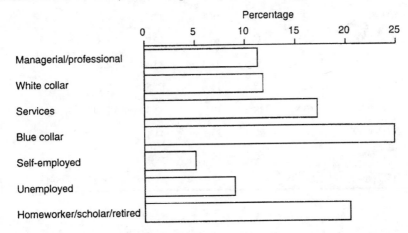

Figure 1.4   Occupational Structure of Respondents

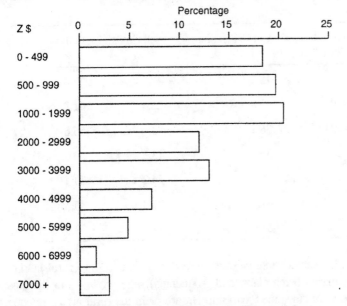

Figure 1.5   Monthly Household Incomes of Respondents

Table 1.1   Income Class Groups by Monthly Household Earnings

Income Group (Z$)	Very Poor	Poor	Lower Middle	Middle	Upper Middle	Upper
0-499	57.6	22.7	10.6	9.1	-	-
500-999	20.8	52.8	18.1	8.3	-	-
1000-1999	25.3	36.0	26.7	10.7	1.3	-
2000-2999	8.9	33.3	27.2	33.3	2.2	-
3000-3999	2.1	18.8	14.6	62.5	2.1	-
4000-4999	3.8	19.2	19.2	42.3	15.4	-
5000-5999	-	22.2	33.3	44.4	-	-
6000-6999	-	66.7	16.7	-	16.7	-
7000 plus	-	-	27.3	45.5	18.2	9.1

Table 1.2   Responses to ESAP by Monthly Household Income

Income Group Z$	Cut Expenditure	Sell Crops	Other
0-499	15.1	47.2	37.8
500-999	35.8	22.4	41.8
1000-2999	36.1	8.2	55.6
2000-3999	36.7	13.3	50.0
3000-4999	36.4	24.2	39.4
4000-5999	41.7	25.0	33.3
5000 plus	51.9	14.8	33.3

Around 40% of households interviewed claimed to have access to rural land on which crops (primarily being maize and groundnuts) were grown. For the most part these crops were consumed, either in Harare or in the rural areas, in equal measure; only about one quarter were sold, mostly in the rural areas. Overall, therefore, there was a relatively limited flow of food from rural to urban areas. Indeed, almost two-thirds of the households interviewed sent food to the rural areas, usually sugar, cooking oil, and flour.

The survey was obviously conducted during a period of economic hardship and ESAP has had a substantial impact on the lives of the respondents. Over 80% of households had suffered financial difficulties of one form or another, whilst some 16% had experienced job losses. One of the many responses to the difficulties created by ESAP has, according to common consent, been an increase in urban agriculture. As Table 1.2 indicated this has been particularly important for the low-income groups as a potential source of revenue. However, whether this potential is realized, and how it links into urban agriculture as a more basic subsistence activity for self-consumption, is an area which needs further investigation. This need was, indeed, one of the important considerations which prompted this survey.

House Garden Cultivation

Although the survey was primarily aimed at investigating illegal, off-plot agriculture, it also sought information on garden, or on-plot, food cultivation too, largely for comparative purposes. As this report will reveal, there were important differences between the two. Overall, 61% of the respondents had gardens, 83% of which were used to produce food. A rather more limited proportion (23%) contained animals, 80% of which were chickens. Of course, gardening was less of an option for poorer households, primarily those sub-letting rooms, although many domestic servants occupying quarters in low-density areas did have garden space available to them. Gardening was also less likely where environmental or tenure conditions were a problem, such as Epworth (see Table 1.3). But where garden space was available it was normally used to grow food and this was true across the income spectrum. Moreover, compared to illegal cultivation, most gardens had been used in this way for some time. In general, access to garden or on-plot space to grow food did not seem as constrained as ENDA (1994) indicated in their report. However, the ENDA report was perhaps oriented more towards low-income households.

For the most part, garden plots were under 20 metre^2 in size, and there was not consistent correlation with household income. Cultivation was a thoroughly domestic task, and head of household or spouse provided most of the labour input and taps providing the water supply. Almost all cultivators used some form of fertilizer, for the most part this was organic, although 13 % employed chemical fertilizers (much higher in some areas); a further 40% used pesticides.

Table 1.3 Populations Growing House/Garden Food

Monthly Household Income (Z$)		Area of Residence	
0-499	72.0	Kambuzumah	90.9
500-999	73.3	Epworth	53.8
1000-1999	88.9	Sunningdale	65.6
2000-2999	79.4	Warren Park	89.7
3000-3999	88.6	Glen Norah	100.0
4000-4999	87.5	Mabelreign	100.0
5000 plus	92.5	Hatfield	70.4
		Rolf Valley	77.8
		Borrowdale Park	100.0
TOTAL	83.1	TOTAL	83.1

These features are quite different from those of off-plot cultivation, where fertilizer and pesticide use is scant, as illustrated below. However, neither garden nor illegal cultivation made much use of herbicides. Expenditure on chemical fertilizers and pesticides for garden use was usually under Z$50 per year in each case, but tended to rise with income, particularly in the case of pesticides (Table 1.4). Although, as might be expected, maize was grown in many gardens, the most popular crops were leafy vegetables or tomatoes (Table 1.5); a pattern confirmed in ENDA's studies (1994). This is not surprising, perhaps, given the space limitations, but it forms an interesting contrast to the balance of crops grown in illegal plots. This suggests that each type of cultivation plays a different role in the household's economy.

There are also different patterns evident in terms of the use that is made of garden produce (Table 1.5). Whilst most crops are self-consumed (or given away to family or friends), rather than sold, the proportion of sales varied across the major products. Some, such as tomatoes or cabbages clearly had more market potential than others. Overall, 22% of households sold some produce, mostly from their home (about two-thirds). The remainder was sold to friends or near local retail centres (see the example of rape in Fig. 1.6). Over 60% of this direct retailing was undertaken by the spouse, usually a female, with the main purpose being to raise additional income for the family. The main 'problem' perceived by the households is that so many other people are trying to sell surplus garden vegetables that prices were generally low.   The retailing of crops therefore involves a value-judgment on the part of the seller as to whether the household receives more value from self-consumption or sales. Pests were also a problem in house-gardens, hence the use of pesticides by those who can afford these.

Table 1.4   Use of Chemical Fertilizer and Pesticide by Monthly Household Income

Income Group Z$	Fertilizer Use %	Pesticide Use %
0-499	5.6	5.9
500-999	44.2	40.0
1000-1999	31.1	28.9
2000-2999	19.4	42.9
3000-3999	46.2	56.8
4000-4999	28.6	50.0
5000 plus	50.0	50.0

Table 1.5   Garden Cultivation - Use of Main Crops Grown

	% Self Consumed		% Selling	
	100%	80-100%	60% or more	(n)
Rape	59	71	20	(160)
Maize	64	80	27	(84)
Tomatoes	41	58	35	(78)
Spinach	53	70	10	(38)
Sweet Potatoes	52	78	14	(31)
Cabbage	39	49	60	(28)
Beans	56	89	25	(27)

Animals were kept by a relatively smaller number of families, some 23% overall, and in this respect the difference between residence in a house and residence in a room or flat was very marked. Thus, while many of those living in rooms had access to some garden space for cultivation, very few were allowed by their landlords to keep animals. The socio-spatial distribution of animals also reflected this pattern, with their incidence being much lower in the low-density, high-income areas then the high-density, low-income areas. For example, only 10% of farmers in Borrowdale Park kept animals, compared to circa 40% in Warren Park and Glen Norah.

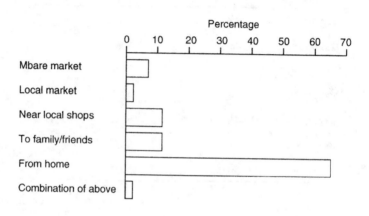

Figure 1. 6   Selling Pattern for Rape

Illegal Cultivation: Organization of Production

Three-quarters of those interviewed were working one plot during the growing season, whilst another 17% were operating two. The remainder farmed three or four. The great majority of these plots (88%) are located in the same suburb in which the respondents reside and around the same high proportion claimed to farm the same plot each season. For the most part this is organized by the cultivators themselves, although around one-quarter claimed that they had have received assistance from local politicians or councillors in this matter. Such assistance, where it occurred was usually related to income levels, with the better off benefitting from such (contacts). Almost all urban farmers cultivate as individuals, with less than 5% belonging to a cooperative despite recent policy initiatives in this context.

Those households cultivating more than one plot tend to be in the low-middle income range earning between Z$1,000 and Z$2,000 per month. Heads of household are concentrated in manual occupations, and are concentrated in Kambuzumah, Warren Park and Mabelegn. For the most part, off-plot gardens are much larger than house gardens. More than 60% of the primary plots are over 50 metre^2. The larger plots tend to be in the more peripheral areas of the high-density suburbs such as Kambuzumah and Warren Park (Table 1.6). In contrast to house-garden cultivation, off-plot activities tended to be more recent in their establishment. Some 70% of the primary plots have been cultivated for less than five years. Additional plots usually represented even more recent developments (Table 1.7). The main reason given for increasing illegal cultivation through plot acquisition was the need for food rather than for cash. To a certain extent this is borne out by data on the use to which crops are put.

Table 1.6   Size of Principal Illegal Plot by Area

	0-49m^2	50-99m^2	100-149m^2	150-199m^2	200m^2 plus
Kambuzamah	15.7	23.5	21.6	-	39.2
Epworth	52.3	-	2.3	-	45.4
Sunningdale	100.0	-	-	-	-
Warren Park	15.4	7.7	20.5	17.9	38.3
Glen Norah	32.6	20.9	14.0	14.0	18.6
Mabelreign	30.4	43.5	15.2	4.3	6.5
Hatfield	97.7	2.3	-	-	-
Rolf Valley	18.9	35.1	16.2	16.2	11.5
Borrowdale Park	2.3	62.8	20.9	9.3	4.7

In contrast to garden cultivation, the main source of water supply is natural precipitation. Farming has, of course, been affected by drought and unreliability in recent years. In terms of labour input, over 70% of families relied on their own contributions alone but some 15% did hire labour, mostly from the neighbours in their local area and often in return for a share of the crop as well as for cash payment. The propensity to hire showed a slight positive correlation with the size of household income.

Most households had cleared their land before starting cultivation, usually of shrubs, and used fertilizers to increased their yields. In contrast to garden cultivation, the great majority (circa 80%) used chemical rather than organic fertilizers, usually compound D and Ammonium Nitrate (ENDA, 1994). This was common in all the surveyed areas. Whilst expenditure on fertilizers was usually under Z$100, it could range much higher. This was usually related to household income (Table 1.8). Few cultivators used pesticides (9%) and even fewer used herbicides, presumably because of cost. However, the widespread use of chemical fertilizers clearly poses potential environmental problems.

Table 1.7   Length of Plot Cultivation by Plot Rank (%)

Years of Cultivation	Plot 1	Plot 2	Plot 3
1	5.3	11.6	10.0
2	17.3	19.8	20.0
3	21.3	14.0	20.0
4	15.7	12.8	-
5	10.4	11.6	15.0
6	6.7	4.7	-
7	6.4	7.0	-
8	2.4	4.7	-
9 plus	14.4	14.0	35.0

Only one fifth of the respondents claimed to have experienced soil erosion on their plot, with most stating that this was only light. However, this may have been a face-saving response by those who felt guilty about causing erosion. Most of those experiencing erosion had tried to do something about this. The principal measures adopted were ground coverage, contour ploughing or ridging. There is some variation by location in propensity to experience erosion hazard. Only 10% of Warren Park and Hatfield residents claimed to experience soil erosion, whereas in some areas such as Mabelreign this was much higher.

Table 1.8 Plot Expenditure on Fertilizer by Monthly Household Income*

Income Group (Z$)	Up to Z$49	Z$50-99	Z$100 Plus
0-499	44.4	40.0	15.5
500-	48.3	24.1	27.6
1000-	34.5	31.0	34.5
2000-	23.7	58.1	18.2
3000-	20.9	50.0	29.1
4000-	20.0	8.3	71.7
5000 plus	20.8	25.0	54.2

*Excludes those not using fertilizer

Almost all respondents, as might be expected, were aware that their cultivation activities were illegal and claimed to know the relevant bylaws. However, whereas almost 80% were aware of the laws against cultivation within 30 metre of a stream, only one third were unaware that they also needed permission from the land owner (private or public) to cultivate. In this context, many had experienced the consequences of their illegal actions and one third had had their crops slashed, with a similar proportion knowing of others who had suffered the same fate. There was, however, a clear and intriguing variation in the degree of slashing across the various study locations (Figure 1.7). Those in the low density suburbs experiencing far lower rates of slashing than those in the high density suburbs.

Theft too posed a problem for off-plot cultivators with almost 60% having experienced this, a much higher proportion than that reported by ENDA (1994) There were variations, but the spatial distribution did not follow a similar pattern to that of slashing. Sunningdale and Warren Park experienced almost twice as much theft as Mabelreign (Figure 1.7). Many other problems were experienced by growers but the most persistent concern was with water supply, particularly in Mabelreign and Borrowdale Park.

By and large, cultivators feel that they get very little assistance from outside agencies despite the optimistic views held in this regard by city councillors. Well over four-fifths claimed to have received no help from government, Harare City Council or NGOs. They were of the opinion that there were areas where assistance would be welcome, particularly in the field of cultivation itself. There was little interest in other forms of help, such as direct financial aid, although the poorest households did place emphasis on the latter (Table 1.9).

Illegal Cultivation: The Crops and Their Use

Crops cultivated in off-plot activities differed considerably from those grown in gardens, largely in terms of relative importance rather than the particular items grown. Maize was overwhelmingly the most important crop (Table 1.10) and was mostly for self-consumption, although almost one-third of the cultivators sold 60% or more. Leafy vegetables were generally less important in off-plot cultivation and there was a more noticeable tendency to sell produce, particularly the more specialist crops such as pulses or tomatoes, although these were not grown on a widespread scale.

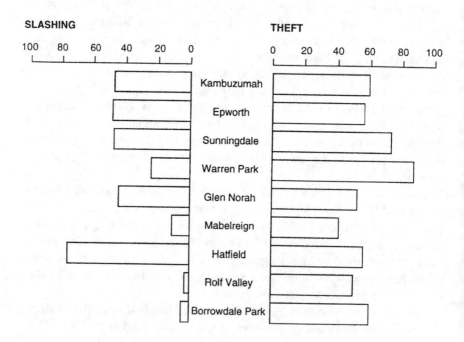

Figure 1.7   Percentage of Households Experiencing Slashing and Theft on Plots, by Area

Table 1.9   Types of Assistance Requested by Income

Monthly Household Income (Z$)	Finance/Fund Assistance	Agricultural Assistance	Others
0–499	42.2	25.1	32.9
500–999	12.5	51.1	35.9
1000–1999	4.8	58.0	37.1
2000–2999	-	47.1	52.9
3000–3999	14.3	34.2	51.4
4000–4999	20.0	40.0	27.3
5000 plus	23.8	38.1	38.1

Undoubtedly, the recent expansion of grinding mills within Harare has been welcomed in the context of self-consumption of maize produced in off-plot activities. Following the removal of the subsidy on roller meal (cheaper maize flour) in 1993, the price has risen from Z$5.82 per 5kg bag to about Z$10.00. This has resulted in a rapid expansion in smaller hammer mills producing coarser but more nutritious (UNICEF 1994) *mugayiwa* (better maize flour) for about Z$5.50 per 5 kg. The mills not only process maize grown by Harare residents but also maize bought by them or by vendors from the GMB (Grain Marketing Board). In a separate survey of millers in Harare, 70% of which were established after deregulation in 1993, it was established that cultivators comprised half of the customers of the mills. Vendors accounted for a full third. The remaining patrons were operators of small shops. So remarkable has been the proliferation of hammer mills (small-scale flour mills) that the charges for their use have even come down over the last year in some districts. However, as Table 1.11 reveals, there is still some unevenness in the use of the mills, presumably reflecting their frequency and proximity to cultivators.

Retailing of off-plot cultivation is, as yet, relatively underdeveloped, despite the fact that many families see this as a way of raising their household income during difficult times. Households want to sell more of what they grow but tend to end up consuming most. The reasons for this weakly developed retail sector appear to relate mainly to lack of experience in this field, but they are also explained by lack of assistance in developing this type of activity, particularly in the context of intermediate services, such as transport.

Table 1.10   Illegal Cultivation: Proportionate Use of Main Crops

Crop	80% plus self consumed	60% sold	30% plus given away	(n)
Maize	65	30	30	(374)
Sweet Potatoes	21	20	50	(173)
Groundnuts	-	31	60	(43)
Beans/pulses	33	44	33	(17)
Rape	20	30	-	(17)
Tomatoes	40	40	-	(12)

Almost one third of the growers sold food directly to consumers, largely on an informal basis. The propensity to sell varies slightly with income and much more so with location. In operation, it indicates that, among illegal cultivators, the poorest households have more need to consume the food they grow and that higher up the income scale there is slightly greater tendency to raise income through retailing (Figure 1.8). By far the leading crop sold in this way (in terms of the numbers who sell rather than the proportion sold) is maize. Figure 1.9 shows how this operates.

In contrast to the direct retailing of garden crops, there is less retailing from home or within the circle of family/friends and more emphasis on selling at recognisable retail locations. Relatively little capital is required for such retailing and this tends to be raised by the retailers and/or their families. In contrast to gardening, direct retailing of crops has been undertaken over a shorter period of time (Table 1.12), an indirect indication of the recent expansion of such activities. This is particularly true for the poorest households interviewed (under Z$500 per month), 58% of whom had taken up direct retailing within the past year.

Overall, relationships with other retailers were usually good or very good, but this was, understandably, less true of relationships with retailers at the lower end of the market, such as hawkers who clearly felt the edge of competition. This rivalry was mentioned as the main problem involved in such retailing activity.

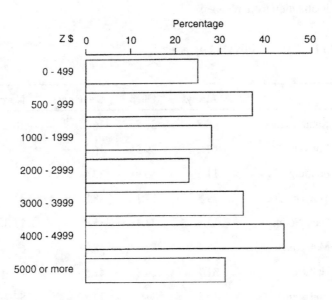

Figure 1.8 Percentage of Households Directly Selling Illegally Grown Crops, by Monthly Household Income

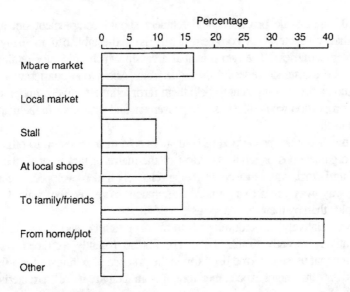

Figure 1. 9 Main Ways of Direct Retailing of Maize

This has been confirmed in separate surveys of food hawkers, indicating an area that needs attention from planners.

Table 1.11   Use of Mills (%) by Area

	Always	Often	Sometimes	Never
Kambuzamah	40.8	32.7	16.3	10.2
Epworth	44.2	39.5	16.3	-
Sunningdale	11.8	55.9	32.4	-
Warren Park	29.3	17.1	48.8	4.9
Glen Norah	13.3	33.3	35.6	17.8
Mabelreign	35.6	8.9	48.9	6.7
Hatfield	31.7	26.8	41.5	-
Rolf Valley	10.5	7.9	23.7	57.9
Borrowdale Park	55.6	11.1	26.7	6.7
TOTAL	31.2	25.5	32.0	11.3

Informal, small-scale producers and retailers should complement one-another rather than compete. This complementarity is well-established in many other developing countries. The two principal areas in which cultivator-retailers felt they needed assistance reflected their duel role. About one quarter would like more land or better equipment to help them farm more effectively, and a slightly smaller proportion would like to see improvement and assistance in the marketing process itself.

A much smaller proportion of cultivators sold their crops on to other more formal organizations or retailers. Most of the maize in fact went to the Grain Marketing Board, with other outlets being relatively underdeveloped. Selling on in this way was an activity undertaken much more by the male head of households than by their female spouse.

This relatively underdeveloped form of retailing had been taken up comparatively recently (Table 1.13), but not so recently as direct retailing, suggesting that those involved had been in the practice of selling on for a number of years. As one might expect, therefore, it is an activity more characteristic of the better educated, medium income households who want to sell and have developed the necessary contacts to do so.

Table 1.12 Illegal Plots: Length of Time in Direct Retailing by Monthly Household Income

Income Group (Z$)	Under 1 year	2-3 years	4-5 years	Over 5 Years
0-499	57.9	21.1	5.3	15.8
500-999	14.8	22.2	48.1	14.8
1000-1999	-	13.6	36.4	50.0
2000-2999	10.0	20.0	60.0	10.0
3000-3999	17.6	17.6	11.8	52.9
4000-4999	9.1	36.4	18.2	36.4
5000 plus	27.2	36.3	-	36.3

Table 1.13 Illegal Plots: Years Retailing by Monthly Household Income

IncomGroup (Z$)	Under 4 Years	5 Years or More
0-499	-	100.0
500-999	62.5	37.5
1000-1999	46.2	53.8
2000-2999	50.0	50.0
3000-3999	42.9	57.1
4000-4999	57.1	42.9
5000 plus	37.5	62.5

It also clearly indicates the potential for a productive and stable commercial relationship than presently exists between producers and more formal outlets.

With encouragement and assistance, this form of retailing outlet can be made more accessible to producers. The principal problems affecting this form of selling-on are, therefore, rather different from those affecting direct retailing of plot produce. Transportation is by far the most important concern, and was raised by almost one-third of respondents both as a major problem and as an area in which they would like assistance.

This is, of course, an activity in which the private sector could be encouraged to become involved in conjunction with the state. Improved transportation is one of the more apparent areas of success under deregulation and a shift from passenger to commodity transport is well worth encouraging.

Conclusions: Food Cultivation in the Household Economy

The importance of cultivation for urban households can be seen in Table 1.14 which indicates the proportion of household food consumption which originates from self-production. For almost one quarter of those interviewed, particularly the lower-income groups, it comprised 60% or more. This is a high proportion. Similarly, income from food retailing played an important role, albeit at a lower level (Table 1.15), for many of the needier households. It is worth noting in this context that, ironically, the poorest households cannot afford to risk selling much of the food they grow. It is needed to supplement their own diet.

Despite the growing importance of urban agriculture as a source of food and income (only one quarter of those interviewed claimed that this had not increased in recent years), the continued rise in the cost of food has put many families under severe pressure. Expenditure on food and beverages thus continues to be substantial as a proportion of the household budget. Indeed, for more than one third of respondents it was in excess of 70% of total expenditure, particularly low-income households. This is a very high proportion and puts immense pressure on the family's ability to purchase and satisfy other basic needs, such as adequate shelter, health care or education. There is, therefore, real pressure to satisfy the necessary food requirements of many households.

Whilst households are clearly concerned about the impact of ESAP and called upon the government to provide more jobs, control inflation or help financially, increased urban cultivation has been shown to be an important strategy through which families have sought to cope with increasingly difficult circumstances. At present there are two ways in which this coping strategy operates.

First, by increased production of food for home consumption. This primarily involves garden production of leafy vegetables and maize, but increasingly is being supplemented by maize production from illegal plots. Here the provision of small grinding mills has clearly had an impact. Second, there is expanded production of food for sale. This occurs in both garden and off-plot cultivation but, as yet, is retailed largely through informal selling in an already crowded food market system. A more stable and ultimately more rewarding form of retailing would be to integrate the informal small-scale urban production more closely with the more established retailers (both formal and informal) or with a set of intermediaries. There would seem to be considerable scope for reorganization and improvement here, in both the private and public spheres, particularly in facilitating collection and re-distribution systems for commodities that are to enter the marketing system. This urgently needs detailed investigation.

Table 1.14   Proportion of Food Consumed from Self-Production
by Monthly Household Income

Income Group (Z$)	None	Under 20%	20-39%	40-59%	60-79%	80-100%
0-499	-	27.5	15.9	31.9	15.9	8.7
500-999	4.1	20.5	27.4	19.2	13.7	15.1
1000-1999	1.3	18.2	44.2	14.3	5.2	16.9
2000-2999	-	18.6	39.5	16.3	14.0	11.6
3000-3999	2.2	15.6	44.4	24.4	4.4	8.5
4000-4999	11.1	14.8	55.6	11.1	7.4	-
5000-5999	-	22.2	38.9	11.1	22.2	5.6
6000-6999	-	16.7	33.3	33.3	16.7	-
7000 plus	-	18.2	45.5	9.1	-	27.3

Certainly, almost all producers were aware that they could produce more and make a positive contribution both to their own situation and to the urban food supply system in Harare as a whole, but only if they had more assistance on marketing and cultivation including better access to improved technology, from seeds to rotivators. It is, therefore, possible to intervene much more positively than has been the case to date in the area of urban food production, with mutual benefits for all, and it is to stimulate further discussion on these matters that this preliminary overview of some of the socio-economic aspects of the situation is presented.

Table 1.15   Proportion of Household Income Obtained from Food Retailing by Monthly Household Income

Income Group (Z$)	None	Under 20%	20-39%	40% plus
0-499	65.0	10.0	10.0	15.0
500-999	43.3	17.9	11.9	25.9
1000-1999	42.0	10.1	26.1	21.7
2000-2999	55.3	18.4	10.5	15.8
3000-3999	39.5	7.0	34.9	18.6
4000-4999	41.7	8.3	37.5	12.5
5000-5999	29.4	17.6	23.5	29.4
6000 plus	38.4	23.1	23.1	15.4
TOTAL	46.8	13.0	20.2	19.9

References

Andrae, G. and Beckman, B. (1985), *The Wheat Trap,* London: Zed Books.

Atkinson, S. (1991), *Nutrition in Urban Programmes & Planning,* London University: Urban Health Programme, London School of Hygiene and Tropical Medicine.

Drakakis-Smith, D. (1992), 'And the cupboard was bare: Food security and food policy for the urban poor', *Geographical Journal of Zimbabwe,* vol. 23, pp. 38-58.

Drakakis-Smith, D. (1994), 'Food systems and the Poor in Harare under Conditions of Structural Adjustment', *Geografiska Annaler,* vol. 76B, pp. 3-20.

Drakakis-Smith, D. and Kivell, P. (1990), 'Urban food distribution and consumption: The case of Harare', in A.M. Findlay, R. Paddison and J.A. Dawson (eds), *Retailing Environments in Developing Countries,* London: Routledge, pp. 156-80.

Drakakis-Smith, D. and Tevera, D. (1993), *Informal Food Retailing in Harare,* Occasional Paper No. 7, Kulturgeografiska Institutionen, Goteborgs Universitet.

Drakakis-Smith, D. Bowyer-Bower, T. and Tevera, D. (1995), 'Urban poverty and urban agriculture: An overview of the linkages in Harare', *Habitat International,* vol. 19, pp. 183-193.

ENDA (1994), *Urban Agriculture in Harare,* unpublished research report ENDA, Zimbabwe.

Gibbon, P (1995), *Structural Adjustment and the Working Poor in Zimbabwe.* Uppsala: Nordiska Afrikainstitutet.

Gibbon, D. (1992) 'The World Bank and African Poverty 1973-1991', *Journal of Modern African Studies,* vol. 30, pp. 193-220.

Goodman, D. and Pecklift, M. (1991), *Refashioning Nature: Food, Ecology and Culture,* London: Routledge.

Gutman, P. (1986), 'Feeding the city: potential and limits of self-reliance', *Development and Change.,* vol. 4, pp. 22-26.

Jackson, J. (1978) , 'Trader hierarchies in Third World distribution systems', in P. Rimmer, D. Drakakis-Smith and T.G. McGee (eds), *Food, Shelter and Transport in Southeast Asia and the Pacific,* Canberra:. Research School of Pacific Studies, Australian National University.

Jackson, J. (1979) , 'Retail development in Third World cities', in J. Jackson and M. Rudner (eds)' *Issues in Malaysian Development,* Singapore: Hutchinson.

Le Heron, R. and Roche, M. (1995), 'A fresh place in food's space', *Area.,* vol.. 27, pp. 23-33.

Maxwell, D. and Zziwa, S. (eds), (1992), *Urban Agriculture in Africa: The Case of Kampala,* Nairobi: ACTS Press.

Mazambani, D. (1982a), *Aspect of Periurban Cultivation and Deforestation Around Salisbury, 1955-1980,* Unpublished MA Thesis, Department of Geography, University of Zimbabwe.

Mazambani, D. (1982b), 'Periurban cultivation in Greater Harare', *The Zimbabwe Science News,* vol. 16, pp. 134-8.

Mbiba, B. (1994), 'Institutional responses to uncontrolled urban cultivation in Harare: Prohibitive or accommodative?', *Environment and Urbanization.,* vol. 6, pp. 188-202.

Mbiba, B. (1995a), 'Classification and description of urban agriculture in Harare', *Development Southern Africa,* vol. 12, pp. 75-86

Mbiba, B (1995b), *Urban Agriculture in Zimbabwe,* Aldershot: Avebury.

McLeod, S. & McGee, T.G. (1990), 'The internationalization of the food distribution system in Hong Kong', in D. Drakakis-Smith (ed.), *Economic Growth and Urbanization in Developing Countries,* London: Routledge.

Mosha, A.C. (1991), 'Urban farming practices in Tanzania', *Review of Rural and Urban Planning in Southern and Eastern Africa.,* vol. 1, pp. 83-92.

Mougeot, L. (1994), 'African city farming in a world perspective', in A. Egziabher et al., (eds), *Cities Feeding People,* Ottawa: IDRC, 1-24.

Rogerson, C.M. (1992), ' Feeding Africa's cities: The role and potential for urban agriculture', *Africa Insight,* vol. 22, pp. 299-234.

Smit, J. and Nasr, J. (1992) , 'Urban agriculture for sustainable cities: Using wastes and idle land and water bodies as resources', *Environment and Urbanization,* vol. 4, 141-152.

Tinker, I.(1987) , 'The case for legalizing street foods', *Ceres,* vol. 20, pp. 26-31.

Tinker, I.(1994), 'Urban agriculture is already feeding cities', in A. Egziabher et al., (eds), *Cities Feeding People.* Ottawa: IDRC, pp. vii-xiv.

Tinker, I. (1997), *Street Foods: Urban Food and Employment in Developing Countries,* New York: Oxford University Press.

UNDP (1991), *Cities, People and Poverty, Strategy Paper,* New York: UNDP.

UNICEF (1994), 'The Impact of Maize Market Liberalization in *Zimbabwe's* Urban *Areas,* unpublished report, Harare: Ministry of Public Service, Labour and Social Welfare.

Wekwete, K.H.(1993), Urban Agriculture in Southern and Eastern Africa, In: L Mougeot and D. Masse (eds) *Urban Environmental Management,* Ottawa: IDRC, 98-110.

World Bank (1991), *Urban Policy and Economic Development: An Agenda for the 1990s.* Washington, D.C.

Yeung, Y.M. (1988), 'Agriculture land use in Asian cities', *Land Use Policy,* vol. 5, pp. 79-82.

2 Vegetable Production in the Maseru Urban Area: The Past, the Present and the Future

HOPOLANG PHORORO

Introduction

Traditionally, agriculture in Lesotho focused on subsistence production of basic crops such as maize, wheat, sorghum, peas and beans. In most cases, these crops were produced under irrigation, using funds provided by donors. Such projects involved large tracts of land. However, over the past twenty years, large arable holdings have been purchased for planned urban development projects to accommodate the rapid migration from rural to urban zones, as well as the natural population growth of Maseru's urban area and its periphery. Migration has been blamed for the declining agricultural productivity, but certain studies indicate that the use of good arable land for urban purposes is not necessarily bad for farming. A considerable amount of agricultural activity continues in urban Maseru. In terms of value per unit area, this form of activity is considered by many observers as more productive than traditional, unimproved, cultivation of field crops.

Urban agriculture is not new. Vegetable production has taken place on agricultural land in the urban and peri-urban areas for a long time. This form of past land use is now threatened and may die out completely. This paper seeks to reveal the reasons why it is no longer possible to continue it. The main difficulty is, clearly, that much of the farmland is taken up for residential and institutional purposes. However, despite this trend, there is an increasing occurrence of vegetable cultivation on residential plots in Maseru. The importance of the activity in the urban landscape, its significance to the generation of added earning capacity and the role that this form of urban farming plays in meeting food and nutrition requirements, and in generating income, will be addressed. Competing land uses have a significant impact on the allocation of land for residential purposes. They thus affect the cultivation of vegetables on the residential plots. The conclusion of this paper is that the present trend will accelerate. In the future, thus, vegetable production will take place on gardens on even smaller residential plots. Innovative methods of producing will have to be sought.

The Past Processes

The production of vegetables began in the 1930s when the Basotho were encouraged by the Department of Agriculture to establish backyard gardens, primarily on land that was said to be infertile and subject to soil erosion. The cultivation of a variety of vegetables such as cabbage, spinach, radish and potatoes was encouraged. The production was mainly for household consumption and small surpluses were sold. One reason for the relatively late introduction of vegetable production by government was that earlier, emphasis was placed on the production of staple crops such as maize, sorghum, wheat, peas and beans. Land that is currently built up in the urban and peri-urban areas was used for agricultural purposes. The cultivated fields were owned, or held, by individual farmers and by the government.

During the 1930s land was abundant and conditions were favourable to extensive crop cultivation. The traditional land tenure system was also favourable because it recognized the right of all Basotho to have access to land for growing subsistence crops The fact that there was no freehold ownership of land did not pose a problem, because households were able to farm the land as they desired, and the risk of land being expropriated was low. The communal land was allocated to a person when he got married. The chief or the headman of the village gave him three fields for growing crops for household consumption and for sale. The household had exclusive rights over the crops that it produced, but after the harvest the land reverted to communal grazing (Maseru Development Plan, undated). In addition to the fields, the household was provided with residential land, and in most cases it was on these plots that the vegetable gardens were cultivated.

Lesotho imports about 75 percent of its vegetables from South Africa. The high volume of these imports indicates that there is a strong potential market which can be met by domestic production (Phororo and Prasad, 1996). The Government of Lesotho became increasingly concerned with the growing dependence of Lesotho on vegetable imports from South Africa, and in 1978 there was a policy reorientation: from the production of grain crops to vegetables. Most of the supply of vegetables came from intensively cultivated, state owned, irrigated farms. These projects were sponsored by government or donor agencies, which provided the funding; or on privately owned commercial farms. Little attention was paid to the vegetables that were cultivated on residential home gardens.

Policy makers placed great emphasis on the projects sponsored by government and the donor funds. These farms were given ample resources. They involved large scale irrigation, and their objective was to achieve self-sufficiency in the consumption of the common vegetables, such as cabbage, potatoes, onions and tomatoes. Targets were set and in some cases they were achieved. However, the general performance of these projects has not been encouraging. Problems of management and of a technical nature, and the lack of sufficient attention to marketing, were the major causes for the setbacks and poor performance.

The Present State of Vegetable Cultivation

Maseru is the capital city of Lesotho, and has the highest urban population in the country: The 1986 figure was 98,017. It represented 44 percent of the total population (Bureau of Statistics, 1992). This urban centre is the most developed in terms of education, health, employment opportunities, and infrastructure development. Therefore, it is clear that the market created by the local people and those who commute into it to use its facilities, makes cultivation on its residential plots more profitable than in similar plots in other urban centres. However, most urban towns, particularly those close to the South African border have also become administrative centres or transit stops for people planning to work in firms and the mines in South Africa. These centres grew and attracted an increasing number of people because they offered better job opportunities and possibilities of earning cash incomes than other localities.

By 1979, the population pressure in Lesotho had intensified to the extent that it was no longer possible for new households to get land even in the rural areas. Thus, the agricultural land in peri-urban areas had to be converted for residential purposes (Maseru Development Plan, undated). Other reasons given for the conversion of agricultural land included soil erosion. Many farmers left their land uncultivated when their households became increasingly dependent on income earned from the modern sector in South Africa. The threat of government repossessing land as a result of the Land Act of 1979 was also cited as a factor (Phororo, 1996). The pressure on land is so serious that thirty percent of families have no rights to land, and most of those who have land do not have more than one field averaging half a hectare. Gone is the customary land tenure of the three fields system. Instead, the emerging pattern is one of increasingly dense, crowded, settlements. The population density increased from 478 persons per square kilometre in 1986 to 707 persons per square kilometre in 1992 (Sechaba Consultants, 1995).

The increasing number of residential plots in the urban and peri-urban areas was partly a response to the growing pressure on the land. A large, and growing, number of households were involved in some form of agriculture. This agriculture entailed every conceivable product: from orchards to vegetable gardening, poultry and dairying raising, and this trend is increasing in all the towns of Lesotho. The same trend is found in many other countries in Africa, Asia, and South America, and the growing interest in it in recent decades, has been manifested by the large volume of research which has been undertaken on urban and peri-urban agriculture. Researchers agree that households engage in urban and peri-urban agriculture to supplement their income from wages, or even as a survival strategy. As a result of the World Bank's Structural Adjustment Policies (SAP) which were imposed particularly on African countries, the supply of new jobs has slackened and, therefore, many households realize a real decline in wages and have to engage in additional economic activities. However, despite the fact that it plays a vital economic role, the growing sub-sector of urban and peri-urban agriculture has been ignored by the government of Lesotho, as also by other African countries. This sub-sector contributes to improved nutrition, higher income, employment opportunities, or to a combination of these benefits.

Urban and peri-urban agriculture takes place in defined boundaries within the residential plots, but many plots are located in urban spaces which are zoned, or function, as public land, such as parks, roadsides, steep slopes and flood plains (Phororo, 1996). The type of activity, whether it is poultry production, dairying or vegetable production, is constrained by the plot sizes. The following discussion provides a closer look at the various forms and plot sizes, and on related spatial characteristics of this agricultural system.

Vegetable Cultivation on Peri-urban and Urban Residential Plots

A study undertaken by the Lesotho Agricultural Production and Institutional Support (LAPIS) Project in 1992 indicated that in the summer season of 1991/92, rural home gardeners planted vegetables on 5,140 ha, urban gardeners planted on 121 ha and institutional farms (state farms and projects) cultivated on 2,639 ha. The yield harvested was 21,800 tons of cabbage, potatoes, onions, carrots, tomatoes, spinach, and rape. Only 2,600 tons were sold, probably mostly from institutional farms, and the majority was for subsistence (Phororo and Prasad, 1996). This study reveals the importance of home gardens and suggests that vegetable cultivation on home gardens is the most common form of urban and peri-urban agriculture in Lesotho. In 1994, it was found that 67 percent of the households were engaged exclusively in vegetable production, two percent of the households kept livestock as a main agricultural activity, and 31 percent were involved in mixed farming, i.e., in both livestock and vegetable production (Phororo, 1996). Vegetable production is most common on home gardens, because the residential plots, particularly in new settlements, are small (100 m^2). In older settlements, the plots are larger (1,200 - 2,500m^2) and permit livestock and poultry rearing (Maseru Development Plan, undated). Thus, the size of the plot does constrain the type of agricultural activities that can take place. Another factor that influences vegetable production on home gardens is political. The urban bylaws discourage the rearing of livestock on urban plots for hygienic and aesthetic reasons. Despite the negative attitude of the government's officials, there are a number of good reasons to promote the expansion of home gardening. Explanations have been outlined above, but in the following section this subject will be treated in greater detail. It focuses on the reasons why vegetable production is an important component of urban and peri-urban agriculture.

Why Households Keep Vegetable Gardens?

Vegetable production from gardens plays an important role in providing nutrition for households and it is for this reason that, in the rural areas, the government has always encouraged home garden cultivation. In the urban and peri-urban areas, on the other hand, agriculture has not been encouraged, probably because it was convenient to depend on the vegetable supply from South Africa, which is fairly close and easily accessible. South Africa was considered to be a stable source, and there has been no perceived need for encouraging local households who cultivated garden plots at their own initiative to expand production. According to Gay (1994), production from home gardens in both rural and urban areas contributed 11 percent to GNP in 1979. He also found that nearly half of the vegetables consumed in Lesotho were produced locally. About 22 percent of this supply came from home gardens. The other half represented imports from South Africa.

The production of vegetables in urban and peri-urban areas in Lesotho is mainly for subsistence purposes: to supplement household food supply. A small surplus is sold in neighbouring areas to generate a small income. In a study on Urban and Rural Gardens, Phororo (1996) indicated that in the Maseru urban area, 12 percent of the respondents mentioned that wages and salaries in conjunction with the sale of vegetables was an important source of income. This implies that the sale of vegetables complements salaries and wages. However, the sale of vegetables is not an important reason for cultivating them. It functions, rather, as an activity which generates an additional small income once the basic consumption need is met. In other African countries, for example in Tanzania, the urban poor (the middle class by the standards of other countries) cultivate in order to supplement their incomes as "insurance" against economic deterioration and high inflation rates. Thus, they engage mainly in livestock keeping and, to a lesser extent, in vegetable production. By selling the produce they supplement their income (Mlozi et al. 1992). This form of urban farming can be thought of as a survival strategy, but as explained below, this is not the case in Lesotho.

The Maseru Development Plan (1987) mentioned that, depending on the income group, households engage in urban cultivation to save money, to make money, and as a hobby. The low income households had gardens to save or to make money, middle and high income households had gardens to save income, while a smaller number cultivated vegetables as a hobby. The low income households are those residing in high density housing, usually unplanned and unserviced sites where access to inputs is difficult. They have very few options to earn salaries or wages and have the least access to land. Therefore, they produce only small amounts of vegetables. Hence, only small quantities are sold by them. Middle and high income households have the greatest access to land, but their primary reasons for cultivating vegetables is not for generating income. They save money, as do low income households, by not having to purchase the vegetables which they can conveniently get them from their own gardens. Thus, in terms of generating incomes, very small amounts are earned from the sale of vegetables.

Furthermore, because these households cultivate to meet consumption needs and are not interested in commercial activities, they do not bother to record the quantities sold and the incomes generated (Phororo, 1996).

Does urban and peri-urban agriculture generate any employment opportunities in Lesotho? Limited opportunities on a part-time basis are available. Part-time employment is generated in the urban and peri-urban areas because the household head and spouse have full-time jobs and are unable to partake fully in gardening activities. However, the gardener is not only involved in looking after the garden, but has other duties to perform, such as washing cars or livestock rearing (in the case of mixed farming), and therefore, is not strictly employed to cultivate vegetables. Phororo (1996) indicated that 40 percent of the households employed paid labour and the other 60 percent relied on household members to undertake specific gardening activities. The children assisted under the supervision of the adults, especially in watering. The women did the thinning, harvesting and planting, and the men did the ploughing, digging and sowing. Since all members derived benefits from the garden, they were all expected to be involved in the cultivation of vegetables.

Considering the extent to which households are involved in vegetable cultivation on small plots, in the Maseru urban area, this activity cannot be recommended for the generation of employment opportunities, except in cases where large scale production takes place mainly for sale. This situation is relevant in other African countries, where urban farming supplements incomes. Households are barely making ends meet and are hardly able to have an additional burden by employing paid labour. Bibangambah (1992) argues that urban agriculture is a symptom of economic decay and, no matter how much the term is glamorized, it represents the invasion of cities and towns by subsistence agriculture and rural poverty. Thus, it should not be recommended as a major source of employment and income. Bibangambah suggests that this form of decay accompanies the collapse of the modernization process and the reversal of the developmental process by regressive forces which compel people to search for extreme means of survival. In most cases, this involves a retreat into subsistence agriculture in an urban setting. Urban output has to ensure the minimum physiological consumption requirements needed for survival. The question is, thus, if it is productive enough to accomplish this purpose.

Food is a very significant item in the household budget. Therefore, if there is a way of saving money by cultivating vegetables, family spendings can be greatly reduced. In 1990, nearly half of the developing countries' households spent 50 to 80 percent of their average income on food in (Mougeot, 1993). Access to an urban garden provides households with a wide variety of vitamin rich vegetables and is, therefore, highly important nutritionally. Phororo (1996) indicated that in urban towns and rural villages, 9 different vegetables were planted during the summer months and only 5 were grown in the winter season. In the Maseru urban area, households cultivated vegetables such as spinach, cabbage, tomatoes, and carrots on plot whose size ranged from 60 to 132 m^2. Cabbage was the most popular vegetable. It was cultivated during both the summer and winter because of its low production costs, high yields, and high marketability. Vegetables such as lettuce, onions, green beans, beetroot and green peppers were grown by less than 20 percent of the producers (Phororo, 1996).

The government of Lesotho has strongly advocated gardening in the rural villages, in order to meet two basic needs; firstly, to achieve household self-sufficiency in vegetable production and, secondly, to improve nutrition. Several donor-funded projects, such as the Semonkong Rural Development Project and the Small Scale Intensive Agricultural Production Project, have been established. The policy addressed the issue of decreasing local vegetable supplies through setting up communal or home gardens. However, in comparison with individual home gardens, communal gardens have not been too successful, because it was not easy to reach joint decisions, and often no consensus among community members could be reached. In many cases producers have parted on bad terms. The establishment of communal garden projects in the urban space was also problematic due to the lack of sufficiently large tracts of agricultural land. Home garden production is, indeed, the only option available for urban agriculture.

Competing Urban Land Uses

Land, particularly in the urban areas, has several competing uses: residential, commercial, institutional, industrial, agricultural, and recreational. This competition is found in the Maseru Urban Area, the most important urban centre in Lesotho. The ststistics on existing land uses can give some idea on the relative position of agricultural land in the city.

Table 2.1 shows that residential land constituted the largest (58.3%) percentage of the existing land use in urban Maseru. It included site and service schemes, which contained medium cost and high cost plots. Some of the land allocated for residential purposes was converted to commercial uses because no land was available for the expansion of the Central Business District (CBD). The older settlement areas have larger plot sizes, as mentioned previously, and their density is low. A serious shortage of land exists in the Maseru urban area, especially in areas around the CBD. In 1985 commercial activities in the CBD occupied 80 percent of the retailing and wholesaling land. Agriculturally defined land covered the state farms, schemes, feedlot complexes and areas used for agricultural demonstration plots and for education purposes. The land in the urban areas is viewed as transitory. Much of it is being illegally converted for residential purposes.

Table 2.1   Existing Land Uses in the Maseru Urban Area, 1979

Type of Land Use	Area (km^2)	% of Total Land
Residential	80.40	58.30
Agricultural	36.90	26.70
Institutional	10.50	7.60
Industrial	4.10	3.00
Formal open spaces		
Recreational	3.90	2.80
Commercial	2.20	1.60
TOTAL	138.00	100.00

Source: Maseru Land Use Map, 1979 (The areas and % of the total land are approximate).

Most of the institutional land in urban Maseru is held by the government for various ministries and departments. Administrative offices are located on economically viable and prime land (Maseru Development Plan, undated). The remaining land uses account for a very small percent of the total; there are two operational industrial areas in the Maseru urban area. Open spaces for recreational purposes are very limited and, the increasing land shortage within the urban zone, suggests that solutions are still lacking (Maseru Development Plan, undated).

The Future

It is clear from the above that even though the residential land accounts for 58 percent of the total land in the Maseru urban area, the competing land uses must not be ignored and the increasing population will have to be accommodated. Agricultural land in the urban area is likely to decrease in the future because field owners will continue to sell off land to builders. Agricultural use is perceived, therefore, as transient. The illegal construction problem results in unplanned and unserviced peripheral settlements. The upgrading of these settlements to acceptable urban standards is costly because provision of infrastructure services requires encroachment on private plots. Field owners fear that if, and when, their agricultural lands are required for public purposes, they will get little or no compensation. They are inclined, therefore, to continue to sell off the land.

The shortage of land in the CBD means that more residential land will be encroached upon, resulting in smaller plot sizes. This will affect the households involved in agricultural activities. The activities will be restricted to vegetable production on residential plots and fewer households will be engaged in livestock and poultry rearing. This trend is already observed in the Site and Services development areas. However, with more residents in urban areas actively engaged in intensive vegetable production, it is possible that production will increase and, in any case, it will not necessarily decrease (Transformation Resource Centre, 1987). Innovative ways of cultivating high value vegetables on restricted areas of land will have to be used. Permaculture is one such viable option. It 'is a design system for creating sustainable human environments' (Mollison, 1991, 1). Mollison observes that permaculture uses the inherent qualities of plants and animals, combined with the natural landscapes and structures, to produce a life-supporting system. Given that land will be a constraint, care must be taken to intensify food production and to minimize waste space by using stacked or clumped plantings. A variety of vegetables can be grown in containers such as plastic garden pots, half filled sacks, and plastic bags. They can be placed on verandahs, concrete floors and balconies. The production of vegetables in this manner enables urban dwellers to be converted from consumers to producers, even if on a small scale.

Conclusions

Vegetable cultivation on home gardens has been practiced by the Basotho for many years. The satisfaction of home grown vegetables, the pride of cultivating a garden and the fact that a vegetable garden enhances the surroundings are factors that have encouraged Basotho to cultivate home gardens (Phororo, 1996). The production of vegetables in the rural areas, where ample land was available, was encouraged for purposes of feeding the towns. Towns were not centres of production, but more of administration and industrial activity, but even in the 1930s the government encouraged vegetable growing in urban areas. Rising population pressure has resulted in reducing the number of people having their own land, and the traditional three fields land tenure system was abandoned. The result was that there has been an exodus from rural areas to Lesotho's urban towns and to South Africa. The migrants who move to Maseru in recent years expect to be accommodated, but there is no agricultural land available for them, because the land, which was in 'transitory' use, had been gradually sold off by its original owners, the farmers, to various businessmen and contractors. The latter bought it for the purpose of converting it into residential land. Illegal land allocations has resulted in 90 percent of Maseru being associated with unplanned urban sprawl, with no planned infrastructure or services. However, this has not eliminated the incidence of agricultural activities on residential plots.

Vegetable cultivation is the most common farm activity in the towns. It requires little land and inputs are not as costly when compared to poultry and livestock rearing. Several types of vegetables are cultivated on urban gardens. They are grown in order to save money, generate income, and meet nutritional needs. The cultivation of gardens on the residential plots is primarily done for subsistence. If there is a surplus it can be given away, or even better, it can be sold. However, the data on competing land uses indicate that land for residential purposes is becoming more and more scarce, as land is demanded for institutional purposes. Zoned agricultural land in the urban areas is virtually absent, and there can be no reliance on allocation of land for vegetable production, Residential plots will become smaller as more people move into peri-urban areas. Viable options such as permaculture, which enables even the land deficient household to produce a limited variety of vegetables for subsistence, is a potential future trend for solving the problem. However, production of vegetables, even if it is only for subsistence, should be encouraged, because it reduces the dependence on

South African imports. Lesotho can, thus, benefit from a reduced currency outflow and from greater national savings.

References

Bibangambah, J.(1992), 'Macro-level Constraints and the Growth of the Informal Sector in Uganda', in J. Baker and P.O. Pedersen (eds), *The Rural-Urban Interface in Africa: Expansion and Adaptation.*, Uppsala: Nordiska Afrikainstitutet, pp. 303-13.

Bureau of Statistics.(1992), *1986 Population Census Analysis Report Volume IV (Population Dynamics, Prospects and Policies)*, Maseru: Lesotho Government.

Gay, J., Gill, D., Green, T., Hall, D., Mhlanga, M., and Mohapi, M. (1994), *Poverty in Lesotho 1994: A Mapping Exercise*, Morija: Sechaba Consultants.

Maseru Development Plan (undated), *Maseru Development Plan*, Working Paper No. 4: *Land Tenure*. Maseru: Physical Planning Division.

Maseru Development Plan (1987), *National Settlement Policy*, Working Paper No. 10: *Agriculture*, Maseru: Physical Planning Division.

Mlozi, M., Lupanga, I., and Mvena, Z. (1992), 'Urban Agriculture as a Survival Strategy in Tanzania', in J. Baker and P.O. Pedersen (eds), *The Rural-Urban Interface in Africa: Expansion and Adaptation.* Uppsala: Nordiska Afrikainstitutet, pp. 284-94.

Mollison, B. (1993), *Introduction to Permaculture*. Harare: Fambidzania Training Centre.

Mougeot, L. (1993), 'Urban Food Self Reliance: Significance and Prospects', *IDRC Reports*, No. 21, 2-5.

Ngqaleni, M.(1989), *A Vertical Systems Analysis of Vegetable Marketing in Lesotho*. Unpublished M.Sc. Thesis, University of Saskatwen, Canada.

Phororo, H. (1996), *Urban and Rural Gardens: Income Generation?* Draft Final Report prepared for the Regional Project on Gender, Households and Environmental Changes, Roma: ISAS.

Phororo, H and Prasad, G. (1996), *Vegetable Marketing Study*, Working Paper No 7, Roma: ISAS.

Sechaba Consultants Staff (1995), *Lesotho's Long Journey: Hard Choices at the Crossroads*, Morija: Sechaba Consultants.

Transformation Resource Centre. (1987), 'Moving to the Cities', *Work for Justice* 14. Lesotho: Mazenod Printing Works.

3 Commercial Horticulture by Kenyan Smallholders

TJALLING DIJKSTRA

Introduction

Kenya belongs to the middle-income countries of Sub-Saharan Africa. It has one of the fastest growing populations of the continent, having witnessed a 40 percent population increase in ten years' time (Kenya CBS, 1994). Overall, its average population density is not particularly high when compared to other African countries. However, the largest part of Kenya consists of sparsely populated dry lowlands, and 18 percent of the land accommodates 80 percent of the population. Population concentrations are found in the highland areas of central and western Kenya and along the shores of Lake Victoria and the Indian Ocean.

Over 80 percent of the people live in rural areas. Agriculture is their main activity and source of cash revenues. Traditional export crops for smallholder production are coffee, tea, pyrethrum and cotton. Many farmers have turned away from those crops, though, because of low producer prices and excessive delays in payment by the marketing boards which until recently monopolized the trade (see e.g., Dijkstra, 1990). Horticulture has become a popular alternative because it brings fair prices and immediate returns. The market prospects for vegetables, fruits and tubers are favourable due to ongoing urban growth.

Almost all horticulture in Kenya is rain-fed and concentrated in the highland areas. The only exceptions are small-scale production of citrus fruits and mangoes in the coastal region, and some large-scale farms and settlement schemes with irrigated production near rivers and lakes in the dry lowlands. The large-scale farms concentrate mainly on production for export. Most are owned by multinational companies or Nairobi businessmen, and they specialize in the production of pineapples, cut

53

flowers, strawberries, etc. Some small-scale out-growers are contracted, for instance for French beans and so-called Asian vegetables (chili peppers, okra, eggplants, etc.), but they are relatively few in number.[1] Although horticultural exports are important to Kenya in terms of foreign exchange, they make up only five percent of the total volume of horticultural commodities marketed in the country (HCDA, 1990). In short, commercial horticulture in Kenya is first and foremost rain-fed production for the domestic market by smallholders in the highland regions.

Commercial Horticulture in Nyandurua, Kisii and Taita

Three regions in the Kenyan highlands known for their horticultural output were selected to study commercial horticulture among smallholders in more detail: Nyandarua District in the central highlands, Kisii District in western Kenya, and the Taita Hills halfway between the central highlands and the coast.

Commercial horticulture did not develop overnight in the research areas, but evolved gradually over the past decades. Favourable agro-ecological circumstances and increasing land shortage in the production areas, in combination with growing urban demand and improvement of interregional road networks have fostered the development process. Substantial purchasing power of consumer groups in large urban centres such as Nairobi and Mombasa allowed long supply lines with transport distances up to 1000 km. In Nyandarua, commercial horticulture developed without much competition from other income-generating activities, while in Kisii coffee and tea competed for the same land, and in Taita employment opportunities competed for the same labour.

Seventy percent of Nyandarua District is suitable for horticulture. The remaining parts have to cope with frequent night frosts, unreliable rain and waterlogging. Eighty percent of Kisii District is suitable for the enterprise, with the remaining part lacking appropriate soils. Horticulture is possible in the entire Taita Hill area, except for the steepest slopes (Jätzold and Schmidt, 1983).

Household surveys were carried out in the areas suitable for horticulture, to assess the importance of horticulture as a source of income. The fieldwork took place between 1990 and 1992 as part of a research project on horticultural production and marketing in Kenya, which in turn was part of the Food and Nutrition Studies Programme. This program was a joint effort of the Ministry of Planning and National Development, Nairobi, and the African Studies Centre, Leiden, The Netherlands. It was financed through Dutch development aid. The horticultural project was carried out by researchers of Egerton University, Njoro, and the African Studies Centre, Leiden, in collaboration with district officers of the Central Bureau of Statistics of Kenya (Dijkstra and Magori, 1991, 1992a, 1992b, 1994a, 1994b, 1995a).

To start with, officers of the CBS (Central Bureau of Statistics) listed all households in randomly selected clusters and recorded whether household members had sold horticultural commodities in the agricultural year under consideration. The findings were remarkable. In Nyandarua, over 95 percent of the rural households in the areas suitable for horticulture had sold horticultural commodities, and in Kisii 79 percent. In Taita, where the lowest involvement was found, still 63 percent of the listed households had sold horticultural commodities. In all three research areas, high participation in commercial horticulture was revealed not only in clusters near all-weather roads, but also in those which were regularly cut off from the world by heavy showers. Impassable roads were a recurrent problem for such clusters, but this kept few rural households from embarking on the enterprise. Commercial horticulture was not just something for the rural elite on prime locations, but an income-generating activity for the majority of the rural population in the surveyed areas.

The omnipresence of commercial horticulture is already one indication of its importance. It might, however, be just a side activity in terms of money, at best generating some petty cash for the households involved. To investigate its impact on the household cash income, we drew a systematic sample from the listed households that sold horticultural commodities in each region.[2] According to the survey results, horticulture was on the average the most important source of cash revenues on the farm in all three regions. A traditional cash crop like coffee, which was grown in Kisii and Taita, hardly figured, due to low prices on the international market which caused farmers to neglect their coffee trees. The only export crop of some income significance at the time of the survey was tea, which was grown in Kisii. Besides horticultural commodities, livestock contributed substantially to the farm revenues, especially in Nyandarua, where graded cows were found in most compounds and the selling of milk to the national dairy cooperative (Kenya Cooperative Creameries) was common. Cereals and beans were of little account in the research areas, either because they were hardly grown (Nyandarua) or because they mainly served for private consumption (Kisii, Taita).[3] Off-farm employment was a major contributor to household cash income in all three regions, but only in Taita did it exceed the importance of horticulture.

Although the averages provide an indication of the importance of commercial horticulture to the income of the households involved, they do not tell the entire story. Horticultural sales could be relatively insignificant at the lower end of the income distribution scale, and more important at the upper end. According to the survey results, this was, however, not true. As a percentage of the total household cash income, commercial horticulture was of roughly the same importance for all income categories in Nyandarua, while being of distinctly greater consequence for low-income horticultural farmers in Kisii and Taita. This reaffirms that the horticultural enterprise was a core activity for broad segments of the rural population, including the poorer households (for details see Dijkstra, 1997).

Problems in Horticultural Production

Although commercial horticulture was a successful income-generating activity in the research areas, the enterprise faced serious problems. During the household survey we also investigated these problems. Some of them figured in all three research areas while others were region- or location-specific.

A widespread problem at the production stage concerned produce losses from pests and diseases. The latter often became rampant due to of lack of crop rotation and diversification. Although the relative importance of crops in terms of value and acreage is not always the same, the composition of the average horticultural cash income gives an indication of the lack of diversification. At the time of the survey, about 85 percent of the average horticultural cash income in Nyandarua and Kisii came from two crops, namely potatoes and cabbages (Nyandarua), and bananas and kale (Kisii). Farmers had been cultivating these commodities on the same plots for years, and bacterial wilt, late blight and eelworms (in the case of potatoes) and banana weevil, nematodes and Panama disease (in the case of bananas) were a constant and ever-increasing threat. Taita was the only area with a somewhat more diversified assortment. The two most important crops, tomatoes and cabbage, supplied less than half of the average horticultural cash income, while 85 percent of the revenues came from a total of nine different crops. The assortment of the Taita farmers even included fairly unknown vegetables such as baby marrow, cauliflower and lettuce, which were in demand from tourist hotels along the Kenyan coast.

Disease and pest problems were exacerbated by failing crop protection. Either farmers lacked knowledge, usin, the wrong chemicals or spraying too late, or they had the knowledge but not the money to buy the proper pesticides and fungicides. Credit to buy horticultural inputs was generally hard to obtain. Neither commercial banks and the Kenya Cooperative Bank nor the Agricultural Finance Corporation (a parastatal) were willing to issue loans to small-scale horticultural farmers, even when the latter possessed a title deed that could serve as security.

While chemical and fertilizer use were already low in the 1980s, the situation worsened in the early 1990s. Input costs rose sharply at that time due to the depreciation of the Kenya shilling and decreasing subsidies on farm inputs as part of Structural Adjustment. Pesticides, fungicides and fertilizers more or less doubled in price within two years' time. Farmers responded by cutting back on their use, leading to a further increase in pests and diseases.

Many horticultural farmers shied away from buying certified seeds in the early 1990s because of recurrent quality problems. The germination rate of seeds produced by the Kenya Seed Company, which still possessed a monopoly at that time, had deteriorated. Farmers and retailers blamed the seed company for supplying poor quality, while the seed company blamed the retailers for improper storage and the farmers for "burying the seeds," that is, sowing them too deep.

Quality problems also occurred in the case of chemicals. Farmers were offered fake pesticides and fungicides in some rural markets, causing them to lose faith in such inputs. Well known is the story about Royco soup which was once sold as a pesticide in one of the local market places of Kisii. The dried soup was sold in the chemical's original packaging material. Once sprayed with this solution, the crop smelled nice while the pests flourished away.

Problems in Horticultural Marketing

The marketing of horticultural commodities is left entirely to the private sector. Private traders provide intermediary groups between rural producers and rural and urban consumers [4] Urban consumers are the most significant group because of their purchasing power and high food demands. The main suppliers to urban centres are the collecting wholesalers, who are locally called middlemen.

Middlemen buy directly from farmers, or, alternatively, use purchasing agents and assembling traders as intermediaries. A purchasing agent works on behalf of one specific middleman, receiving a commission, while an assembling trader operates independently, buying and selling on his or her own account. Assembling traders may sell their commodities in the marketplace or near the farms, while purchasing agents are usually only found near the farms. The strength of both types of intermediaries is their knowledge of the local situation through day-to-day contact with the farmers, which is possible because they are part of the local community. They know which farmers produce what kinds of crops, and they are capable of identifying marketable produce. Moreover, they are able to predict when crops will be harvestable, either by looking at their own crop, or asking the opinion of the farmers. A middleman can use this knowledge to plan his produce collection trips. Optimum planning is especially important during periods of produce scarcity, when various buyers compete for the same small marketable surplus.

Assembling traders who bring their produce to the local marketplace also take care of the transport from the farms to the somewhat better roads that usually connect marketplaces with the outside world. They use smaller trucks, tractors and hired manpower where the bigger trucks of the middlemen would get stuck. They may also store produce brought to their house by local farmers until the middleman arrives.

Purchasing agents and assembling traders visit the farmers and inform them about the planned collection date of the produce, in order to ensure timely harvesting and, if necessary, packing. Labourers may also have to be hired to do the work. The agent bargains with farmers on behalf of the middleman about the buying price, while the assembling trader strikes his own deal. Farmers may have to be paid an advance, to make sure they do not sell their produce to another trader.

As noted, both the agents and collecting traders deliver to middlemen (though agents may also deliver to assembling traders). These middlemen are the connection between the relatively isolated production areas and the large consumer centres elsewhere in the country. On arrival in the urban centres, they generally sell their load from the back of the truck, either to distributing wholesalers who are based in the wholesale market or to retailers who come to visit this same wholesale market.

The middlemen play a vital but also a very risky role. The problems they have to face can be illustrated by looking at middlemen trading in cooking bananas between Kisii and Nairobi. The most important problem the middlemen have to face is lack of trucks for hire. Large trucks can be hired only in Nairobi, where they are in high demand. In Kisii town smaller trucks are sometimes available, but the costs are relatively high and the owners request a deposit. In Nairobi the need for a deposit is negotiable, especially when the truck owner knows the middleman from previous business. A middleman who is well known to the owner may just have to call Nairobi one week in advance and request that the truck come to Kisii on a specified day. Payment then takes place after the middlemen has arrived in Nairobi with the truck and sold the bananas. Hiring prices fluctuate seasonally, depending on the scarcity of trucks for hire, which is related to harvesting periods throughout Kenya and specific periods of high demand, such as the approach of Christmas. Instead of hiring a truck a middleman could in theory buy one. Most horticultural traders, however, lack capital for such an investment. Moreover, getting a loan from a bank is usually impossible or very costly because of the risky nature of the middleman business and the requirement of collateral.

Apart from scarcity of trucks for hire, banana middlemen also have to cope with poor road conditions in the production areas. After a shower, a truck driver may refuse to enter an area because the access road is too muddy. The middleman then has to find a smaller truck or people to carry the bunches to the large truck, and at the same time persuade the driver to stay. If the truck gets stuck, the middlemen has to look for another truck to pull it out or find people to collect stones to put under the wheels of the truck. Both alternatives will cost money, while the middleman's returns further diminish because of quality deterioration of the bananas. Once harvested, the bananas start to ripen. Once loaded, they start to heat up, and they are grilled by the sun and lashed by the rain. If the transportation process takes too long or the handling is too rough, black spots appear on the skins of the bananas which are the forerunners of rot. Eventually, the selling price of the bananas in Nairobi may drop by as much as 75 percent.

Theft is another problem to the middlemen. It may occur at any stage of the trade. First, if not supervised closely the labourers who do the loading may hide some of the harvested bunches in the bush instead of carrying them to the truck. A middleman needs at least two persons he can trust, one on the farm and one near the vehicle. Once en route, the truck may be attacked by bandits that operate between Gilgil and Naivasha in Nakuru District and target trucks that go slow while climbing the escarpment. Especially during the night, when low temperatures favour transport of perishables, the dangers of robbery are real. The bandits load the bananas into another vehicle and damage the truck. Should the middleman arrive safely in Nairobi, theft may occur in the wholesale market. The middleman agrees with a wholesaler on an average buying price per bunch or couple of bunches, after which the fruits are unloaded by labourers who are hired by the wholesaler. The bunches are counted when entering the wholesale store, and many will disappear between the truck and the store if the middleman does not supervise the process closely.

Besides theft, oversupply can also be a problem upon arrival in Nairobi. This is partly a consequence of fixed market days in the banana producing areas. Mogunga market, which is situated along the tarmac road and borders an important banana production area, operates on Sundays. Many middlemen who come to the market to buy bananas take the fruits to Nairobi. As a consequence, Nairobi regularly has an oversupply on Mondays. Whenever that happens, potential buyers are in a strong bargaining position and many refuse to pay on delivery. They may pay one week later, or even refuse to pay at all, whereupon the middleman has to find a policeman to intervene. A middleman who is not able to sell his bananas at a reasonable price in the wholesale market will sometimes take the truck to retail markets elsewhere in the capital in order to sell the bunches to retailers. This is, however, a costly and risky affair because of extra transport charges and the chance of being left with part of the load.

In summary, being a middleman is not easy. The rewards a middleman receives for taking the risks are, however, substantial, and farmers might be able to get a larger share of the cake when transporting their produce to Nairobi themselves. However, very few horticultural farmers travel to large urban markets to sell their commodities, even if such markets are located within their district. According to the household survey, in Taita 3 percent of the farmers does so, in Nyandarua 2 percent, and in Kisii and Taveta less than one percent. [5] Farmers do not like selling their produce in large towns because they do not have the confidence to deal with urban customers (either traders or consumers). This stems partly from the more sophisticated appearance of urban people. It is also related to the supposed unscrupulous bargaining methods of urban traders and to fierce competition that is thought to exist in urban market places. Most of these ideas are preconceived, which does not mean they are wholly unfounded. An often very real problem to the farmers is a language barrier, especially when the town is outside their tribal area. In a local market almost everyone speaks the local language, while in a large town farmers will be addressed in Kiswahili or English. Proficience in the trade language is essential because prices are determined through bargaining. Another problem is finding a selling spot. Market places in rural areas and small urban centres usually do not have stalls, and anyone wanting to sell produce displays her commodities on the ground. (Almost all horticultural traders in rural markets are women.) Market places in large urban centres have permanent stalls which have to be rented on a monthly basis. Only professional traders in business throughout the week can afford to pay the rent. Sometimes selling on the ground does occur, though illegal, but the traders involved know the police and pay regular bribes.

Lack of a stall should not in theory have to keep farmers from carrying their produce to town. They could also offer their entire lot for sale to professional wholesale or retail traders who are present in the urban market place. This is, however, a risky option because of the perishability of the commodities. If the farmer cannot sell her produce to traders on the day of arrival, the quality will deteriorate rapidly. Moreover, she will have to find a place to spend the night and store the produce. She will therefore be eager to sell her produce immediately upon arrival and return home. Urban traders know this, and when a farmer offers produce for sale they will use the time factor in the bargaining process.

Farmers might organize themselves into a marketing cooperative to increase their bargaining position, bringing their produce to town and presenting it to urban traders as a group. This is rarely done, however. The Kenyan cooperative movement has acquired a negative image due to financial and organizational mismanagement, and farmers are now reluctant to participate in any new initiative.

The vast majority of the horticultural farmers choose to sell their commodities either at the farm or in a local market place. Selling at the farm may also imply selling along a road near the farm, because many farms are not accessible to vehicles. The local market place may be located either in the rural area or in a small urban centre. The latter is not as urban as suggested because a population centre is called urban in Kenya when it has over 2,000 inhabitants. Both in rural areas and small urban areas, markets are periodic, and selling on the ground is allowed. For that matter, the market places are often poorly developed, and many of them change into a large mud pool after a heavy shower. Middlemen buy their commodities in these periodic markets and near the farms (see Dijkstra, 1997).

Most of the horticultural farmers depend on the middlemen, not only for selling their produce but also for up-to-date information on prices and on supply and demand conditions on the urban markets. A potential source of independent price information to the farmers is the radio. A few times a week the Kenyan Broadcasting Corporation, in collaboration with the Ministry of Agriculture, broadcasts commodity prices, data which have been collected in major urban wholesale markets like Nairobi and Mombasa. Although these prices give only a rough idea what farm-gate prices to expect, they are supposed to improve farmers' bargaining position in dealing with middlemen. Unfortunately, fewer than 5 percent of the horticultural farmers listened to the broadcasts at the time of the survey. First, a radio or money to buy batteries was often lacking. Second, if farmers had a working radio they usually listened only to their regional station that broadcasts in the local language, whereas the price reviews were on the national network in Kiswahili.

Lack of independent market information is a potential disadvantage, as it allows traders to manipulate buying prices at the expense of the producers. The situation is particularly risky for farmers in less accessible production areas, as on the higher slopes of the Aberdares (Nyandarua) and the Taita Hills. Due to high precipitation and the absence of all-weather roads, these areas were often difficult to reach at the time of our survey, and a limited number of middlemen tried their luck irregularly. These middlemen could theoretically agree on a kind of price cartel that would artificially lower farm-gate prices. It must be noted that such cartels were not found by our survey, but conditions were favourable for them.

Poor access unfavourably affected the prices paid to the farmers. Middlemen's transport costs are passed on to the farmers and reflect things like their truck getting stuck in the mud. Any delay would inevitably lead to high physical losses due to the perishability of the commodities. Losses further increased because many traders used substandard packing materials. Transportation of tomatoes by basket, cabbages by gunny sack, and bananas by unprotected bunch is far from ideal. Improper packaging did not arise from traders' ignorance, but from the scarcity and high costs of suitable packing materials such as wooden boxes and cartons in the production areas. In the end, farmers suffered most, as middlemen lowered buying prices in accordance with expected produce losses.

Conclusions

Smallholder horticulture in Kenya has evolved gradually over recent decades. In the first half of the 1990s, it had become the most vital source of cash revenues on the farm in the survey areas. Not only prosperous households and farmers located near all-weather roads, but also poorer households and farmers living at more isolated locations, had embarked on the enterprise. Horticulture had brought rising incomes to broad sections of the rural population and diversification within the agricultural sector - two key aspects of rural development.

Continued growth in Kenya's urban population will lead to a further rise in the demand for horticultural commodities. Market prospects are good, and commercial horticulture is expected to be a key source of income for the surveyed households in the years to come. The sustainability of the horticultural enterprise is, however, threatened from within. The rise of commercial horticulture initially led to diversification in the agricultural sector. When it proved profitable, farmers started to forget other agricultural crops. This is not necessarily a problem, since horticultural crops are extremely varied in nature. However, farmers tend to limit themselves to a few horticultural commodities, making their farming as poorly diversified and as vulnerable as before. It is vulnerable at the production stage due to pests, diseases and input problems, and at the marketing stage because of lack of market information and dependency on middlemen.

Middlemen play a crucial role when it comes to marketing horticultural commodities and most farmers cannot do without them. The traders perform well within an often hostile market environment. The constraints they have to face involve a poor infrastructure, poorly developed market places, scarcity of transport means, theft, lack of capital, and produce losses due to scarcity and high costs of suitable packing materials.

Notes

1   For a discussion on Kenyan producers and traders of horticultural export commodities see Jaffee (1987) and Dijkstra and Magori (1995b).

2   The sample sizes were: Nyandarua 229, Kisii 144 and Taita 87 households.

3   For the present article, beans are not regarded as a horticultural commodity, with the exception of those that are eaten fresh (e.g., French beans). Most types of beans are dried before being stored or sold, in contrast to other

vegetables that are usually traded and consumed fresh. Dried beans, like maize, encounter other marketing problems than fresh produce because of their lower perishability.

4   In addition to the household surveys, trader surveys were carried out in the research areas. Horticultural traders were interviewed while buying in the production areas and selling in rural and urban markets. In total, approximately 800 traders were interviewed.

5   According to the definition of the Kenya Central Bureau of Statistics, a large urban centre has over 10,000 inhabitants.

References

Dijkstra, T. (1990), *Marketing Policies and Economic Interests in the Cotton Sector of Kenya.* ASC Research Report No. 40, Leiden: African Studies Centre.

Dijkstra, T. (1997), *Trading the Fruits of the Land: Horticultural Marketing Channels in Kenya,* Aldershot: Ashgate.

Dijkstra, T. and Magori, T.D. (1991), *Horticultural Production and Marketing in Kenya Part 1: Introduction, Research Objectives and Methodology,* Food and Nutrition Studies Programme Report No. 41, Nairobi: Ministry of Planning and National Development, Leiden: African Studies Centre.

Dijkstra, T. and Magori, T.D. (1992a), *Horticultural Production and Marketing in Kenya Part 2A: Horticultural Production in Nyandarua District,* Food and Nutrition Studies Programme Report No. 47, Nairobi: Ministry of Planning and National Development, Leiden: African Studies Centre.

Dijkstra, T. and Magori, T.D. (1992b), *Horticultural Production and Marketing in Kenya Part 2B: Horticultural Marketing in Nyandarua District,* Food and Nutrition Studies Programme Report No. 48, Nairobi: Ministry of Planning and National Development, Leiden: African Studies Centre.

Dijkstra, T. and Magori, T.D. (1994a), *Horticultural Production and Marketing in Kenya Part 3: Taita Taveta District,* Food and Nutrition Studies Programme Report No. 51, Nairobi: Ministry of Planning and National Development, Leiden: African Studies Centre.

Dijkstra, T. and Magori, T.D. (1994b), *Horticultural Production and Marketing in Kenya Part 4: Kisii & Nyamira,* District Food and Nutrition Studies Programme Report No. 52, Nairobi: Ministry of Planning and National Development, Leiden: African Studies Centre.

Dijkstra, T. and Magori, T.D. (eds) (1995a), *Horticultural Production and Marketing in Kenya , Part 5: Proceedings of a Dissemination Seminar at*

Nairobi, 16-17th November 1994, Food and Nutrition Studies Programme Report No. 53, Nairobi: Ministry of Planning and National Development, Leiden: African Studies Centre.

Dijkstra, T. and Magori, T.D. (1995b), 'Flowers and French Beans from Kenya: A story of export success', in: S. Ellis and Y. Faur (eds), *Entreprises et Entrepreneurs Africains,* Paris: Karthala, Orstom, pp. 435-444.

HCDA (1990), *Horticultural Development and Marketing Policy Guidelines,* Nairobi: Horticultural Crops Development Authority.

Jätzold, R. and Schmidt, H. (1983), *Farm Management Handbook of Kenya.* Vol. 2: *Natural Conditions and Farm Management Information (Part A: West Kenya, Part B: Central Kenya, Part C: East Kenya).* Nairobi: Ministry of Agriculture.

Jaffee, S. (1987), 'Case Studies of Contract Farming in the Horticultural Sector of Kenya', IDA Paper No. 83, Binghampton, NY: Institute of Development Anthropology.

Kenya CBS (1994), *Kenya Population Census 1989,* Vols. 1 and 2, Nairobi: Central Bureau of Statistics.

4 The STOAS Mutual Fitting Approach - Developing Horticultural Gardens in Cities: The Dar-es-Salaam Project

GEORGE G.D. LULANDALA

STOAS (Foundation for the development of Agriculture, Education, and Training) Agriprojects Foundation believes that knowledge (head) and skills (hands and legs) alone are not enough to strengthen horticulture projects in Africa. Attitude and commitment are needed to apply the two

Introduction: Urban Poverty in Africa

Acute urban problems risk spiralling out of control if the current African continental trend toward higher unemployment and underemployment is not reversed. Unemployment is the main cause of urban poverty. Urban poverty, characterized by the deterioration of living and working conditions, overcrowding, the spread of disease, crime and malnutrition, is increasingly prevalent. Although the creation of jobs and protection is not the sole means of alleviating the urban crisis, it is the most direct and effective means available. A relatively low cost way of achieving this is by investing in horticultural gardens in the urban and peri-urban informal sector. This, along with the many related secondary and tertiary activities which accompany agricultural production sector (such as small-scale peddling, petty trading, unregistered backyard food factories), can eliminate much of the unemployment and underemployment, and at the same time help to solve nutritional problems. The principal Secretary of the Ministry of Agriculture estimates that, if well planned programmes are implemented, horticulture is capable of employing up to 60 percent of the urban labour force.

The Dar-es-Salaam: Resources and the Agricultural System

Dar-es-Salaam Region in Tanzania covers an area of about 1,393 sq. kilometres and has a population of 2.8 million, which is increasing at a rate of about 5.8 percent per annum. Dar-es-Salaam has tropical coastal weather, with a mean annual temperature of 26°C (79°F) and an average relative humidity of 81.5 percent. The rainfall climatograph belongs to the bimodal model. The short rains start in October and last until December, while long rains last from March to May. Dry periods are usually experienced between June and October.

The Coastal Zone is suitable for growing tropical fruits, vegetables, and ornamental flowers depending on the availability of water. Soil types and rainfall regimes determine the potential land-use patterns of specific areas.

Dar-es-Salaam's soils are varied in nature, but they can nevertheless be classified into the following four broad categories: 1. fertile soils, but with low potential due to shallow rooting depth; 2. soils of low fertility but with moderate potential; 3. soils of low to medium fertility with moderate, potential, occurring mostly in the west and south of Dar-es-Salaam; 4. various alluvial and colluvial soils of considerable agricultural potential but requiring special management (e.g. flood control and drainage).

Soil characteristics, coupled with good climatic conditions, make Dar-es-Salaam a location endowed with a high potential for the production of a wide range of fruits, vegetables, ornamental flowers, and tree planting (Table 4.1). Thus, the nutritive importance of fruits and vegetables for the city residents need not be over-emphasised. These crops are excellent sources of vitamins A and C; iron; calcium; and protein (Manyafu, 1971; Oomen and Grubben, 1978)

Tables 4.2 and 4.3 indicate the nutritional values of the various vegetables and fruits commonly grown in Tanzania while Table 4.4 shows the reasons for growers or producers to engage in fruits and vegetable production in Dar-es-Salaam City.

The population influx into Dar-es-Salaam City, Tanzania, as well as the unusually high growth rate, is threatening food security. It results in heightening competition over the relatively small number of added jobs, and depresses the residents' incomes and the nutritional level. Consequently, the health of the majority of people, especially that of the children and women are badly affected. The large, and rising, population puts an high demand on the finite resources, and the disadvantaged groups (youth and women) become more marginalized.

Table 4.1a   Horticultural Production Potential in Dar-es-Salaam City Vegetables - Area (hectares) and Quantity (tons)

Crop	1989	/90	1990	/91	1991	/92	1992	/93	93	/94	Potential Yiald Tons/ha
	Ha	Tons	Ha	Tons	Ha	Tons	Ha	Tons	Ha	Ton	Potential Yiald Tons/ha
1. Tomatoes	812	3860	832	4190	855	4475	612	3060	368	1840	15.0
2. Fresh Pulses	350	1023.3	470	1296	570	1596	440	1320	310	2730	3.0
3. Okra	642.8	1194.2	654	1290	679	1510	478	956	277	154	7.0
4.Chin. Cabbage	10	200	8	160	10	200	10	200	-	-	20.0
5. Eggplant	10	300	12	360	12	360	12	300	11	270	25.0
6. Amarathus	16	160	16	160	18	185	20	300	20	300	15.0
7 Sweet and Hot Pepper	-	-	-	-	10	50	32	160	57	285	5.0
8. Onions	-	-	-	-	4	40	5	50	5	50	10.0
9. Cucumber (Matango)	-	-	-	-	7	70	9	225	10	100	15.0
10 Water melon	-	-	-	-	8	180	9	360	10	200	20.0

Table 4.1b Horticultural Production Potential in Dar-es-Salaam City Fruits - Area (hectares) and Quantity (tons)

Crop	1989/ Ha	1990 Tons	1990/ Ha	1991 Tons	1991/ Ha	1992 Tons	1992/ Ha	1993 Tons	1993/ Ha	1994 Tons	Potential Yield Tons/ha
1. Citrus	687	10016	580	8750	620	7300	5995	26980	579	26055	4.0
2. Pineapple	804	15085	194	3880	662	12390	1317	10536	655	5240	12.0
3. Banana	1081	12586	1694	13628	1657	1324	830	16600	537	9960	20.0
4. Pawpaw	-	-	-	-	120	480	80	320	52	260	5.0

The resulting environmental degradation has to be reconciled with the need for food security, but in the long run it reduces the quantity of the food supply.

Table 4.2   Nutritive Values of Common Indigenous Leafy Vegetables (100 gm Fresh Weight of Edible Portion)

Vegetable	Protein gm	Ca gm	Fe gm	B-Carotene gm	Vit. C gm
Amaranthus sp	5.0	410	8.9	5,716	50
Manihot utilissima	6.1	300	7.6	14,437	310
Cucurbita pepo	3.0	475	0.8	8,375	80
Ipomoea batatus	3.2	160	6.2	2,700	70
Vigna unguiculata	5.7	255	5.7	7,616	56
Gynandropsis gynandra	6.1	-	-	15,916	-
Corchurus olitorium	5.6	270	7.7	8,750	55
Solanum nigrum	5.6	215	4.2	7,625	30
Launae cornuta	4.6	130	3.1	1,430	-

Sources: Manyafu (1981); Oomen and Grubben (1978).

Despite the fact that the city has an enormous potential for developing horticultural crops, the performance of the horticultural sub-sector has been disappointingly poor. It must be recognized that local horticultural production is critical for the overall city development, for its macro-economic stability, its food security, job creation, and poverty alleviation.

The status of horticultural production in Dar-es-Salaam has been constrained by the following factors:

a   lack of sufficient inputs - this includes the amount and quality of planting materials, fertilizers, and pesticides;
b   inadequate research findings, caused a shortage of technical packages;
c   financial constraints;
d   lack of suitable, high yielding crops and disease resistant varieties or species;
e   inadequate quantity of recommended fruits and vegetable seedlings to meet

the farmers' demand;
f   lack of an organized marketing system for horticultural produce;
g   low ranking of horticultural crops, relative to other field crops in the peri-
     urban areas;
h   high perishability and unimproved harvest handling techniques.

**Table 4.3   Selected Mineral Content in Fruits
(Fresh Weight Basis, 100gm of Edible Portion)**

Fruit	Frotein gm	Ca gm	Fe gm	B-Carotene gm	Vit.C gm
Mango	0.6	25	1.2	2,200	42
Papaya	0.4	21	0.6	950	52
Guava	1.1	24	1.3	290	326
Oranges	0.8	38	1.1	230	46
Cape Gooseberry	1.9	9	1.0	430	11
Avocado	1.4	19	1.4	530	18
Banana	-	9	1.4	120	9

Source: Manyafu (1971) ; Latham (1979).

Table 4.4   Reasons for Engaging in Fruit/Vegetable Production (%)

Reason	Households			Open Spaces		Peri -Urban		
	DSM	Dod.	Ars.	DSM	Ars.	DSM	Dod.	Ars.
Reduce Food Exp	50.0	38.0	50.0	4.8	8.3	14.7	0.0	4.2
Income/Employ	51.4	60.0	62.0	87.1	92.0	91.2	92.0	95.8
Background	5.4	4.0	2.0	19.0	4.2	17.6	16.0	0.0
Home Consump	64.9	70.0	62.0	24.2	75.0	44.1	60.0	45.8
Exercise/hobby	6.8	12.0	20.0	3.2	12.5	5.9	0.0	4.2
Other	5.4	0.0	4.0	0.0	0.0	0.0	0.0	0.0
Total Number	74.0	50.0	50.0	62.0	24.0	34.0	25.0	24.0

Note: Since a respondent can give more than one answer, percentages do not add up to
100 percent (*Key:* Dod. = Dodoma   Ars. = Arusha   DSM = Dar-es-Salaam}.

Source: Kinabo and Nyange (1994).

i   lack of transport for peri-urban producers/growers;
j   lack of storage facilities.

One of the effective and immediate strategies to increase the supply of vegetables and fruits in Dar-es-Salaam is to improve and expand intra and peri-urban community based horticultural crops production areas.

The Dar-es-Salaam Project : Main Objectives

The overall objective of this project is to increase production of vegetables, fruits, flowers, and tree seedlings, to satisfy the city's demand. This is expected to help to improve the economic and nutritional status of Dar-es-Salaam residents, and create new jobs especially for the youth and the women. The specific objectives of this project include:

1   improving the nutritional status of the Dar-es-Salaam residents through increased availability of vegetables and fruits;
2   training and helping farmers raise productivity in limited land areas of Dar-es-Salaam without damaging the environment;
3   promoting production and use of local (traditional) vegetables and fruits, including the creation of awareness of producers and consumers to the nutritional values and adaptation to local environments;
4   encouraging women to participate actively in vegetable, fruit, flower, and tree production, utilisation, and training;
5   creating awareness of the traditional ways of preserving vegetables, without sacrificing the nutritional values, so as to improve availability during off-season periods;
6   helping able bodied people of Dar-es-Salaam raise their incomes through horticultural employment opportunities and sales;
7   promoting the growing of non-traditional crops and flowers so as to diversify horticultural production and income sources through local and international markets;
8   improving the environment through tree planting;
     improving marketing skills, so as to promote production and sale of vegetables, fruits and flowers;
10   providing good quality fruit, seeds, and other planting materials for crops such as coconut, mango, citrus, banana or pineapple.

Target Groups

This project is serving five target groups: individual growers, community-based groups, non-governmental organizations, the private sector, and the city council's gardens. The five gardens are being used for production, demonstration, and training. To assure sustainability, the project gardens have separate bank accounts and their revenues are ploughed back into the project. Local communities, private sectors, women groups, youth groups, community based NGOs, schools, colleges, and religious groups involved in gardening and nutrition are full participant fully in this project.

Description of the Project Management and Structure: Mutual Fitting

The project management approach outlined in Figure 4.1 below is geared towards eliminating unnecessary bureaucracy which would otherwise delay decision making. The approach to the project management is that of involving a mutual fitting principle. Each beneficiary and stakeholder is fully involved in decision making, development, execution, and management, as guided by STOAS Agriprojects Foundation. Beneficiary and stakeholder needs, concerns, and perceptions are reviewed from time to time through the project management and horticultural gardens development committees.

This approach has strengthened stakeholder linkages and has assured a common procedure of achieving a common aim. It has also strengthened teamwork and cooperation at the steering, coordination, monitoring, and development levels. The management structure has initiated an attitude of commitment and accountability at the funding, managerial, execution, and development levels.

Above all, the project management structure is supporting an established and a well defined 'local management structure' to assure mutual fitting and sustainability. All project players are responsible for what goes on in the project, but the execution task is fully assigned to STOAS Agriprojects Foundation in order to effectively initiate and assure change. The project has six major components:

1   Horticultural Technical Services and Networking
2   Production and Marketing
3   Training
4   Input suppliers
5   Pilot Gardens and Input Centres

6   Establishing a local management team to take over the project

The Project's Monitoring and Evaluation

This is a systematic process of judging the project effectiveness trend according to definite steps and purposes. Internally, the project is continuously monitored and evaluated by the project management committee using Bennett's model. This model is preferred because it can also be used for planning, implementation, and evaluation (project development). Also, this approach helps those involved to overcome the anxiety and fear which usually accompany evaluation. It takes into consideration stakeholder needs, apprehensions, and concerns, in order to reduce uneasiness. The approach is well focused and specific. The internal monitoring and evaluation is, therefore being carried out by using the following steps:

1   input;
2   activities;
3   growers/Community/Groups Involvement;
4   reactions of Target groups;
5   KASA change;
6   practice change;
7   project Results and Utilization

For the purposes of the funding agencies, two project monitoring and evaluation exercises are undertaken during the two year project period. These include:

a   internal monitoring and evaluation (mini-evaluation after one year),
b   external monitoring and evaluation (impact assessment to answer
     the question, 'Has the project made any difference to the lives and
     incomes of growers and consumers of horticultural crops in Dar-Es-
     Salaam city'). The project objectives are measured closely during the
     monitoring and evaluation processes.

For the purposes of the funding agencies, two project monitoring and evaluation exercises are undertaken during the two year project period. These include internal monitoring and evaluation (mini-evaluation after one year) and external monitoring and evaluation (impact assessment to answer the question: 'Has the project made any difference to the lives and incomes of growers and consumers of horticultural crops in Dar-es-Salaam city').

The project objectives will be measured closely during the monitoring and evaluation processes.

The mini-evaluation which is undertaken after one year is performed by two members of the project management committee. The final evaluation (impact assessment) is done by a local non-governmental organization (external evaluation). It is selected by NIGP/STOAS through newspaper advertisements and bidding.

The first evaluation takes one week and the second evaluation take two weeks. The internal evaluation concentrates on production which reflects funds expenditure and field operations. It is, thus, more than just an auditing work. The evaluation reports are be presented to the Project Steering Committee through round table reporting and are then circulated by means of a written document. The project steering committee has to approve the strategies recommended for utilizing the results of the evaluation. This is important in order to avoid abandoning the report on the shelves.

Sustainability

Sustainability is the single most important factor if the project is to survive on a long term basis. Commitment, responsibility, action, tangible outcome, and a sense of local ownership are essential to the sustainable development of the project. Eventually the project has to be able to continue the activities on its own without the support of NIGP/STOAS.

The sustainability of this project will be determined by its ability to continue on its own both at the managerial and grass root levels, after NIGP/STOAS pulls out. It should be able to meet production costs and make profit from its own revenue.

Summary

The main essentail features of the project are:

- The management structure supports a local structure (mutual fitting)
- The five pilot gardens have separate bank accounts and their revenues are being ploughed back into the gardens
- The project is being coordinated by a Project Development Coordinator from the City Council of Dar-es-Salaam. When NIGP/STOAS pull out, the title of the Project Development Coordinator will change to

Programme Coordinator

- The project will change to a 'programme' after NIGP/STOAS pull out
- The project management is promoting an early sense of project ownership and hence creating a potential for long term project sustainability
- The project management is pinpointing an efficient marketing system.
- The project is utilizing locally available resources
- Development of *'attitude'* and *'commitment'* towards horticultural development is a priority
- Inputs are available on time
- Using environmentally sound horticultural practices
- Posters are being printed to publicise the benefits of the project.

The Expected Benefits of the Project are:

- Creation of jobs
- Increased productivity
- Increased income through sales
- The city gardens are productive
- City-residents improve their health
- The city council is earning more money
- Increased vegetable, fruits, and flower export
- The government is earning more foreign money
- Livestock keepers have readily available market for their farmyard manure
- The project involves directly the disadvantaged groups
  (youth and women)
- The project has an efficient marketing system
- Growers are being equipped with knowledge and skills regarding production, marketing, utilization, and environmental planning
- Greening of Dar-es-Salaam City.

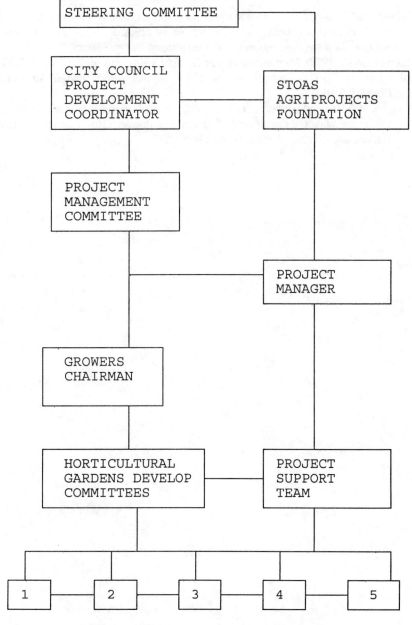

Figure 4.1   Mutual Fitting: Project Development and Management Structure   Key: 1, 2, 3, 4, 5 - Project Pilot Gardens

References

Kinabo and Nyange (1994), *Urban Horticulture in Tanzania, A Situation Analysis of the Production, Marketing, and Consumption of Fruits and vegetables in Dar-es-Salaam, Dodoma, and Arusha,*   Research study, Dar-es-Salaam.

Latham, M.C. (1979), *Human Nutrition in Tropical Africa,* 2nd edition, Rome: FAO.

Manyafu, J.L. (1971), *Indigenous vegetables,* Annual report, Ilonga Agriculture Research Station.

Oomen, H.A.P.C. and Grubben, G.J.H. (1978), *Tropical vegetable in human nutrition,* Comm.unication 69. Department of Agricultural Research Roy Tropical Institute, Willemstad, Curacao: Amst & Orphan Pub.

5 Urban Agriculture, Production and Marketing: The Tanzania Experience

MALONGO R.S. MLOZI

Introduction

Tanzania has an area of 945,087 km^2 and a population of 26 million people. Its rate of growth is about 3 percent per year. The urbanization rate is 3 percent. About 67 percent of the population still lives in rural areas and provides 85 percent of the labour force. The rural inhabitants mostly practice subsistence agriculture. Even in Tanzania's towns most people engage in some agriculture (Mosha, 1991; Sawio, 1993; Stevenson et al., 1994; Mlozi, 1995). Urban farming is, in fact, a widespread phenomenon in developing countries (Sanyal, 1985; Kleer, 1987; Tricaud, 1987; Yeung, 1988; Freeman, 1991; Drakakis-Smith, 1992; Maxwell and Zziwa, 1992; IDRC, 1994; May and Rogerson, 1995). Most researchers agree that people undertake it to produce their own food and earn some extra income.

This paper presents research findings of an urban agriculture project conducted in five towns in Tanzania. The organization of this paper is as follows: First, the introduction which explains the background to the project. The next section provides the main reasons for the persistence of markets for agricultural products within the subsistence economy. The third section offers a brief discussion of the market flow of agricultural products. This is followed by a section on the methods used for this study. The fifth section discusses the results of the study and the sixth provides the conclusions and policy implications.

The Persistence of Markets for Agricultural Products

Traditionally, people in towns have depended on rural areas for their food needs.

79

Today this is not the case as some towns meet specific food needs from within their environment. A case in point is the city of Dar-es-Salaam that produces most of its eggs and broiler meat. For example, Mosha (1991) estimated that the city produced 90 percent of the common leafy African spinach. Not all food production within cities is subsistence; much is grown for commercial sale within the informal and formal sector (Drakakis-Smith, 1992: 259). In Tanzania, the existence of markets for agricultural products in the country's towns is based on socioeconomic and political factors inherent in the country's milieu. These factors manifest themselves at four levels: the government, the Ministry of Agriculture, the city councils, and individuals. For example, at the government level is the basic economic crisis of the country that has eroded the real income of the people living in towns (Maliyamkono and Bagachwa, 1990; Bukuku, 1993; Mans, 1994; World Bank, 1995).

Marketing of Agricultural Products

In Tanzania's towns, urban agricultural products come from two sources: from livestock and crop enterprises. In the towns, the marketing of agricultural products is mainly based on several factors. There are deliberate government policies that encourage people to produce their own food and pay for it from their own income. Some people opt to sell agricultural products after they have failed to obtain employment in the withering formal sector. Others, who come from the rural-urban migrant sector, fail to get more desirable urban jobs. Consequently, many of them find their livelihood by engaging in food selling, e.g., by hawking cooked food and by running food-eating places that use agricultural products. The growth of hotels, restaurants, formal and informal food catering services in the towns have created a market for agricultural products. The presence of various government institutions such as hospitals, schools, army barracks, and colleges have all created a growing demand for agricultural products. The annual increase of the urban population has also created demands for several agricultural products. Certain agricultural products (eggs, milk, vegetables) from within the towns are cheaper than those produced in distant areas, because of the added transportation costs.

In Tanzania, there are two sources of agricultural products which are sold in the urban markets. First, agricultural products come from household compounds of all socio-economic classes. In the city of Dar-es-Salaam and Dodoma, Stevenson et al. (1994) found that people sold 34 percent of the vegetables from their household compounds. Most agricultural products from the household compound reach the markets and the consumers through four kinds of business-people: wholesalers, retailers, hawkers, and vendors (Figure 5.1). The hawkers and vendors usually sell their agricultural products directly to the consumers (Stevenson et al., 1994; Drakakis-Smith, 1992; Jones-Dube, 1992; Rasmussen, 1992). The elite agriculturalists, on the other hand tend to sell their products (milk, eggs and broiler meat) to tourist hotels and government institutions. Other agriculturalists in medium and low quality housing areas sell their products in the open markets, to food-eating places, to food-cooking hawkers (*Mama nitilie, youth*), and directly to the consumers.

The second source of agricultural products is the gardens, plots, and various open spaces that are not part of the urban dwellers' household compounds. In these areas, common products include African spinach, tomatoes, cabbage, onions, eggplants and green peppers. The growers then sell these products to four intermediary traders: wholesalers, retailers, hawkers and vendors. The two latter groups are the majority (Figure 5.1). Producers in the open spaces of Dar-es-Salaam sell 85 percent of the vegetables that they grow (Stevenson et al., 1994, p. 40). Some agriculturalists in these areas also sell their products in the open markets directly to consumers, or to retailers, restaurants, food eating places, cooked-food hawkers, and vendors. Most farmers in these areas are people of low socio-economic status (SES) who live in low quality, high density, housing. In Tanzania's towns, the amounts of retailing, wholesaling, or contract selling of agricultural products depend not only on the size of the town, but also on the size and the type of the agriculture enterprise. Other important factors are the availability of infrastructure and capital, and the SES of the operators.

Methodology

The Urban Agriculture Project at Sokoine University of Agriculture started in 1986 and was active until 1991. It investigated the nature and the origin of food production activities within the urban centres and their peripheries in Tanzania. The research covered the following six towns: Dar-es-Salaam, Dodoma, Mbeya, Morogoro, Kilosa and Makambako (Figure 5.2).

The original sample size was 1820 (Dar-es-Salaam, 700, Mbeya, 320, Dodoma, and Morogoro, 300 each, and Kilosa and Makambako, 100 each). However, 65 questionnaires had to be discarded because of incomplete, responses, or for other deficiencies. The final sample consited, therefore, of 1755 respondents.

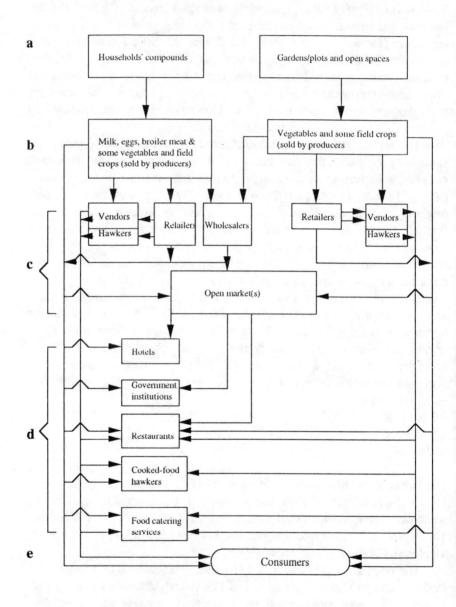

Figure 5.1   The Flow of Urban Agricultural Products to the Markets and the Consumers

a - Source; b - Producers; c - Distributors; d - Processors; e - Consumers

The researchers selected respondents by means of disproportional stratified sampling as described by Blalock (1972), Babbie (1990) and Henry (1990), on the basis of low and high densities in their areas.

Within the low and high density areas, the selected respondents included political and non-political leaders, and farmers and non-farmers. Females were also included, but they comprised only about 26 percent of the total (Table 5.1). To improve the research exercise, researchers selected agriculture or livestock extension workers in each town and trained them to interview and fill in questionnaires that they comprehensively filled during each respondents' interview process. Quantitative data were analysed at Sokoine University of Agriculture using the SPSS to obtain descriptive statistics.

Table 5.1 Sampling Ratios

Criterion	Ratio
High/Low density	5:1
Farmers/Non-farmers	2:1
Non-political leaders/political leader	3:1
Men/Women	4:1

The Findings of the Marketing Survey

Of 1,755 respondents who practiced urban agriculture, 74 percent (1302 respondents) were males (see Table 5.2). This was because of the high ratio of males in the sampling procedure (Table 5.1). Of 1,755 respondents, 73 percent (1,218) lived in low quality housing areas (high density or small plots).

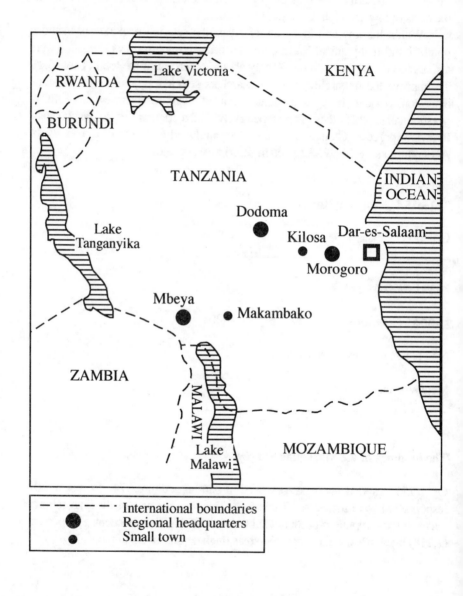

Figure 5.2   The Location of the Surveyed Towns in the Study of Urban Agriculture

In these crowded areas respondents raised a small number of livestock (cattle, chicken, goats) and cultivated small plots of selected vegetables and field crops. However, it was found that of the 1755 respondents, 57 percent (999 respondents) reported that they raised livestock in their household compounds (Table 5.3). Of them, i.e., the respondents with livestock, about 54.4 percent (543) said that they both sold and consumed livestock products (milk, eggs, broiler meat). The others, 37.6 percent of the 999 (376) said that they used their livestock products for household use only (Table 5.3). This implied that most people in the five towns raised livestock primarily to meet their own food needs. This   is quite common among many other agriculturalists living in the low quality housing areas.

**Table 5.2   Characteristics of Respondents - by Gender and Town
(n=1755)**

Gender		D'Sal -aam	Dodo- ma	Mbeya	Moro -goro	Kilo -sa	Maka -mba- ko	Total
Male	%	38.3	15.4	17.4	17.7	5.1	6.1	100
	No.	(499)	(201)	(227)	(230)	(66)	(79)	(1302)
Female	%	39.5	15.8	17.8	15.2	7.0	4.4	100
	No.	(179)	(72)	(81)	(69)	(32)	(20)	(453)
Total		(678)	(273)	(308)	(299)	(98)	(99)	(1755)

Source: (for this and subsequent tables) Survey data.

Another survey, which was concerned with the mode of marketing, found that of the 1755 respondents, 36.6 percent (642 respondents) said that they sold their livestock products through the retailing channel (Table 5.4). This study also found that most agriculturalists sold directly to customers when the latter came to their homes to buy the products, especially when they bought in small quantities. Some livestock keepers sold their products in the open markets only when the products were abundant. For example, only 520 livestock raisers (about 30 percent of all the respondents) said that selling livestock products in the open market was the more profitable method. The study also found that the elite agriculturalists commonly used wholesalers and contract selling for marketing products such as milk, eggs and broiler meat. Some of them sold these products to the tourist hotels, schools, hospitals, and private restaurants. However, this was a small group. Of the

1755, only 101 interviewees (6.8 percent) sold their livestock products on contracts to hotels. This practice was more common in the city of Dar-es-Salaam than in the smaller towns (Table 5.4).

Table 5.3   Use of Livestock Products - by Town (n=999) *

D'Sal	Dod	Mbe	Mor	Kilo	M' mb	Total
40.7	13.1	20.8	16.6	1.8	7.0	100.0
(221)	(71)	(113)	(90)	(10)	(38)	(543)
26.6	18.1	17.8	19.1	6.2	12.2	100.01
(100)	(68)	(67)	(72)	(23)	(46)	(376)
42.5	2.5	23.8	28.7	0.0	2.5	100.0
(34)	(2)	(19)	(23)	(0)	(2)	(80)
(355)	(141)	(199)	(185)	(33)	(86)	(999)

* In this and the subsequent tables the following codes are used: D'Sal = Dar-es-Salaam; Dod = Dodoma; Mbe = Mbeya; Kilo = Kilosa; M'mb = Makambako.

Table 5.4   Ways of Selling Livestock Products - by Town (n=642)

Ways		D'Sal	Dod	Mbe	Mor	Kilo	M'mb	Total
Retailing	%	39.3		14.2	19.7	1.0	8.1	00.0
	No.	(116)		(42)	(58)	(3)	(24)	(295)
Open market	%	74.4		6.8	10.5	2.3	1.5	100.0
	No.	(99)		(9)	(14)	(3)	(2)	(133)
Wholesaling	%	30.8		38.3	16.7	1.7	8.3	100.0
	No.	(37)		(46)	(20)	(2)	(10)	(120)
Contracting	%	50.0		33.3	3.7	0.0	7.4	100.0
	No.	(27)		(18)	(2)	(0)	(4)	(54)
Ret & whol*	%	20.0		42.5	7.5	5.0	0.0	100.0
	No.	(8)		(17)	(3)	(2)	(0)	
Total		(287)	(76)	(132)	(97)	(10)	(40)	(642)

* Retailing and wholesaling (see note for Table 5.3).

Our research has revealed that 470 of the respondents (26.8 percent) indicated that they did not use the contract system to sell their products because the total amount they had was too small, and they could not meet the threshold quantities required for using this system (Table 5.5). One of the main problems was that the livestock growers had no marketing organization of their own for selling livestock products. Such a system could have overcome at least some of the shortcomings they faced. The massive failure of the cooperative drive which was sponsored by the Tanzanian government may account for the low incentive for cooperation.

Table 5.5   Reasons for no Contract Selling of Products, by Town (n=470)

Reason		D'Sal	Dod	Mbe	Mor	Kilo	M'mb	Total
Small prod.	%	34.6	8.7	15.6	25.7	2.8	12.6	100.0
	No.	(124)	(31)	(56)	(92)	(10)	(45)	(358)
Avail. mkts	%	52.4	14.3	23.8	1.6	0.0	7.9	100.0
	No.	(33)	(9)	(15)	(1)	(0)	(5)	(62)
Low prices	%	50.0	15.6	18.8	15.6	0.0	0.0	100.0
	No.	(16)	(5)	(6)	(5)	(0)	(0)	(32)
Transport	%	57.1	0.0	42.9	0.0	0.0	0.0	100.0
	No.	(8)	(0)	(6)	(0)	(0)	(0)	(14)
Delay pay	%	33.3	33.3	33.3	0.0	0.0	0.0	100.0
	No.	(1)	(1)	(1)	(0)	(0)	(0)	(3)
Total		(182)	(36)	(84)	(98)	(10)	(50)	(470)

* Small prod. = small producers; Avail. makts = availability of markets (see note for Table 5.3).

Table 5.6   Where Agricultural Products are Sold, by Town   (n=730)

Where sold		D'Sa	Dodo	Mbe	Moro	Kilo	M'mb	Total
Bus/people*	%	45.2	11.6	20.0	16.7	1.1	5.4	100.0
	No.	(294)	(76)	(130)	(109)	(7)	(35)	(651)
Cooperative	%	10.5	1.8	48.2	31.6	3.5	3.5	100.0
	No.	(6)	(1)	(28)	(18)	(2)	(2)	(57)
Others	%	0.0	27.3	18.2	45.5	0.0	9.0	100.0
	No.	(0)	(6)	(4)	(10)	(0)	(2)	(22)
Total		(300)	(83)	(162)	(137)	(9)	(39)	(730)

* business people (see note for Table 5.3).

Of the 1755 respondents (730, i.e., 41.6 percent) said that they sold their livestock products to business-people (Table 5.6). The study found that this was so because business-people paid cash money in advance. Most livestock keepers used this cash to buy other enterprise inputs (feed, medications, forage).

From tthe answers provided by some respondents, (457, or about 35 percent) it can be concluded that many growers were quite satisfied with the markets for their agricultural products in the towns. This includes the formal as well as the informal ones. However, our findings clearly indicate that the majority of the growers found the marketing system unsatisfactory (Table 5.7).

Table 5.7   Satisfaction with Markets for Agricultural Products, by Town (n=619)

		D'Sal	Dod	Mbe	Mor	Kilo	M'mb	Total
Yes	%	46.4	13.3	19.3	15.1	1.5	4.4	100.0
	No.	(212)	(61)	(88)	(69)	(7)	(20)	(457)
No	%	38.9	6.8	22.8	17.9	1.9	11.7	100.0
	No.	(63)	(11)	(37)	(29)	(3)	(19)	(162)
Total		(275)	(72)	(125)	(98)	(10)	(39)	(619)

Source: Survey data (see note for Table 5.3).

Conclusions

This article has discussed factors that sustain markets for urban agricultural products in Tanzanian towns. Several factors intensify the marketing of urban agricultural products and these in turn bring about an increase in the production.Products come from household compounds, from gardens and from open spaces in the towns. The growers consumed most of the livestock products at home, while farmers sold most of their produce. Direct sale by farmers to customers was not common, however. It was found, rather, that farmers sold their crops to retailers, even though the marketing process was complex, and a number of marketing agents could be involved.

Several factors are involved in the   production and the marketing operations, and this complexity tends to intensify and exacerbate the problems. The production system comes from the households compounds, from gardens, and from several open spaces in the towns. For simplicity, the marketing of the urban agricultural system as a whole can be described as being affected by four hierarchical levels: 1. the national government; 2. the ministry; 3. the city council, and 4. the individuals (Figure 5.3).

Policy Implications

In the country's towns, urban agriculture and the marketing of its products will continue to exist. There is a need, therefore, to adopt policies to improve it:

1   The government, using the city councils' health personnel, ought to check on the quality of livestock products, such as milk, so that customers get milk of acceptable quality.
2   The government ought to liaise with interested Non Governmental Organizations (NGOs) so as to provide loans to urban agriculturalists to improve their enterprises. The ultimate results should be to improve husbandry, to raise the quality of the produce and to increase total yields.
3   The government ought to hasten the privatization of institutions such as Ubungo Milk Processing Plant in the city of Dar-es-Salaam, so that people raising dairy cattle can sell their milk there. This can insure that customers get high quality milk products.
4   The MALCD (Ministry of Agriculture, Livestock, and Cooperative Development) ought to use its extension workers to teach urban agriculturalists to establish cooperatives for marketing their products so that they increase their share of their profit margins.
5   Urban agriculturalists ought to form area-based marketing organizations for selling their agricultural products, in order to increase profits. Such producer organizations can decrease the number of retailers, hawkers, and vendors who also adulterate milk to earn unjustified profits. MALCD and specific NGOs should help producers to form areas-based organizations.

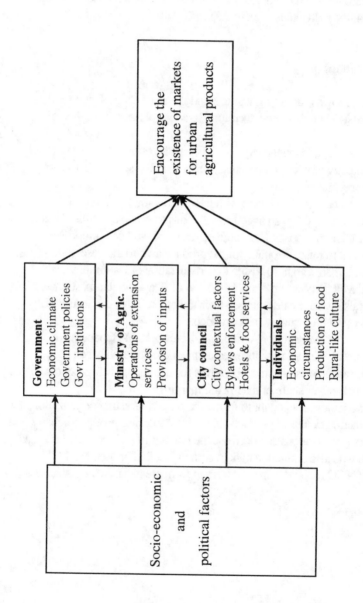

Figure 5.3   The Four Nested Contextual Levels that Encourage the Existence of Markets for Urban Agricultural Products

Acknowledgment

The author wishes to thank the International Development Research Centre (IDRC) of Ottawa, Canada for funding this research project and Sokoine University of Agriculture for allowing time-off for the researchers. The author also thanks his co-researchers Drs. Z. S. K. Mvena and I. J. Lupanga for making this research a success. Thanks also are due to the agriculture and livestock extension workers who assisted in filling the questionnaires during the entire study period. The author also thanks the urban dwellers and urban agriculturalists who took part in the study.

References

Babbie, E.R. (1990), *Survey Research Methods,* 2nd. ed. Belmont: Wadsworth Publishing Company.

Blalock, H.M. (1972), *Social Statistics.* New York: McGraw-Hill.

Bukuku, E.S. (1993), *The Tanzania Economy: Income Distribution and Economic Growth,* Westport: Praeger.

Drakakis-Smith, D. (1992), 'Strategies for meeting basic food needs in Harare', in J. Baker and P.O. Pedersen (eds), *The Rural-Urban Interface in Africa: Expansion and Adaptation.* Uppsala: Scandinavian Institute of African Studies, pp. 258-83.

Freeman, D.B. (1991), *A City of Farmers: Informal Agriculture in Open Spaces of Nairobi, Kenya,* Montreal: McGill-Queen University Press.

Henry, G.T. (1990), *Practical Sampling,* Newbury Park: Sage Publication.

International Development Research Centre (IDRC), (1994), *Cities Feeding People: An Examination of Urban Agriculture in East Africa.* Ottawa: IDRC.

Jones-Dube, E. (1992), 'The influence entrepreneurs on rural town development Botswana', in J. Baker and P.O. Pedersen (eds), *The Rural-Urban Interface in Africa: Expansion and Adaptation.* Uppsala: Scandinavian Institute of African Studies, pp. 148-70.

Kleer, J. (1987), Small-scale agricultural production in urban areas in Poland, *Food and Nutrition Bulletin,* vol. 9, pp. 24-28.

Maliyamkono, T.L. and Bagachwa, M.S.D. (1990) *The Second Economy in Tanzania.* London: James Curry.

Mans, D. (1994) , Tanzania: Resolute action, in I. Husain, and R. Faruqee. (eds), *Adjustment in Africa: Lessons From Country Studies.* Washington, D.C.: The World Bank, pp. 352-426.

Maxwell, D. and Zziwa., S. (1992), *Urban Agriculture in Africa: The Case of Kampala,* Nairobi: ACTS Press.

May, J. & Rogerson, C.M. (1995), 'Poverty and sustainable cities in South Africa: The role of urban cultivation', *Habitat International*, vol. 9, pp. 165-81.

Mlozi, M. R. S. (1995), *Information and the Problems of Urban Agriculture in Tanzania: Intentions and Realizations*, Ph.D. Dissertation. The University of British Columbia, Vancouver, Canada.

Mosha, A. (1991), 'Urban farming practices in Tanzania', *Review of Rural and Urban Planning in Southern and Eastern Africa*, vol. 1, pp. 83-92.

Rasmussen, J. (1992), 'Entrepreneurial milieu in smaller towns-the case of Masvingo, Zimbabwe', in: J. Baker and P.O. Pedersen (eds), *The Rural-Urban Interaction in Africa: Expansion and Adaptation*, Uppsala: The Scandinavian Institute of African Studies, pp. 171-86.

Sanyal, B. (1985), 'Urban agriculture, Who cultivates and why? A case of Lusaka, Zambia', *Food and Nutrition Bulletin*, vol. 3, pp. 15-24.

Sawio, C..J. (1993), *Feeding the Urban Masses? Towards Understanding of the Dynamics of Urban Agriculture and Land-use Change in Dar-es-Salaam, Tanzania*, Ph.D. Dissertation, Clark University, Worcester, Massachusetts.

Stevenson, C..J. Kinabo and Nyange, D. (1994), *Urban Horticulture in Tanzania. Research Report,* Dar-es-Salaam, Tanzania: German Agency for Technical Cooperation (GTZ), mimeo.

Tricaud, P.M. (1987), *Urban Agriculture in Ibadan and Freetown,* Tokyo: The United Nations University, The Food and Energy Nexus Programme, Research Report No. 23.

World Bank. (1995), *African Development Indicators*, Washington, D.C.: The World Bank.

Yeung, Y.M. (1988), 'Agricultural land use in land use in Asian cities, *Land Use Policy*, vol. 5, pp. 79-82.

6 Trade in African Rural Development: The Case of Zimbabwe

POUL OVE PEDERSEN

Introduction: The Role of Trade in Rural Development

In much of the development literature, and especially the literature on rural development in Eastern and Southern Africa, trade and traders have been seen as the scapegoats of development. Rural traders and middlemen were often seen either as agents of exploitative central economic powers or as superfluous profiteers in their own right. This negative view of rural traders has in part been based on Marxist theory; but in Eastern and Southern Africa it has merged both with the understandable, strong aversion to Asian and other foreign traders who dominated rural trade during the colonial period and in many areas also after independence, and finally with a traditional belief that business which leads to change in lifestyle and separation from traditional rural consent might be caused by sorcery and witchcraft (see e.g. Bourdillon 1987; The Herald, Tuesday, January 24, 1995, on a case of abduction and killing of children for body parts to be sold to businessmen and traditional healers).

From a second viewpoint much of the literature on informal activities and petty trade has seen trade as an activity with easy access requiring few qualifications and little capital. Therefore, people with no other means of living would be engaging themselves in the same informal trading activities leading to superfluous multiplication of functions (see e.g. Raikes 1994). Consequently, growth in the informal trade is seen as a response to crisis in the economy and therefore, anti-cyclical.

From a third viewpoint the economic literature has tended to see trade and services as secondary, derived functions of production which are expected to develop pro-cyclically. Therefore, a rapid growth in trade is seen

93

as problematic and difficult to understand in the African situation where production stagnates.

These different attitudes to trade are partly contradictory, although they all tend to see the growth of trade in a rather unfavourable light. The purpose of this paper is to try to resolve some of these seemingly contradictions in the understanding of the role of trade in rural development. The paper is based on arguments put forward in new institutional economics (see e.g. Williamson 1981), network theories (see e.g. Johanson and Mattson 1986) and newer theories of enterprises and enterprise systems (see e.g. Whitley 1992 and Whitley and Kristensen 1996 and Pedersen 1997b), where the division of labour between enterprises, and thus the content of and functions carried out by individual enterprises, are seen not as predetermined, but as the result of enterprise strategies and their mutual adaptation to each other and the social and institutional context in which they operate. Therefore, the content and functions of enterprises will vary with e.g. region, country and sector.

According to this viewpoint the sharp empirical and theoretical distinction between trade and production is fictive. A large part of the trade is carried out, not by trading enterprises, but by production enterprises, and commodity flows which in one production system are externalized and considered as trade may in another system be enterprise internal and, therefore, not considered as trade. Thus, many small enterprises which we classify as producers also retail their own products, and often spend more resources and earn more value added as traders than as producers.

Furthermore, trading activity may consist of several other individual functions than the simple exchange of goods, such as:

1   marketing activities;
2   aggregation and disaggregation of goods into larger or smaller consignments;
3   packing and repacking of goods;
4   forwarding;
5   custom clearance;
6   storage;
7   financing;
8   insurance and risk minimization;
9   transport and communication.

The trading enterprise may also play an important role in the organization of production. Especially in the early phases of industrialization, outwork and subcontracting are often organized by trading enterprises rather than by production enterprises (see e.g., Weijland 1994 and Pedersen 1991).

These functions of the trading system may be carried out by the trading enterprise, the producer or the consumer, by separate enterprises specialized in transport, finance, storage etc. or not at all. In the industrialized and newly industrialized economies these functions are known as the logistic system which is increasingly seen to play an important role in the functioning of the economy. This paper will show that they also play an important role in the structuring of the African rural economy, even though they are not always carried out by specialized enterprises.

The different segments of trading activities are part of what in the new institutional economics have been known as transaction costs. The new institutional economy would, therefore, expect them to be distributed in the *vertical production chain* in such a way that the transaction costs are minimized. However, the different functions require resources which are often scarce in African rural areas, such as capital, transport capacity, safe storage space, and packaging. Therefore, they are often bottlenecks in the production and distribution system. This means, on the one hand, that they are open for attempts to monopolization, profiteering, corruption and other irregular practices. On the other hand, however, they lead to a *horizontal market segmentation* based on access to different sources of scarce resources, such as different formal and informal sources of trading capital and credit (e.g. banks, stock exchange, supplier credit, money lenders, donors and NGOs, private loans or individual savings), different locations, different means of transport (e.g. own truck, truck for hire, car, matatu or bus, scotchcart, bicycle or walk) or different storage facilities. Where economists have usually seen market segmentation as a sign of market inefficiency, we shall argue that it may lead to a more efficient use of scarce resources which would usually not be available to a monopolist, whether public or private.

Contrary to the traditional view of African rural trade, which has tended to see rural trade as overdeveloped and rural traders and middlemen as superfluous, we shall argue that it is precisely because trade plays such an important role in the development process that profiteering and corruptive practices have become associated with it.

In the following sections of the paper we shall present four cases of how trading functions are organized and what imact they have had on development in rural Zimbabwe, namely clothing trade and production, distribution of fertilizer, distribution of fruits and vegetables in the district service centres, and finally the development of general dealers in small rural business centres. The cases have been chosen to illustrate the processes of vertical specialization and horizontal market segmentation in the rural economy. They are based on extensive studies of the structure and development of two district service centres, Gutu and Gokwe, and some smaller rural business centres in the communal areas of Zimbabwe since independence and especially during the first half of the 1990s (see also Pedersen 1992, 1993, 1994, and 1997a).

Before independence rural trade in the communal areas was not well developed. Most agricultural produce was used for subsistence, as access to outside markets was not developed. Rural money incomes were mostly based on remittances from migrant workers. Most industrial consumer goods were bought in the large towns and brought home by the migrant workers. Since independence the Government of Zimbabwe has pursued a policy of rural development comprising of investments in rural infrastructure and agricultural services and the development of a network of district service centres in the communal areas. This has resulted in a rapid increase in marketed agricultural produce and a corresponding increase in the rural money incomes, thus leading to increasing commercialization of the rural economy and a rapid growth in the number of non-agricultural activities. It has also led to an increasing retail trade in goods and services in the rural areas, and, especially in the district service centres. Wholesale trade and industrial production has also grown, but to a more limited and unsatisfactory extent. It is in this context that the four cases to be presented below should be seen.

Clothing Trade and Production in Gufu and Gokwe

A. Retail Trade

The supply of clothing to the small town market is dominated by retail trade, and local production plays a relatively minor role. The retail sector is dominated by branches of large national and regional retail chains, which during the second half of the 1980s started to establish branch stores in the district service centres. In Gutu there are about 10 chain stores, and in Gokwe even more. However, there are also locally owned clothing shops, and many general dealers sell some clothes and fabrics; finally, a little is sold on the small open air market - mostly pieces of cloth and low quality dresses. Some of the branch stores specialize in clothes only, but many of them have a second speciality line, e.g. furniture, enamel kitchenware, shoes and records, towels and bedspreads, blankets and suitcases, or fabric and buttons.

There is a certain segmentation of the market, both according to income groups and types of clothes. Most of the chain stores cater to the middle income groups, but even so there appears to be a visible difference between stores catering primarily to rural customers and others catering to more 'urban' customers, mostly civil servants. The large chains tend to operate with uniform prices all over the country, and, in general, do not give credit. In Gokwe (which has a higher income level than Gutu) a few of the chain stores cater especially to high income groups (civil servants and traders). They sell higher quality goods at higher prices and typically give credit. In Gutu, some of the locally owned shops perform this service. Many of the general dealers and the smaller locally owned shops cater mostly to middle to lower income groups. In order to compete, they often give credit to known and trusted customers.

School uniforms are an important market segment which most shops try to serve, but in which especially one chain has specialized. This chain has branch stores in both Gutu and Gokwe. It sells school uniforms and sports clothes of relatively high quality and high price. It tries to sell directly through the schools through campaigns and student competitions.

A special small market now developing is the market for sports clothes. In Gokwe a very small retailer has specialized in sports clothes, which it tries to sell both to individuals and through schools and sports clubs. In Gutu, a new large book-binding enterprise with 30 employees rebinds old books for the schools and as a sideline activity prints school names and logos on T-shirts for the schools' sports teams.

B. Clothing Production

Clothing production in the small centres consists of knitters, tailors and a few larger workshops which could be called industrial.

In Gutu there are three fairly large clothes-making workshops with 5, 15 to 20 and 30 to 35 employees respectively. In Gokwe there is none. Their most important market is school uniforms. The smallest of the three produces mostly school uniforms, but also dresses which are sold retail from the workshop. It does not attempt to get larger orders, because at its present size it would not have a sufficient capacity to fill them. The two largest workshops both attempt to reach other markets as well, because the market for school uniforms is highly seasonal. However, it is difficult for them to get into the local retail market, because it is dominated by chain stores which have no competence to buy locally. In order to get into the local market, both of the large workshops have established their own retail outlets in Gutu centre (one of them also has an outlet in Buhera centre about 60 km away) and have salesmen travelling in the rural areas. However, the local market is not sufficient for either of the two enterprises and both attempt to develop specialities which can bring them into a larger, regional or national market. This has become difficult because the dominance of retail chains which serve as their own wholesalers has left little room for clothing wholesalers. Instead, both of the enterprises have diversified into protective work clothes for the urban enterprise market and for the mines. Here they can obtain orders which are sufficiently large to satisfy their needs but which are too small to be interesting to the large factories.

The small tailor businesses operating in the centres are mostly one-person enterprises operated by men. Some of them have rented a shop or part of one while others are operated on rented shop verandas. They do mostly repair work, but some of them also produce school uniforms. There are about five of these small tailors in both Gutu and Gokwe. They have no employees and mostly no apprentices (although some train their own children or nephews).

In addition to the independent tailors some of the local shops selling clothes employ a tailor who mostly fits industrial clothes to customer size. Some of the knitting enterprises also do some dressmaking. One woman in Gutu operates a small retail shop where she sells women's and children's dresses produced by two young women. She also sells second-hand clothes. In addition, she operates a hairdressing saloon, and her husband has a dry cleaning outlet. In Gokwe, one woman tailor specializes in bedspreads and cushions, while a man produces travel bags.

The small knitting enterprises which knit jerseys and sweaters on knitting machines are all operated by women. There are more than 15 knitting enterprises in Gutu centre but only half as many in Gokwe. Including the owner/manager, they employ one to four persons. The market for knitwear is highly seasonal, concentrated in the few winter months, and few of the women can afford to produce stocks for the rest of the year. In order to counteract the seasonality of the market, some combine knitting with dressmaking, and many take in paying apprentices. A few also operate hairdressing salons, and one operates together with her husband's radio, TV and watch repair business. In Gutu, many of the small knitting enterprises are run by the wives of the larger general dealers in the centre and operated on the shop premises. Knitwear is mostly sold from the shop or through saleswomen travelling in the rural areas. Only one of the interviewed enterprises in Gokwe sells some of its production through other retailers.

In general, it seems to be easier for the small-scale knitters to compete with the retail sector than it is for the small tailors. The obvious reason is that the small knitters often produce jerseys of a similar or even better quality than the large industries, while the quality produced by the small tailors is usually lower. Therefore, the tailors have to engage in price competition for adequate prices to a larger extent than the knitters. On the other hand, only a small part of the small tailors, dressmakers and knitters operate in the business centre. Many more, especially women dressmakers and knitters, are likely to operate from their home. Therefore, the fact that some disappear from the centre may not mean that they have closed. It may mean that they have moved their business home to save rent.

In addition to the training in tailoring and knitting taking place in the small production enterprises, a number of enterprises especially in Gutu and to a smaller extent in Gokwe, offer training on a larger scale in dressmaking and knitting. These training centres are all run by women, mostly as private enterprises, but some are run by churches or cooperatives.

C. The Effect of Retail Chains on Development and Restructuring of the Clothing Sector in the District Service Centres

The development of the clothing sector in the district service centres has been heavily influenced by the establishment of branch stores of large retail chains during the later half of the 1980s. Many of the national retail chains operate with fixed prices all over the country. This has forced local traders to reduce their prices and has set in motion a process of restructuration, specialization and market segmentation in the clothing sector. The general dealers' clothing sales have probably gone down, while some locally owned, specialized clothing shops have been opened. While most of the chain stores cater to the middle income market, the locally owned clothing shops have tended to cater to the higher income market of civil servants and business people. Some of the small general stores, on the other hand, sell low quality goods, often supplied from informal workshops owned by family members.

The reduced price differences between the district service centres and the large towns have made it possible for the small towns to recapture an increasing part of the rural market which was earlier supplied directly from the large towns by work migrants. As a result the local market has increased much more than rural incomes. The branch stores have also led to increasing competition for the small local tailors, who have been left with little more than the market for repair work.

The dominance of the clothing market by large retail chains has also reduced the local market for the larger local producers. The retail chains procure their goods nationally and operate as their own wholesalers. As a result the local branch managers usually are not allowed to buy goods locally. Local producers, therefore, have a very limited local market and are forced to go directly to the national market. The dominance of the retail chains on the national market also means that the wholesale sector for clothing is not very developed. The larger local producers, therefore, are forced either to sell their products through their own retail shops or through travelling salesmen in the rural areas, or produce for the enterprise or institutional niche markets where small to medium-sized orders can be obtained.

Fruit and Vegetables Trade

In both Gutu and Gokwe, fruit and vegetables are sold mostly by market vendors at the market place, although some general dealers and supermarkets also sell them. In both towns, the district councils have built roofed stalls for the market vendors, but especially in Gutu, licensed market vendors also operate outside the stalls. In both towns, the number of licensed vendors is around 75, although there are probably a few more in Gutu. In addition, there are a number of unlicensed vendors who mostly operate in the residential areas.

In Gutu, locally grown fruits and vegetables only make up a small part of the supply. Most of the fruits and vegetables sold at the market come from Harare by bus. Groups of three to five vendors often send a representative to Harare to buy for the whole group. This is hardly the most efficient way of distributing fruits and vegetables.

In 1990, a newly established fruit and vegetable wholesaler in Gutu attempted on a regular basis to ferry truckloads of bananas, oranges or other fruits and vegetables into Gutu to supply the market vendors, and a second wholesaler was about to open. None of the wholesalers had transport of their own, and by 1994 both had closed again. In addition to the wholesalers a white commercial farmer in Masvingo district regularly brought truckloads of cabbages and other vegetables to the market in Gutu as well as to other centres in the province.

Also in Gokwe many fruits and vegetables are brought in from Harare by the market vendors, or by a wholesale outlet established in 1990 (also closed by 1994). But here local produce covers a larger part of the supply than in Gutu. This is partly due to the climate in Gokwe, which is better for vegetable growing; but probably the characteristics of the market vendors also play an important role. In Gutu, the market vendors are all women; mostly single or divorced women living in the high-density residential area of the town, and without close relations to the potential vegetable growers. In Gokwe, a number of the vendors are male vegetable growers from the nearby rural areas, and also many of the women vendors grow vegetables themselves. This guarantees a direct link between the vendors and the growers. A link of this kind does not exist in Gutu. If the local supply of fruits and vegetables to the markets in the district service centres is to increase, this linkage obviously must be developed. The new vegetable wholesalers in Gutu and Gokwe claimed that this was their long-run intention. At the time of the interviews, however, they received all their supplies from Harare and from commercial farmers. Among the market vendors in both Gutu and Gokwe, there was considerable resentment toward the wholesalers, who were seen as competitors rather than as providing a service. Nevertheless, there seems to be an urgent need for a better capitalized wholesale organization in Gutu both to organize the link to the potential local producers and to organize transport from the larger markets.

Distribution of Farm Inputs, Especially Fertilizers

The most important farm inputs are fertilizers, seeds, chemicals, and stockfeed. It is characteristic for these products that they are produced for the national market by only a few producers and that the market has been partly regulated. In the communal areas, farm inputs are distributed directly from the producer or via wholesalers, large general stores, specialized farm input traders or cooperatives; however, competition between the different distribution channels varies from product to product and from area to area. To give an impression of the distribution system and its dynamics, we focus especially on fertilizer, which is probably the most important of the farm inputs in both value and amount.

Fertilizer in Zimbabwe is produced by only two large industrial enterprises: ZFC (Zimbabwe Fertilizer Corporation) and Windmill, both with headquarters in Harare. Fertilizer is sold at a price ab producer's gate, and the buyers pay for the transport. The producers have no transport capacity of their own, but they do help both farmers and traders organize transport. Windmill distributes 3/4 of its sales directly to communal farmers and only one fourth through traders and cooperatives. ZFC sells a much larger share through traders and farmers' cooperatives.

Fertilizer distribution appears to be very different in our two districts, Gutu and Gokwe. In Gutu centre, there is a large and apparently growing trade in fertilizer. The cooperative MCU has, partly with support from an agricultural rural development programme (the CARD programme financed by GTZ), managed to increase its sales several times; two new specialized dealers in farm inputs have recently been established, and a third opened just after the first field work took place (April 1990). The large general dealers, who have traditionally distributed the fertilizer, claim that their sales have not decreased (this may not hold true). In Gokwe centre, on the other hand, fertilizer sales appear to be very limited. The local farmers' cooperative is apparently almost bankrupt, and neither wholesalers, large general dealers, hardware stores, or any others appear to sell much fertilizer. Several outlets sell chemicals especially for cotton farmers, but they sell hardly any fertilizer.

This difference between the two centres is contrary to our expectation, because Agritex, the extension services, claims that the use of fertilizer ought to be larger in Gokwe than in Gutu, because the former has a wetter climate. This is also supported by Sunga et al. (1990), who show that while only 10 percent of the farmers in the dry areas (natural region IV and V) use fertilizers, 25 percent or more of the farmers in areas with more rain use it.

The explanation of this apparent paradox is that because individual farmers in Gokwe use more fertilizers than farmers in Gutu it pays for them to buy directly from the producers. In this way they can take advantage of scale economies, i.e., fill a truck, even if they purchase their fertilizers individually or in small groups. In Gutu, where both fertilizer use and farm size is smaller, more farmers will need to collaborate in order to fill a truck and organize direct delivery of fertilizer from the producer. Consequently, it is easier for local traders and the cooperative to compete in Gutu.

The recent growth in fertilizer sales in Gutu also seems to have been spurred by GTZ and the CARD programme support to the Gutu branch of the Masvingo Cooperative Union (MCU). GTZ has provided MCU with working capital in the form of a revolving fund of Z$100,000, but at the same time required it to reduce its mark-up to 15 percent. This has made it possible for MCU to improve its distribution of farm inputs in Gutu district and at the same time reduce its prices. The result is that MCU was able to increase its fertilizer sale rapidly during the early 1990s. Some of this increase is likely to be a genuine increase in fertilizer use, but some of it is likely to be due to reduced direct sales from the producers and reduced local sales, especially from the small general dealers.

MCU gets its fertilizer from ZFC and has become the sole distributor for ZFC in Gutu. Windmill delivers to the private traders, either directly or through a large businessman in Masvingo who operates as a sort of agent or intermediary for Windmill. The success of MCU has forced Windmill and the local traders to become more competitive, in order to maintain their market share. The price for a bag of AN-fertilizer ab producers' gate is Z$20.30 (1990). The price of transportation to Gokwe or Gutu would typically be around Z$5, but earlier, private traders took up to Z$32 for a bag. MCU in Gutu now charges about Z$27, and private traders have, therefore been forced to reduce their price considerably.

Part of MCU's strategy has been to open 5 depots and 10 sub-depots in the district, and thus improve delivery service. This has also forced private traders to improve their distribution service. Only the larger traders, however, have been able to do this, and this has probably led to concentration of private fertilizer sale in the hands of specialized farm input dealers, and among the largest of the general dealers. It has also led to market segmentation, where private traders concentrate on segments of the market which are not supplied by MCU.

Membership of MCU is not open. It is largely limited to full-time communal farmers, many of whom are master farmers with relatively large fertilizer use and relatively easy access to AFC credit. On the other hand, very few part-time farmers and farmers with supplementary non-farm-jobs are members of MCU. It is among the latter that the large general dealers with rural branches have their customers. The small holders buy relatively little fertilizer, but they often need the credit which general dealers may give; they also need the close access to rural stores. They are, therefore, willing (or forced) to overpay for fertilizers in order to receive the services of the traders.

Finally, most of the market for specialized farm input, which is handled by the large dealers, is among small commercial and resettlement farmers who order relatively large amounts of fertilizer, and are, therefore, relatively easy to supply. Thus, they are able to keep both costs and prices relatively low. Consequently, there is considerable market segmentation based on relative advantages, not in product or in production, but in credit and delivery services.

After introduction of structural adjustment policies in the early 1990s, the price of fertilizer rose. To counteract these price increases and the negative effects of the serious drought in the 1991-92 season, the government distributed, in 1992-93, large amounts of fertilizers to peasant farmers free of charge. According to one farm input supplier, the free distribution of fertilizer in Gutu amounted to twice ordinary pre-drought sales (but Gutu may have received more than most other areas), while sales remained at about half the pre-drought level, or the same as during the drought year. In 1993-94, the promised government handouts were not forthcoming in time, and in spite of price increases, local sales in Gutu appear to have more than doubled relative to the pre-drought level. The growing demand resulted in a new addition to the existing farm input suppliers, as a local trader converted his clothing shop to a fertilizer store. Fertilizer sales appear to have continued to grow in 1994-95 although only slowly.

The reason for the rather dramatic increase in fertilizer sales is that the price of maize rose after the drought even more rapidly than the price of fertilizer. As a result, the fertilizer price in terms of maize equivalent fell by about fifty percent. This rapid increase in maize price, however, has only benefited the larger communal farmers, small-scale commercial farms and resettlement farms producing a marketable surplus. Small communal farmers who did not produce enough for subsistence have been hit by price increases of both maize and fertilizer. The increased sale of fertilizer, therefore, is likely to have been concentrated on the larger farms. Their increasing incomes have resulted in increasing investments in farm implements and in the production of chicken and pigs, and, therefore, also increased sales of stockfeed. This development has benefited the development of specialized farm input suppliers.

Rural Business Centres Network: Three Cases from Gutu District

Under the district service centres, a carefully planned network of small rural business centres exists. The small rural centres are typically located about 10 km apart. They play an important role in the distribution of consumer goods and the collection of cash crops, especially from the smallest communal farms. There are very detailed plans for these small centres, but few public investments have been made there. The network of centres was intended to comprise different levels of a hierarchy, and the centres also vary in size, but in reality most of the centres are dominated by general dealers.

Such rural service centre networks, characterized by a few large centres and a large number of rather undifferentiated centres, are found in many developing rural areas (Johnson 1970). In an African context, Berg (1981) in Zambia and Musyoki (1987) in Kenya have described such rural service centres that vary in size but not in function. However, there are few more detailed studies of such small rural centres and their businesses. In order to get a clearer picture of the small rural business centres and the way they function we have surveyed three such small centres in Gutu district. The three centres, Chisheche, Gonya and Mataruse, are located along the road (and bus route) running eastward from Gutu centre, respectively, 8, 30 and 75 km from the centre. The first shops in the three centres were established in 1976, 1960 and the 1950s and by 1990 they had grown to 18, 18 and 8 shops, respectively.

A. The Nature of Businesses in Rural Business Centres

Most of the businesses in the three small centres today are run by local people without businesses elsewhere, but some of them run more than one business in their centre, typically a general dealer shop together with either a butchery, a bottle store or a grinding mill. Thus the 44 businesses operating in the three centres in 1990 were run by only 32 businessmen.

Most of the businesses are operated by the owner and/or his family. Only in Gonya and Mataruse a few of the larger businesses employ 2 to 4 people in addition to family labour. Except in the grinding mills, which are considered men's work, most of the people who work in the shops are women.

Only few producers and wholesalers bring their commodities directly to the shops, and most of the owners, especially in Gonya and Mataruse, have to fetch commodities from wholesalers in Gutu centre or in Masvingo. This represents a problem, because many of the shopowners do not have cars, or if they have, they are often old cars which breakdown frequently. In addition, many owners who work outside Gutu use their cars during the week. Consequently, goods are often transported by bus.

In terms of sales there is a considerable difference in the size of the individual businesses. The businessmen who operate the largest businesses are typically those who have been operating for a long time. They have had more time to accumulate capital, and, therefore, tend to be better stocked. Often, they have also been engaged in grain trade (as approved buyers for the Grain Marketing Board). Due to lack of both capital and transport, the smaller businessmen have only been able to do this on a very limited scale, if at all.

Especially before the mid-1980s a large majority of the new local businessmen were active or retired civil servants. In many cases, their wives are also teachers, nurses etc. Thus, most of the businessmen have earned the money they invested in their businesses as wage earners, mostly in the public sector.

In addition to their jobs and businesses, all the businessmen also have smaller or larger communal farms. These farms contribute important additional income to the household economy, but they also tend to increase cash flow problems, because capital resources are bound to these farms for a large part of the year and thus cannot be invested in commodity stocks. Thus, chronic cash flow problems are the key problem in most of these businesses. This problem can be solved only if credit is available to them, which it generally is not. However, even if they could obtain credit, it is doubtful whether it would be a good idea to borrow under the existing circumstances. It would solve their cash flow problems, but it would also increase their costs and reduce their ability to withstand the large fluctuations in turnover which are likely to prevail as long as the economy of the communal areas are so closely linked to agricultural cycles.

Of the 44 business activities located in the three rural business centres in 1990, 25 were general dealers with very little specialization, and the specialized functions, butcheries, bottle stores and beer halls, are probably specialized because it is required by the licensing regulations and not for any economic reasons. The general dealers basically sell groceries, though some of them also have limited supplies of such goods as textiles and kitchenware. The textile goods often are of own production or delivered by other small entrepreneurs in the family.

The lack of specialization, in the usual sense of the word, does not mean that everyone sells the same goods and serves the same market. Rather, each shop to some extent has its own secluded market zone. It consists of the owner's extended family and people from his home area or work place who tend to patronize his shop.

At the same time, the generally low level of cash flow, the frequent breakdown of transport facilities, and the limitation in availability of goods in the wholesale stores, result in a very limited, unequal and fluctuating supply of goods in the shops, depending on which goods the individual shop has been able to procure during a particular week.

Consequently, although most customers may have their preferred shops, they will in fact often need to circulate between the shops in order to buy what they need. Therefore, over time all the shops get their share of the market, at the same time as the many competing general dealers with different resources increase the probability of permanent supply in the centre. Thus, although all the centres are dominated by general dealers, there is still a certain unplanned differentiation between both dealers and centres, but a differentiation caused by supply factors rather than demand factors. Differentiation comes, not as the result of a decision to specialize, but rather from lack of financial resources for fully stocking the shops, from insufficient transportation, and from limited and unstable supplies. All of these constraints prevent shop owners from acquiring the goods they would like to stock. Thus, the general dealers in the small centres do supplement each other to some extent.

B. Change and Stability in the Business Communities in the Small Rural Business Centres

Although we have been able to identify some changes in the business community in Chisheche, Gonya and Mataruse during the last 30 years, these changes have been surprisingly slow. Of the 30 businessmen who have been operating businesses in Gonya and Mataruse during the 30 year period 1960-1990, 17 still operate in the centres. The 13 which were closed during the period had been in operation in an average of almost 12 years, and the 17 businesses still in operation in 1990 had been so for more than an average of 11 years. Four of them were more than 28 years old, and only four were less than 5 years old.

In Chisheche, which developed mostly during the 1980s, the average age of the enterprises is obviously much lower than in the two older centres. But also here there have been relatively few changes in ownership.

This high degree of stability is quite surprising when one considers that the businesses have been operated in an environment with very large both economic and political fluctuations caused by frequent droughts, commodity shortages, unstable deliveries, changing policies, and a war of independence.

The reason for this high degree of stability is found in the investment strategy and cost structure of businesses in the small rural centres, where

1   original investments are usually based on own savings and treated as sunk costs, so that no interest needs to be paid;
2   current investments are often small;
3   alternative income for the labour applied is often very low or even zero;
4   the owner or his wife often have other sources of income.

As a result, most businesses are able to survive for long periods even with a very low turnover. If the shopkeeper has a large family, the wholesale discount which he realizes as a retailer for his family's own consumption may be enough to justify his keeping the shop open. In addition, there is a certain prestige in having a shop, and as costs are limited, it may be kept going even if incomes are low.

On the other hand, the success of a businessman depends to a large extent on his ability to stock his shop. Businessmen operating on a very low level may well survive, but they are not likely to be able to stock their shops satisfactorily, and will, therefore, have low turnover and income.

Often the old businessmen use their shops as a pension scheme, and thus gradually destock it until little more than the building is left. This life-cycle change of shops in the small business centres is one of the reasons for the very great differences in turnover of the shops found in most centres. It is probably also an important reason why so few of the businesses in these small centres are taken over by the children. In fact, in our three centres, there seems to be only one instance where a shop has been taken over by one of the owner's children.

To take over one of the old shops and run it successfully requires considerable capital, partly because the new owner will have increased costs if he has to buy or rent the shop, and partly because a younger owner with a family is likely to require a larger income than the old shopkeeper.

Consequently, the shop is likely to be either closed or taken over by someone with a larger capital who is better able to secure a larger share of the market.

Contrary to Gonya and Mataruse, which have been dominated by one or a few large shops, Chisheche has until 1990 had a much more equal structure. The take-over in 1990 of one of the shops by a businessman from Gutu centre seemed for a time to change this. This new businessman in Chisheche was able to stock his shop much better than the old ones, and in 1992 it seemed that he would be able to take over a considerable share of the market from the other shops. This would have created a more skewed enterprise structure in Chisheche, similar to the one found in Gonya and Mataruse.

However, when we visited Chisheche in early 1995, the shop had been destocked and turned into a bar, which has a much more rapid turnover and therefore requires less operational capital. There were two reasons for this change. First, a serious traffic accident meant that the owner was unable to work for a long period and that he lost his file of debtors. Unable to reclaim this outstanding debt, he lost his shop at his original home in a neighbouring district. Secondly, he had made large investments in renovating a restaurant in Basera, which earned much less than he had hoped for due to drought.

Though these are very specific problems experienced by an individual businessman in Chisheche, they are also typical of the problems of many small businessmen which make it difficult for them to expand their businesses. The example shows first that the businessmen's risks are not only the normal business risks, but also personal risks which are high in the developing countries and for which there is no social security. The example also illustrates an observation that we made in many more cases, namely a tendency of many small businessmen to invest what they earn in fixed capital so that even small fluctuations in the economy leave them without sufficient working capital. As few of the small businessmen are able to obtain credit, this often forces them to reduce their activities.

The Structure of Rural Production and Distribution Systems

Typical for the distribution systems presented above is that in each sector there is a number of parallel subsystems of production and distribution operating at the same time. These parallel subsystems range from semi-subsistence activities where the household and its neighbours consume a large part of the produce, over more market-oriented micro, small and medium-scale producers to large urban industries, and from small market traders, over general dealer stores, more specialized shops to regional, national or even international retail chains.

In one end of the market system we find the small, often household-based, non-agricultural activities, either producers or traders. They usually sell directly to a very local and mostly low-income consumer market. However, when they expand or when their local market shrinks they may attempt to expand their market area by hiring travelling salesmen or travelling themselves in the rural areas. They often barter their goods for grain or other agricultural produce. They may also sell to traders operating in the larger towns or exporting to the neighbouring countries. We only found a few examples of this in our investigation, but trade liberalization has apparently resulted in an increasing small scale/informal import/export trade (often barter trade) between neighbouring countries in Africa, though the extent of this border trade is still little known.

These small rural enterprises operate on markets which, due to seasonal fluctuations and frequent droughts, are often very unstable, and most of them are highly undercapitalized. For capital they generally rely on their own savings or loans from the family. Few of them have access to the formal financial institutions, and even if they had, there is a great risk that they will not be able to repay the loans in time of crises. As a result, most of them suffer from recurrent cash flow problems which, together with frequent transport problems and lack of supplies, mean that they are not able to stock their stores or to obtain the necessary production inputs on a regular basis. Therefore, a certain multiplication of traders and producers seems necessary in order to guarantee a regular supply of the market. On the other hand, the multiplication of traders and producers also reduces the market and earnings of each enterprise, and thus becomes a source of the cash flow problems. Therefore, there must be a limit to the multiplication of activities.

On the other end of the rural market system there is the large national retail chain with branch stores in the larger district service centres. They cater mostly for the rural middle income market and tend to concentrate on commodities which can give them a rapid turnover. They tend to cream off the more stable part of the market. Besides clothing, chain stores are also operating in hardware and furniture. In Zimbabwe the retail chains have generally operated with fixed national prices which were lower than the prices kept by the local rural traders. Therefore, the rural traders were forced to lower their prices or leave those market segments where the branch stores were established. On the other hand the reduced price differences between rural and urban areas meant that the district service centres captured a large part of the market share which earlier went to the large towns. This has benefitted the local traders, which in spite of the development of the branch stores have also been able to expand, albeit in other market segments. Thus most of the traditional general dealers have been reduced to groceries, while others have attempted to specialize in market segments not served by the chain stores.

As a result a considerable market segmentation has developed between the different producers and traders. This segmentation is based on differences partly in product and product quality, but more importantly in delivery services, such as credit, transport, size of consignment and location of outlet. This market segmentation based on delivery services secure a more efficient use of scarce resources in the distribution system from different sources which would not be accessible to a single distributor. Where economists have usually seen market segmentation as a sign of market inefficiency, we would, therefore, see it as a sign of efficient use of scarce resources in the distribution system.

The retail chains operate their own wholesalers, who buy directly from the large industrial producers or, occasionally, even have their own production facilities. This means that branch stores are usually not allowed to buy locally, and, therefore, do not represent a potential market for local industries. At the same time the dominance of retail chains in a number of sectors (especially clothing and hardware) mean that an open wholesale sector serving the small and medium-scale industries is little developed. The large industries often sell directly to the large retailers, which leave the small rural retailers in a vacuum. The lack of effective wholesalers and sales agents also is a major problem for the small and medium-sized industries attempting to expand into the larger regional, national or international markets. Instead, many of the small-scale industries are forced to organize their own retailing by opening producer outlets or hiring travelling salespersons to operate in the rural areas. Others attempt to produce for enterprise or institutional niche markets, where they can obtain orders of a size which are satisfactory for them but too small to be interesting to the larger industries. However, in general, the absence of 'open' wholesalers and sales agents who have sufficient capital resources to support growing small-scale industries, appears to be a major hindrance to the growth of production in rural areas and small rural centres.

The Role of Trade in Rural Development Revisited

In conclusion we would argue that trade should not be considered a derived function of production but an integral part of the production system.

In comparison with production, trade requires, in most cases more, rather than less, capital, per value added. To start a small production enterprise producing for orders often requires only the tools, because custumers often deliver the raw materials so no stocks are required. To start a trading business providing the same income level in most cases will require a larger amount of operating capital. It is of course true that one can start trading with very little capital, but then usually also with very little profit.

The assumption that trade requires few qualifications is also more than doubtful. Trade requires complex organization of networks and resources to be profitable, and lack of commercial training is probably as serious as lack of technical, vocational training.

In rural economies as the African ones, where instability and regional differences are large and where infrastructure is little developed and trade and production is highly undercapitalized, there is a large need for an efficient trading system which utilize the available resources efficiently. There is also much room for profiteering and speculation. But problems of profiteering and speculation are clearly not solved by prohibiting or limiting trade, but by developing it and supplying it with the necessary infrastructures and resources to function.

References

Acharya, S. (1983), 'The Informal Sector in Developing Countries - A Macro Viewpoint', *Journal of Contemporary Asia*, vol. 13, pp. 432-445.

Berg, L.M. van den (1981), *Central Place Theory And Planning Of Rural Service Centres In Africa*, Lusaka: Zambia Geographical Association Occasional Study No. 11.

Bourdillon, M. (1987), *The Shona Peoples*, Gweru: Mambo Press (1st ed.1976).

Johanson, J. and Mattson, L.G. (1986), 'Interorganizational Relations In Industrial Systems - A Network Approach Compared with the Transaction Cost Approach', *International Studies of Management and Organization*, vol. 40, pp. 307-324.

Johnson, E.A.J. (1970), *The Organization of Space in Developing Countries*. Cambridge, Mass: Harvard University Press.

Musyoki, A.K. (1987),'The hierarchy of centres and the urban balance strategy in Kenya: The case of Machakos District', *Journal of Eastern African Research and Development*, vol. 17, pp. 74-87.

Pedersen, P.O. (1991), 'A network approach to the small enterprise', in E. Bergman, Gunther Maier and F. Tdling (eds), *Regions Reconsidered. Economic Networks, Innovation, And Local Development in Industrialized Countries*, London: Mansell Publ.

Pedersen, P.O. (1992), 'Agricultural Marketing and Processing in Small Towns In Zimbabwe - Gutu and Gokwe', in J. Baker and P.O. Pedersen (eds), *The Rural-Urban Interface in Africa. Expansion and Adaptation*, Uppsala: The Scandinavian Institute of African Studies.

Pedersen, P.O. (1993), *Clothing Rural Zimbabwe: Sectoral Strategies and Local Development*, CDR Working Paper 93.7, Copenhagen: Centre for Development Research.

Pedersen, P.O. (1994), 'Structural Adjustment And The Economy of Small Towns in Zimbabwe', in P.O. Pedersen, A. Sverrisson and M.P. van Dijk (eds), *Flexible Specialization: The Dynamics of Small-Scale Industries in the South*, London: Intermediate Technology Publication.

Pedersen, P.O (1997a), *Small African Towns Between Rural Networks And Urban Hierarchies*, Aldershot: Avebury.

Pedersen, P.O (1997b), 'Clusters of Enterprises within Systems of Production and Distribution' in M.D. van Deijk and R. Rabelloti (eds), *Enterprise Clusters and Networks in Developing Countries*, EADI Book Series 20, London: Frank Cass.

Raikes, P. (1994), 'Business as Usual: Some 'Real' Food Markets in Kenya', *Sociologia Ruralis*, vol. 34, pp. 26-44.

Sunga, E., Chabayanzara, E., Moyo, S., Mpande, R., Mutuna, P. and Page, H. (1990), *Farm Extension Base-Line Survey Results*, Unpublished manuscript, Harare: Department of Agriculture and Rural Development, Zimbabwe Institute of Development Studies.

Weijland, H. (1994), 'Trade Networks for Flexible Rural Industry' in Poul Ove Pedersen, Arni Sverrisson and Meine Pieter van Dijk (eds). *Flexible Specialization: The Dynamics of Small-Scale Industries in the South*, London: Intermediate Technology Publications.

Whitley, R. (1992), *Business Systems in East Asia - Firms, Markets and Societies*, London: Sage Publications.

Whitley, R. and Kristensen, P. H. (eds) (1996), *The Changing European Firm: Limits to Convergence*, London: Routledge.

Williamson, O.E. (1981), 'The Economics of Organization: The Transaction Cost Approach', *American Journal of Sociology* vol. 87, pp. 548-577.

PART II
THE JOS (NIGERIA)
PERI-URBAN STUDIES

7 Economic Characteristics of Dry Season Gardening: The Jos-Bukuru Example

EMMANUEL O. OMOMOH

Introduction

Market gardening in the Jos-Bukuru area has significant economic potential. This is due to the increasing market demand for fruits and vegetables in Jos-Bukuru, as well as in other Nigerian urban areas. Gardening takes place particularly in open spaces and on idle land, both within the urban area and at the urban fringe. The gardeners in these places have varied backgrounds - former tin-mine workers, civil servants, or other private employees.

Irrigated dry-season gardening was practiced in the low lying *fadamas* (irrigable flood plains) of the local streams for a long time. Recently, however, it has been extended upslope, into the more elevated land, beyond the traditional *fadamas*. This expansion has required a growing amount of water which is obtained from sources such as abandoned mine ponds, surface streams and hand-dug wells, utilizing a combination of the traditional bucket watering (mainly the shadoof) system, and small engine-driven water pumping machines.

The expansion of this form of cultivation is largely motivated by commercial considerations. Most of the farmers involved can now produce vegetables and other food items for their own consumption as well as surplus for sale. Thus, market gardening has become increasingly significant economically in the greater Jos-Bukuru area. It is still, however, dominated by small holdings, small farm sizes and low capital inputs. It is, therefore, prone to various problems arising from the diseconomies of its small scale.

In this report we examine some of the activities of these small-scale gardeners regarding their costs, financial gains or losses and the cost-efficiency of their gardening operations. The report is meant to provide some insight into economic considerations relevant to the question whether market gardening activities in the Jos-Bukuru area are economically viable.

Background

One of the most basic tests of economic operation is that of the efficiency level. The issue of technical and economic efficiency of the peasant farmer is a complex one. Some peasants are poor but may be efficient, making the best of very limited resources or of a harsh environment. However, variations in productivity between one farmer and another suggest that many farmers do not operate in the most efficient way, and that considerable increases in productivity and output can still occur if they improve their operational efficiency.

The capitalist system assumes that in the process of production, efficiency implies that resources are used in a way that minimizes production cost per unit of produce (Sender et al., 1986). According to this definition, efficiency is perceived as a relationship between input and output. However, peasant economies do not necessarily operate according to the economic laws assumed by neo-classical economists. Measuring the cost of most of the inputs is often not practicable. Besides, the low level of technology, coupled with the high degree of manual labour, means that efficiency has a meaning which differs substantially from that which it takes in advanced economies. For example, risk minimization and family subsistence, rather than profit maximization, constitute fundamental principles. The peasant farmers tend to be more interested in improving food security by decreasing the risk of failure. Those who are desperate, sacrifice the long term prospects for short term survival. And those who are insecure and fear loss or displacement, may not invest for the future at all. Invariably, the small farmers, particularly those operating close to the subsistence margin, can hardly afford most of the needed resources. Therefore, they are often unwilling to give up the prospect of immediate production to ensure long term benefits.

Thus, it is difficult to apply the capitalist approach to peasant economies. Although often unquantifiable, the satisfaction derived from engagement in economic activity is at least as important as the level of profit is to 'economic man'. True, peasants do not necessarily enjoy hard manual labour, but they consider themselves efficient if they can satisfy their families' food requirements, and provide them with a minimum level of social welfare.

The simple economic model of profit maximization does not hold even in capitalist societies. Many people are not 'maximizers', but 'satisfiers' i.e., they are not necessarily interested in 'making as much money' as they can. Others, such as the hobby farmers, may derive satisfaction from the very act of farming and have no special economic goals, or set goals that are unrelated to output levels, in their agricultural work (Daniels, 1986). Clearly, in such cases, where the monetary accumulation is not a measure of success, it is very hard or even impossible to calculate efficiency in financial terms.

It is argued, therefore, that an application of a conventional profit-maximization model to peasant agricultural cultivation in tropical Africa would not be useful. In tropical Africa, the peculiar agro-technical methods such as row-intercropping, mixed intercropping, re-intercropping, among others, as practiced by the small-scale gardeners also pose a problem for measuring efficiency. In addition, tools are largely rudimentary and simple. The use of traditional implements such as hoes, cutlasses, buckets and shadoof for watering, etc. makes the farming operations tedious.

Much of the capital inputs are derived from domestic sources or from the farmers' labour and environment. This refers, obviously, to the use of fertilizers, and some of the basic irrigation equipment. The construction of canals and aquaducts, which are the equivalents of irrigation pipes, tiles and sprinklers or dripping equipment is manually done. Thus, land, labour and capital are all combined together into one inseparable production factor. This is a critical issue. The implements, techniques, and know-how, which the farmers utilize, strongly influence the size of harvest and the degree of efficiency. This, in turn, affects how much food is produced.

The distinguishing feature of dry-season agriculture lies in the pivotal role of household labour which is difficult to calculate in terms of market wage rates, profits or losses. However, the farmers regularly make decisions designed to maximize gains and minimize costs. The need to quantify the levels of inputs and outputs such as food supplies, labour hours, land availability and mouths to feed is apparent. Farmers tend to maximize the returns of their relatively scarce factors of production (mainly land, water pumps, and chemical fertilizers) by intensifying inputs of their relatively abundant factors (mainly labour). Thus, in their operations, the small farmers regularly combine relatively large labour inputs (self, family, and hired) with a small holding. This results in relatively high yields as well as greater energy efficiency despite the low capital inputs.

Furthermore, an important conclusion that can be derived from the close link among the factors of production is that land resources are not independent or static factors. Land's long-term productivity is conditioned to a great extent by the farmer's techniques and know-how. Good farmers maintain soil quality by using proper amounts of manure and fertilizers. Those who do not do so and those who use inappropriate technology, can quickly degrade the soils threatening its productive capacity. They also reduce its productivity and their family's food security. There is, therefore, a clear relationship between soil management and efficiency levels.

This observation suggests that it is possible to assess the level of efficiency, even using crude methods. Field studies do reveal that there are wide variations in productivity and farming techniques between one farmer and another. This implies that many farmers are not operating in the most efficient way, and that considerable increases in productivity and output can still be achieved if the farmers could improve their operational efficiency. The efficiency question is of vital importance where the operation is small. Large-scale operations may derive high income even if their margin of profit is low, and their efficiency is below the accepted standards. But the small-scale farmers cannot achieve this. Low margins of profit would threaten small-scale farmers' sustainability. Other factors affecting the level of productivity include the weather, the instability of which may reduce returns.

It is not sufficient to examine the productive phase only. Even the most efficient farmer can see his profit reduced to zero if the local marketing system is improper; if his access to land and water resources is insecure or denied; if the price level is inadequate; or, if government policy is indifferent, not sufficiently supportive, or even negative. Good policies that are inadequately implemented, or left to be implemented by corrupt persons, are powerful constraints, which may interfere with the proper operation of the farm as a viable business.

The Main Focus of this Paper

Not all the foregoing issues can be considered here. We shall concentrate on some questions, which, apart from one, deal with the production phase and focus on quantitative and qualitative indicators, which apply to farm viability and efficiency. We will focus mainly on the following questions:

a   How can efficiency levels be measured in the operations of the small-scale gardeners in the Jos-Bukuru urban area and its environs?

b   Do the farmers have access to the necessary inputs that will enhance productivity?

c   What are the farmers' perceptions about farming and what are their views on their welfare and satisfaction?

d   At what stages in their farming process are the farmers more efficient (or less efficient)?

e   At what scales of operation can market gardening be considered economically viable?

f   What is the relationship between efficiency and price, and, do farmers receive an adequate share of the market price?

Data analysed in this study were collected from field surveys. These took place between November and December 1993, when 146 farmers were interviewed using chance sampling, and in May 1994 (127 farmers interviewed). In addition, ten selected gardeners were closely monitored between January and February 1994. The selected monitored farmers represented all the major social groups living in the irrigable study area.

Sources of Capital for the Gardeners

The success of market gardening activities, to a large extent, depends on the availability of capital to the gardeners. The small-scale operations by the gardeners are largely influenced by the amount of financial capital available to them (Table 7.1).

    The gardeners rely on various sources of funds for their farming activities. Personal savings were relied upon mainly by about 70 percent of the sample farmers. It was gathered from field interviews that most of the gardeners were not accostomed to save part of the returns from current years to finance the succeeding years' operations. Therefore, what is reported as personal savings is usually money realized from sale of rain-fed farming produce. Some gardeners sell the products from their rainy season farming harvests at cheap prices in order to have funds to start dry-season gardening activities. Those who experience crop failure or poor harvests from rainy-season farming normally have to approach their friends and relatives for loans. About 29 percent of the respondents said they took loans from friends and relatives. Farmers are usually granted such loans. They are expected to pay them back before or at the end of the gardening season. However, they lack access to bank credit.

Table 7.1 Sources of Financial Capital Reported by a Sample of Gardeners, 1992/93 Gardening Season

Source	Number of farmers	% of Total farmers	% of Amount
Personal earnings	109	70.3	63
Bank loans	1	0.7	7
Loans from friends and relatives	45	29	30
Total	155	100	100

Source: Field Survey, Nov. - Dec. 1993.

It is important to emphasize that friends and relatives do not ask for any interest or formal documents. The process is simple, but the amounts are small (See Ben-Yami's article in this volume). Some of them expressed unhappiness regarding the difficulties involved in the process of obtaining loans from the banks. It was difficult for the farmers to say exactly how much money they obtained from each source. However, it was reported that personal earnings ranged from 500 to about 60,000 Naira, while loans from friends and relatives ranged from about 300 to about 30,000 Naira.

The inability of the farmers to plan for the resources that will be required for the next gardening season is a major constraint inhibiting their performance and profit margins. As a result, they cannot, for instance, buy the relevant inputs like seedlings, fertilizers, water pumps etc. before the next farming season as a way to avoid the effects of inflation.

Farm Sizes Per Holding and Costs of Renting Land

The following report is based on a second phase survey of 127 farmers who operated during the 1992/93 dry-season. The market gardeners under study fall into three broad categories in respect of their farm holdings. They are:

a   relatively small farmers who operate farm sizes of below 2 hectares;

b   relatively medium-scale farmers who operate 2 to 2.9 hectare holdings;
c   relatively large-scale farmers who operate 3 to 6.5 hectares (Table 7.2).

The 127 farmers cultivated altogether 126.4 hectares of land. The smallest group (group a) constituted about 84 percent, and cultivated about 57 percent of the land. The medium-scale farmers composed about 13 percent three percent of the respondents, with 13 percent of the land. The farms owned and operated by each farmer ranged from 0.04 to 6.5 hectares, the average being about one ha only. About 60 percent of them cultivated farms of around this average size (See Appendix 7.1). The range of farm sizes reported here is similar in all the three zones. In fact, no statistically significant variations in farm sizes were found between the zones. The survey reveals also, that during the farming season in which the study was conducted, most of the gardeners (about 70 percent) rented their land, and only about 30 percent owned it. However, the last figure conceals numerous forms of 'ownership', some of them being no more than rights of use on communal land.

Table 7.2   Farm Holdings and Costs of Renting Land by the Sample Gardeners, 1992/93 Gardening Season

Size of farm holding	=<1.9 ha	2-2.9 ha	3-6.5 ha	Total
Number of farmers	106	17	4	127
% of all respondents	84	13	3	100
Cultivated area (ha)	73	37	16	126
% of total land area	57	30	13	100
Owners of farm land	29	7	-	36
Renters of farm land	77	10	4	91
Cost of land (Naira)	48,540	16,400	10,200	75,140

Source: Field Survey, May, 1994.

It is important to emphasize, in this context, that security of tenure was fairly tenuous. However, accessibility to land by the older gardeners could not be said to constitute a major constraint to market gardening. Generally, gardeners under study did not possess certificates of occupancy on their farmlands or holdings. Thus, the degree of insecurity on farmland is high.

The sample farmers reported a fairly wide range of expenditure on land. The cost of renting land per annum ranged from 50 to 4,000 Naira. The average was 817 Naira. However, land rent varied significantly between the zones, being highest in the central zone and lowest in northern zone. This does not mean, however, that farmland in the northern zone is cheaper than in the other zones. In fact, there is reason to believe that it is becoming increasingly insecure and progressively more expensive for new entrants. The reason for this is that market gardening activities started much earlier in the northern zone, and the farmers there have established fairly strong cultivation rights. The average number of years of cultivation reported by the farmers in this zone was fifteen as against twelve years reported by farmers in the other zones. The duration of the tenancies varied widely, however. The northern farmers had no doubt benefitted from their early start not only by being able to reduce their land cost, but also by being able to exert stronger tenurial rights on their holdings. Their use right was most probably relatively fortified in time by their acceptance in the community and by their ability to foster friendly relationships with members of the land owning communities.

The role played by the social and the ethnic factors is of prime significance for accessibility to land. Much of the *fadama* land, particularly in the northern zone, is now owned by the University of Jos. Originally, most of the land in this zone was claimed by the Anaguta and Jarawa people, who are the traditional inhabitants of the area. These indigenous groups had little or no interest in irrigated farming and were quite willing to give the land out to the mining companies.

However, in the central and southern zones, land is largely owned by a single group, the Birom. Lately they have developed interest in market gardening. Some of them have learned the techniques and acquired the basic skills necessary for dry-season market gardening. There is today, therefore, an increasing number of Birom who compete with the settlers and migrant farmers in the use of *fadama* land during the dry-season.

Overall, the accessibility to land by some gardeners has been changing in an accelerated manner in recent years. However, there are considerable zonal north-south differentials in this change. It has adversely affected the migrant farmers and to some extent, the settler gardeners. There are likely to be fewer migrants in the near future because of the increasing scarcity of farmland in the area. As the available land reserves of the Jos area are being filled up, land price may likely increase. Security of tenure for migrant and settler farmers may decrease. The small farm size will probably become more prevalent and its economic profitability can only be achieved through further intensification of gardening activities.

Land Preparation

One of the most difficult tasks in the process of cultivating vegetables is land preparation. On the Plateau, land preparation is relatively difficult and expensive. This is mainly because the terrain on the Jos Plateau is rugged and the land available for agriculture is limited. Furthermore, mining activities have substantially reduced and degraded the limited available land in the *fadama* plain suitable for agriculture. Unfortunately, the open cast tin mining operations were usually concentrated along the valley channels of old and new streams which are the most valuable land for market gardening.

Because of the increasing use of small petrol-fuelled water pumping machine, it has become possible to extend irrigated market gardening upslope. Thus, three categories of irrigated fields have emerged. These have been identified as following:

a   river flood plain or traditional *fadama*;
b   middle slope irrigated fields;
c   upper slope irrigated fields.

Relatively speaking, the cost of preparing or improving land is enormous. It depends on the type of *fadama* used. The length of time and cost of preparing 1 ha by 7 male labourers, each working 9 hours per day in each field, varies considerably,

Farm workers spent relatively more time in preparing the same piece of land in the middle and upper slope than in the river flood plain or traditional *fadama*. All the activities involved, such as tilling/reclamation, breaking of rocks, leveling and making of ridges are very tedious. Only the male farmers have the strength to prepare the land. The further away a piece of land is from the plain, the more energy and resources it takes to prepare. Tools used are simple. These include hoes of varying sizes, cutlasses, hammers, shovels, diggers, buckets, shadoofs, a small motorized pump, and other tools. Additional activities, such as planting and transporting, weeding, application of fertilizers, watering, harvesting and sale of produce, also make substantial demands on the farmers' resources.

The length of time spent in the farm by the farmers varies slightly. The average number of hours spent per day was nine. The average number of days spent per week was six while the average number of month(s) reportedly spent per gardener in a season was 6.4. The information on the hours spent per day, days per week and month(s) per season clearly suggest that farmers do, indeed, devote a considerable amount of time to their farm work.

Farm Inputs

The scale of a gardening farm depends, to a large extent, on the availability and use of farming inputs. The inputs required are many and the ability of the farmers to buy them varies. Most of the farmers, particularly the smallest of the relatively small-scale operators are still constrained by their inability to afford the basic need of irrigation farming. Hence, their scale of cultivation is still relatively small. Table 7.3 presents some of the farming inputs and their costs.

Most of the farmers have a common practice of growing almost all the different vegetables. For example, it is common to have cabbage, carrot, lettuce, spinach, tomatoes, eggplant etc. grown by the same farmer. These are either cultivated as mono-crops or as multi-crops. Market gardeners usually experience several problems:

- The demand for seeds is high. Consequently, seeds have become costly. Some of the seeds available in the market are imitations. Many farmers have had no harvest because they bought and sowed the fake seeds. Efforts made by the farmers to produce seeds by themselves have proved futile.

- The scarcity and the high cost of fertilizer is by the farmers rated as the most difficult problem. They can hardly operate without the use of chemical fertilizers. The relatively small-scale farmers used per season between 5 and 10 of the 50 kg bags of fertilizers, the medium-scale farmers used between 10 and 30 of the 50 kg bags while the relatively large-scale farmers used over 30 bags of the 50 kg bags per season (Table 7.4). The cost of acquiring fertilizers is constantly rising. Most of farmers do not have direct access to this input except through the middlemen who have taken advantage of the price to exploit them. The middlemen usually buy up fertilizers and sell to the farmers on credit and repayment is made after harvesting. The farmers are, therefore, required to hand over their farm produce to the middlemen who then sell it on the farmer's behalf.

Table 7.3   The Cost of Acquiring Farming Inputs, 1993/94

INPUT	COST (Naira)
20g packet of cabbage seeds (hybrid)	120 – 150
10g packet of carrots seeds (hybrid)	50 - 70
20 g packet of lettuce seeds (hybrid)	70 - 90
100 g packet of spinach seeds (hybrid)	50
10g packet of tomato seeds (hybrid)	20
0.5 litre of herbicides	300
0.5 litre of pesticides	300
Chemical fertilizers:	
- 50 kg of NPK	180
- 50 kg of Super phosphate	150
- 50 kg of Urea	290
Organic fertilizers:	
- a truck load of unsorted compost manure	250 – 400
- a truck load of chicken dropping	300 – 500
- a truck load of ash	180 – 250
Cost of hiring labour (male) daily wage	120 – 150
Cost of hiring labour (female) daily wage	100 - 180
Cost of hiring seasonal labour	6,000-7,000
2' pump hose diameter by 1982	700
2' pump hose diameter by 1991	5,000
2' pump hose diameter by 1993/94	14,000
3' pump hose diameter by 1993/94	18,000
Suction hose (10m length)	500 - 600
30m length of hose for 2' pump	1,000
20m length of hose for 2' Pump	1,200

Source: Field Survey, Nov.-Dec. 1993.

- The availability, use and management of farm labour is crucial for dry season the market gardening. Farmers make use of both family labour and hired labour. The availability of labour, particularly hired labour, is becoming increasingly inadequate. Farmers reported that the cost of hiring farm labour was increasing (Table 7.5). The farmers and their labourers usually arrived at some agreement regarding labour use and it returns.

Table 7.4   Quantities of Chemical Fertilizers and Seeds Used by Sample Gardeners, 1992/93 Gardening Season

Type	Qty. of Chemical Fertilizer (50kg)	Qty. of Tomat. Seeds (10kg)	Qty. of Cabbage seeds (20g)	Qty. of lettuce seeds (20g)
Relatively small scale farmer	5 - 10	5 – 7 packets	1 packet	1 packet
Relatively medium scale farmer	10 - 30	7 – 12 packets	2 - 3 packets	2 - 3 packets
Relatively large scale farmer	30 +	15 & above	5 - 6 packets	5 - 6 packets

Source: Field Survey, Nov. - Dec. 1993.

As shown in Table 7.5, most labourers from monitoring surveys, reported that they received between 100 and 150 Naira per day. Some labourers worked for seasonal pay. These, however, were relatively few. Most of them were migrant labourers, who come at the beginning of the dry season, in most cases, together with their wives. When the gardening season is over they go back to carry out rain-fed agriculture in their states of origin. Such labourer said they received between 6,000 and 7,000 Naira per season. The monitoring surveys revealed that there are some other benefits which the labourers particularly the seasonal labourers get from the farmers. They include feeding and accommodation for the workers and the family, free or subsidized health care cost and some quantities of food at the end of the farming season. Some of those who work as seasonal labourers were the settler farmers' relatives. Apart from the monetary and material benefits seasonal labourers who are distant relations are given more quantities of food, usually maize produced and stored from rain-fed agricultural and in some cases they received new clothes as well.

Table 7.5   Wages Paid to Farm Labour 1992/93 Gardening Season (Two Monitoring Periods)

Amount per day (Naira)	1st Mon. freq.	2nd Month freq.	Amount per season (Naira)	1st Monit freq.	2nd Monit. freq.
50 - 100	-	1	2,000-3000	-	-
101 -150	23	19	4,000-5000	4	3
151 -200	7	4	6,000-7000	14	13
Total	30	24	Total	18	16

Sources: (for this table and Table 7.6) Field Survey, Jan. - Feb. 1994.

- One of the most important inputs into irrigation farming is the pumping machine. Farmers who are able to afford it only need to worry about cost of fuel and maintenance. Those who do not own pumps rent from those who have. However, renting of pumps entails a high degree of uncertainties as this is possible only when the pump owners do not need to irrigate their own fields. The cost of pumps has risen progressively and significantly in recent times, as shown in Table 7.3. The same pump that sold for 700 Naira in 1982 sold for 5,000 Naira in 1991 and by 1993/94 the price had risen to 14,000 Naira and in 1995/96 to 30,000 Naira. The hyperinflation that has persisted in the country for more than a decade now has adversely affected the ability of the farmers to purchase the necessary inputs for irrigation farming.

Besides the various inputs mentioned thus far, farmers spend a lot of money on several other activities. For instance, money is spent on sourcing water by damming streams, constructing earth-dams, expanding or deepening mine ponds and sucking wells. However, most of the farmers find it difficult to calculate exactly how much they spend on the various inputs in the course of a gardening season.

The Output

One of the questions posed at the outset of this paper is, how commensurate are the prices farmers receive for their produce to their efforts? During the 1993-1994 gardening season, a 25 kg basket of tomatoes sold for between 100 and 180 Naira (Table 7. 6). A report from an interview says one of the relatively large-scale farmers produced about 30,000 baskets of tomatoes per season. A medium-scale farmer can produced 10,000 - 15,000 baskets of tomatoes while a small-scale farmer can produce about 3,000 - 8,000 baskets. The smallest of the relatively small-scale farmers produced 500 - 2,000 baskets of tomatoes per farming season.

Table 7.6   Selling Prices of Vegetables 1992/93 Gardening Season

Vegetables	Price (Naira)
Bundle (18kg) of spinach	80 - 100
25 kg basket of tomato	100 - 180
15 kg basket of carrot	120 - 200
8 kg basket of beetroot	100
5 kg basket of greenbeans	60
10 kg basket of pepper	80 - 100
12 kg bag of peas	100
30 kg bag of cabbage	280 - 300
20 kg bag of egg-plant	120 - 150
3 kg basket of lettuce	50 - 70

The law of demand and supply best explains the reasons for the prices farmers receive for their produce. The pattern of cultivation is such that most of the farmers are usually at the peak of harvest at the same time. Hence, markets are flooded with vegetables between the month of February-April. During this period, prices of vegetables fall sharply, because supply is larger than demand. The lack of appropriate storage facilities always compels the farmers to accept the poor prices offered for their produce.

Financial Expenditure and Earning Totals by the Sample Farmers

In this study, we have attempted a grouping of the various farm inputs and their costs as reported by the farmers (see Appendix 7.2). A summary of the findings is provided in Table 7.7.

Table 7.7   Financial Expenditure and Earnings by the Sample Farmers, 1992/93 Gardening Season ('000 Naira)

Type of Farmers	No. of respondents	Total input cost	Total output value	Total profit	Mean profit
Small-scale	79	679	1,698	1,019	12.9
Med-scale	6	121	362	241	40.7
Large-scale	1	22	56	34	34.0

Source (for this and the next table): Field Survey, May, 1994.

It is important to emphasize that information was not available on all items of expenditure as well as output. Generally, irrigated market gardeners do not keep records of their expenses and returns from their gardening activities. This constituted a serious problem in constructing a balance sheet for market gardening in the study area. One main reason for this is that a large majority of the farmers are illiterate. Besides, some of them said records keeping would discourage them from farming if they discovered they were operating at a loss. Inability of the farmers to keep proper records of farming activities is one of the major constraints that they face. Unfortunately, most farmers did not recognize this as a problem. This could be because of their low level of exposure and lack of awareness.

Many of the gardeners who operated beyond 2.4 hectares found it difficult to provide information on how much they spent on farming inputs and even to guess their total turnover or profit. It was observed that some of them feel slightly uncomfortable in saying how much they make as profit. However, personal interviews and field observation shows that many of them do make a profit (Table 7.8).

The total earnings, after deducting production cost, seem to be fairly high. However, for the small-scale farmers, the mean earning was less than 13,000 Naira, or about 560 U.S. dollars at the official exchange rate (which was 23 naira to one dollar). Nevertheless, most farmers had some surplus for investing in irrigated market gardening. Table 7.7 presents the total made by the sampled gardeners in the 1992/93 season. However, there are wide variations among the groups in terms of amount set aside for investment. The relatively small-scale farmers invested no more than 8,700 Naira each. About 11 percent of them reported losses during the 1992/93 farming season. These losses ranged, according to them, from 1,250 to 17,320 Naira. Furthermore, personal information on the input-output relationships of some of the gardeners reflecting the different categories of farmers identified is shown in Table 7.8.

As already pointed out, irrigated gardening in the study area is still dominated by small holdings, small fields and relatively low capital input. Consequently, it is prone to the various problems arising from the diseconomies of scale. At a relatively small scale of operation, many of the gardeners are still capable of acquiring the funds for their farming operations. This situation has affected their urge to expand and, indeed, their productivity.

Similarly, some of the gardeners operating relatively large farms usually run short of some inputs, like fertilizers, irrigation water and seeds at some stage of their cultivation. This has caused many of them to abandon already prepared plots.

Table 7.8   Input-Output Relationships of selected Gardeners, 1992/93 Gardening Season ('000 Naira)

Type of Farmer	Fertil.	Seed	Labour	Total	Out-put	Balance
Small-scale	2,650	0.9	2.0	5.6	5.2	-400
Small-scale	3.5	1.6	3.7	8.7	20.0	+11.3
Medium-scale	8.1	2.4	9.0	19.5	61.2	+41.7
Medium-scale	5.4	1.8	100.0	17.2	49.3	+32.1
Large-scale	11.2	4.1	6.9	22.0	56	+34.0

However, the scale of operation that may be most successful and viable is likely to be the upper quartile of the relatively medium size group. All the gardeners are faced with some constraints regarding inputs. Yet, at a medium scale of operation of one ha or slightly more, the gardeners can manage effectively the various factors of production at their disposal to achieve relatively more sustainable output.

As shown in Table 7.8, a medium-scale gardener who invested 19,490 Naira in gardening activities made a profit of 41,720 Naira, while a large-scale gardener invested 22,000 Naira and made a profit of 34,000 Naira.

Social and Psychological Benefits to the Gardeners

Most of the gardeners (about 70 percent) expressed satisfaction with market gardening. Despite the numerous constraints facing them they are very happy that they can produce sufficient food for their household as well as surplus for sale. About 80 percent of what the farmers and their households eat is produced by themselves. Thus, the food security in the farmers' households is relatively high. This is a source of joy and satisfaction to most of the farmers. One of the farmers at Anglo-Jos happily said: 'I produce nothing less than 30,000 baskets of tomatoes and make a minimum profit of about 600,000 Naira every year from all that I cultivate'. Another farmer at Korot, who is popularly known as 'Serkin-Noma' meaning chief of farming, said 'I made a minimum of 60,000 Naira every year after paying workers and settling other expenses'. Though the accuracy of these statements can be questioned, the high positive perspectives of market gardening by some farmers are noteworthy.

Indeed, many of them are proud to be farmers. They seemed contented and happy. The social welfare and satisfaction of the farmers is also accompanied by some financial profits for some of the gardeners. Looking at this scenario, efficiency or viability of the gardening activities cannot be viewed based narrowly on monetary costs-benefits analysis. The farmer and his family's labour contribution and consumption are also important.

Summary and Conclusions

The paper has provided some insights into the cost and benefits as well as external influences in market gardening, and into the economic considerations involved in household consumption. The contribution made by the market gardeners from the greater Jos area to the availability of crops and vegetables in Nigeria is substantial. The gardeners are making the best out of the available resources, regardless of their farming constraints, to meet the growing market demand for crops and vegetables.

Although the gardeners studied are smallholders operating at very small scales, they are seemingly efficient at managing relatively small farms. The conclusion is that the intensive agricultural system of these farmers achieves relatively moderate production and combines subsistence and market benefits. The clearest benefit farmers derived from gardening activities is their individual household's food security.

However, there is need to enhance the economic sustainability of the gardeners on the Plateau. One of the ways to achieve this is to re-orientate the gardeners to think more of gardening activities as a business than as a way of life.

References

Daniels, T.L. (1986), 'Hobby Farming in America: Rural Development or Threat to Commercial Agriculture?' *Journal of Rural Studies.* Vol. 2, pp. 31-40.

Sender, John and Smith, Sheila (1986), *The Development of Capitalism in Africa.* London: Methuen.

Appendix 7.1   **Farm Sizes and Cost of Renting Land in the Study Area 1993/94**

A. Northern Zone Respondents.	Ethnic Group	Farmer's status on land	Farm sizes (ha)	Cost of renting land per annum (Naira)	No. of years of cultivating the land
Small scale Farmers					
1	Hausa	Owner	0.3	N/A	15
2	"	"	0.55	N/A	15
3	Birom	"	0.8	N/A	6
4	Hausa	Tenant	0.4	100	10
5	"	"	0.7	180	20
6	"	"	0.55	50	25
7	"	"	0.7	120	8
8	"	Owner	0.18	N/A	30
9	"	Tenant	0.6	100	4
10	"	"	1	400	20
11	Fulani	"	0.4	500	10
12	Hausa	"	0.4	120	N/A
13	"	"	0.4	150	N/A
14	"	"	0.7	300	9
Total			7.68	1,920	
Medium scale farmers					
15	Hausa	Owner	2.3	N/A	30
16	"	Tenant	2	1,000	N/A
Total			4.3	1,000	
Large scale					
17	Hausa	Tenant	3.3	1,200	-
Total			3.3	1,200	
Sub-Total			15.28	4,230	N/A

B. Central Zone
Respondents.

Small scale farmers					
1	Birom	Tenant	0.5	300	10
2	Hausa	"	1.9	400	11
3	"	"	1.6	300	5
4	"	"	1.2	1,000	20
5	"	"	1	2,000	29
6	"	"	0.5	600	N/A
7	Birom	Owner	1	N/A	5
8	Hausa	Tenant	1	2,000	15
9	"	"	0.5	1,200	15
10	"	"	1.5	4,000	25
11	"	"	0.7	800	10
12	"	"	0.6	500	10
13	"	"	0.7	300	N/A
14	"	"	0.9	300	N/A
15	"	"	0.9	300	N/A
16	Birom	Owner	0.5	N/A	N/A
17	Hausa	Tenant	0.4	300	14
18	"	"	1.5	1,000	1
19	"	"	1.2	1,000	15
20	"	"	1	400	15
21	"	"	1	1,000	20
22	"	"	1	800	20
23	"	"	0.5	800	1
24	"	"	1	1,000	10

25	"	Free	0.04	N/A	1
26	"	Tenant	0.4	200	1
27	Birom	"	1.5	700	2
28	"	Owner	1	N/A	9
29	"	"	0.5	N/A	7
30	"	"	0.5	N/A	4
31	Hausa	Tenant	0.5	N/A	2
32	"	"	0.5	800	13
33	"	"	0.7	800	20
34	"	"	0.5	800	20
35	Calabar	Owner	0.4	Farm Produce	N/A
36	Hausa	"	1	500	N/A
37	Birom		0.4	N/A	N/A
38			0.8	N/A	N/A
Total			30.89	24,100	
Medium scale Farmers					
39	Hausa	Tenant	2.5	800	30
40	"	"	2.7	1,500	1
41	"	"	2.7	700	26
42	Birom	Owner	2	N/A	4
43	Hausa	Tenant	2	1,400	8
Total			11.9	4,400	
Sub-Total			45.79	30,500	

C. Southern Zone Respondents
Small scale farmers

No.				F/producers	
1	Fulani	Tenant	1	700	24
2	Hausa	"	0.6	400	2
3	Fulani	"	0.8	500	1
4	Birom	"	0.5	300	15
5	Hausa	"	0.7	500	15
6	"	"	1	1,500	16
7	"	"	0.3	200	N/A
8	Fulani	"	0.6		2
9	Hausa	"	0.23	300	24
10	"	Owner	0.69	N/A	16
11	"	"	0.5	N/A	5
12	"	Tenant	1	1,000	22
13	"	"	0.23	500	15
14	"	Owner	0.69	N/A	8
15	Birom	"	0.23	N/A	N/A
16	Hausa	Tenant	0.46	780	8
17	"	"	0.69	780	6
18	Fulani	"	0.46	30	2
19	Hausa	"	0.6	1,000	1
20	Birom	Owner	0.46	N/A	10
21	Hausa	Tenant	0.6	1,000	5
22	"	"	0.46	300	12
23	"	"	1.38	700	9
24	"	Owner	0.92	N/A	N/A
25	Hausa	Tenant	1.38	N/A	N/A
26	"	"	0.23	N/A	45

No.					
27	Hausa	Tenant	0.46	200	N/A
28	Birom	Owner	0.5	N/A	20
29	Hausa	Tenant	0.5	100	5
30	"	"	0.2	500	15
31	"	"	0.5	400	N/A
32	Birom	Owner	0.5	500	16
33	Hausa	Tenant	0.7	500	3
34	Birom	Owner	0.46	N/A	N/A
35	"	"	0.5	700	N/A
36	Hausa	Tenant	0.7	2,000	17
37	"	"	0.46	450	15
38	"	"	1.38	800	15
39	"	"	1.38	900	15
40	"	"	0.46	80	2
41	Birom	Owner	0.23	100	20
42	Hausa	Tenant	1	500	22
43	"	"	1	300	25
44	"	"	1	400	N/A
45	"	"	1	200	10
46	Birom	Owner	0.23	N/A	N/A
47	Fulani	Tenant	0.46	200	3
48	Hausa	Owner	0.46	N/A	6
49	Birom	"	0.46	N/A	2
50	Hausa	Tenant	0.3	700	8
51	"	"	0.5	1,000	N/A
52	"	"	0.6	1,000	N/A
53	Birom	"	0.46	500	25
54	"	Owner	1	N/A	1
Total			34.11		

Medium scale farmers	55	Hausa	Owner	2	N/A	5
	56	Birom	Tenant	2.7	1,500	10
	57	"	"	2.3	2,500	12
	58	"	Owner	2	N/A	-
	59	Hausa	Tenant	2	4,000	20
	60	Birom	Owner	2	N/A	4
	61	"	"	2	N/A	-
	62	"	Owner	2	N/A	5
	63	"	"	2	N/A	1
	64	Hausa	Tenant	2.7	2,000	20
Total				19.7		
Large scale farmers	65	Hausa	Tenant	3	3,000	12
	66	"	"	6.5	4,000	6
Total				9.5	7,000	
Sub-Total	127			63.31	39.790	599
Grand Total				126.38	74,410	1206
Average				1.0	817	12

Appendix 7.2   **Total Financial Expenditure and Earning by the Sample Farmers 1993/94**

Sample number	Input	Output	Balance (Output-input)
Northern Zone			
Small scale farmers			
1	4,500	6,900	2,400
2	7,000	10,510	3,510
3	1,630	1,900	270
4	3,600	1,900	-1,700
5	2,850	6,000	3,150
6	1,500	4,400	2,900
7	4,000	51,500	47,500
8	3,200	N/A	N/A
9	2,300	26,150	23,850
10	6,990	5,340	-1,650
11	750	N/A	N/A
12	4,650	1,000	-3,650
13	4,250	3,000	-1,250
14	180	N/A	N/A
Sub-Total	43,450	118,600	75,330
Medium scale farmers			
15	1,740	1,960	220
16	15,270	26,500	11,230
Sub-Total	17,010	28,460	11,450
Large scale farmers			
17	10,155	N/A	N/A
Total	60,460	147,060	86,780

Central Zone:
Small scale
farmers

1	N/A	N/A	N/A
2	17,905	N/A	N/A
3	7,320	N/A	N/A
4	5,000	22,500	17,500
5	46,000	30,000	16,000
6	46,000	N/A	N/A
7	14,000	N/A	N/A
8	33,800	47,000	13,200
9	21,100	30,000	8,900
10	40,000	60,000	20,000
11	8,650	20,500	11,850
12	17,510	20,000	2,490
13	17,000	N/A	N/A
14	29,600	50,900	21,300
15	20,660	15,700	-4,960
16	3,750	N/A	N/A
17	13,480	65,400	51,920
18	1,000	N/A	N/A
19	28,500	80,000	51,500
20	N/A	15,500	N/A
21	13,900	23,800	9,900
22	4,800	13,585	8,705
23	2,560	6,300	3,740
24	17,680	N/A	N/A
25	N/A	1,200	N/A
26	8,890	20,300	11,410
27	16,495	N/A	N/A

30	1,100	1,500	400
31	9,600	17,000	7,400
32	3,440	16,000	12,560
33	5,760	11,900	6,140
34	5,660	11,900	6,240
35	12,300	30,200	17,900
36	3,000	1,200	-1,750
37	750	6,800	6,050
38	6,500	14,220	7,720
Total	346,550	633,205	286,655
Medium scale farmers			
39	14,720	N/A	N/A
40	660	3,000	2,340
41	14,200	75,150	60,950
42	7,100	43,500	36,400
43	9,490	N/A	N/A
Total	21,960	121,650	99,690
Large scale farmers			
44	4,530	N/A	N/A
Total	368,510	754,855	386,345
Southern Zone			
Small scale farmers			
1	4,320	45,000	40,680
2	1,042	N/A	N/A
3	2,680	12,000	9,320
4	N/A	N/A	N/A
5	3,750	N/A	N/A
6	24,800	N/A	N/A
7	560	1,200	640
8	1,780	2,500	720

9	18,020		15,000	-3,020
10	7,500		N/A	N/A
11	8,750		20,625	11,875
12	2,500		17,475	14,975
13	21,400		17,040	-4,360
14	4,500		17,290	12,790
15	4,640		34,640	30,000
16	5,560		41,040	35,480
17	4,880		22,200	17,320
18	3,400		N/A	N/A
19	5,300		N/A	N/A
20	2,850		15,400	12,550
21	9,425		N/A	N/A
22	4,300		22,500	18,200
23	7,440		53,450	46,010
24	1,130		N/A	N/A
25	23,700		82,000	58,300
26	1,050		4,000	2,950
27	1,420		N/A	N/A
28	19,500		30,400	10,900
29	3,200		N/A	N/A
30	3,074		3,100	26
31	7,260		30,000	22,740
32	2,550		12,000	9,450
33	2,480	20,000	27,000	17,520
34	8,900			18,100
35	2,340		7,500	5,160
36	10,900		30,200	19,300

37	10,050	39,200	29,150
38	14,000	43,000	29,000
39	10,000	12,000	2,000
40	1,850	2,000	150
41	N/A	600	N/A
42	15,500	27,200	11,700
43	1,540	17,000	15,460
44	2,400	25,500	23,100
45	5,410	14,000	8,590
46	2,250	8,250	6,000
47	400	3,300	2,900
48	4,920	18,600	13,680
49	6,700	43,500	36,800
50	3,220	21,300	18,080
51	9,260	68,000	54,740
52	25,450	20,000	-5,450
53	10,254	N/A	N/A
54	13,190	N/A	N/A
Sub-Total	288,884	946,410	657,526
Medium scale farmers			
55	12,500	65,000	52,500
56	7,020	7,100	80
57	16,050	49,140	33,090
58	N/A	N/A	N/A
59	17,500	36,000	18,500
60	2,010	5,440	3,430
61	8,650	35,000	26,350
62	1,610	8,600	6,990

63	N/A	200	N/A
64	5,200	6,000	800
	70,540	212,280	141,740
65	21,900	56,255	34,355
66	45,100	N/A	N/A
Large scale farmers			
Total	381,324	1,214,945	833,621
Grand Total	810,294	2,116,860	1,306,566

8 Women's Participation in Small-Scale Irrigation Farming in Jos-Bukuru Area, Nigeria

RAHILA P. GOWON

Introduction

The dominant position held by women in African agriculture is suggested by the fact that as much as seventy percent of Africa's agricultural workers are female. They also constitute more than ninety percent of the continent's processors of staple foods (Harsch, 1994). This is in addition to their handling of most of the marketing of the agricultural products. Their enormous contributions in agriculture, which are often unnoticed or are taken for granted by most people and governments have been acknowledged by Boutros Gali. He was cited as emphasizing that women's contribution in both agriculture and other sectors of the economy is essential to food security and rural development, since they grow most of Africa's food and sustain rural life (Gellen, 1994).

The women who work the land are generally poor, illiterate and male-dependent. At the same time, they are the main force in the struggle against rural misery, backwardness and urban dependency. Yet, they lack the critical resources such as land, credit facilities, labour-saving implements and the political power needed to maximize their principal role in agriculture as well as in other sectors.

Within the Jos Plateau area, many women are, as expected, involved in rainfed farming. However, the extent of their involvement in dry-season irrigation farming, has not yet been ascertained. This is partly because in this region the latter is a relatively new type of farming.

This report discusses the various activities in which women in the nine areas under study were seen involved regarding irrigation farming, from land preparation to the marketing of the products harvested.

Their participation is described under seven sub-headings:

a   The extent of participation by women
b   Scales of operation
c   Access to inputs
d   Entrepreneurship and management systems
e   Marketing strategies and experiences
f   Three case studies
g   Problems and prospects

The Extent of Participation by Women

The role and status of women in market gardening in the study area, as observed in the field, is secondary to those of their male counterparts. Their impact is hardly seen or felt in the actual farming. However, the reverse is the situation regarding the marketing of the products, in which they compete favourably with the men (Table 8.1). They also form the bulk of the farm labourers, but not for all activities in the gardening.

Table 8.1   Participation of Women in Small-Scale Irrigation Farming

Nature of operation	No. of women involved	Percentage
1. Farm owners	40	4.9
2. Marketers	59	7.3
3. Labourers	713	87.8
Total	812	100.0

Source: Field Survey, 1994/95.

Three categories of farmers were encountered: the settlers, indigenes and migrants. All the women farmers (except one) encountered in this survey were indigenes. Only one woman settler gardener was seen. All the female farmers who have farm holdings were found in the southern zone of the study area (Table 8.2). About 40 out of the 2,000 dry-season farmers in the study area, were women (Ajaegbu, 1994).

Since irrigation farming is essentially a specialized system of farming, most women engage the services of men for land preparation, the construction of water channels and for watering. Women who do carry out some land preparation, only plough and harrow the farm.

Table 8.2   Types of Women Farmers

Farmers Types	Ethnic group	Location	Years. involved in farming	No. of women	Percent
Settler	Hausa	Central Zone	6 years	1	8.3
Indigenous	Birom	Southern Zone	2-10 yrs	39	91.7
Migrants	Nil	Nil		-	-
Total				40	100.0

Source: Field Survey, 1994/95.

As shown in Table 8.3, the numbers of women engaged in the different activities include both women farmers and women labourers. As noted earlier, the latter constitute the bulk of labourers in market gardening. Most of the female labourers are adolescent girls and young women. These figures are by no means exclusive because the same woman could be involved in two or more farming activities.

Table 8.3 Females' Farm Activities (Farmers and Labourers)

Activity	No. of women involved
Land preparation	18
Watering	30
Weeding	120
Harvesting	103

Source: Field Survey, 1994/95.

Those who do the watering normally use the shadoof, buckets, basins and other smaller containers for this purpose. This is because few of them can afford a motorized pump.

The women are generally within the age ranges of 20-55 years. Most of them are married and within the child-bearing ages of 20-40 years. Most of them have been engaged in market gardening for between two and ten years. Four of the women farmers are widows, two of them are divorced and the remaining are married. One of the widows does not have any child (family) while the others (married or divorced ones) have three to seven children.

As can be seen from Tables 8.4 and 8.5, all but one of the women who joined in market gardening did so more than a year ago, but within the last seven years. Furthermore, while elderly women (of over forty years old) are still present in the sub-sector, the younger ones have also been taking to gardening. In all, the women marketers are generally in their middle ages, while the farm labourers are much younger women and adolescent girls.

Table 8.4   Number of Farming Years and Percent of the Women Involved in Farming

Years of farming	No. of women	Percentage
1	4	8.0
2-4	20	50.0
5-7	16	42.0
Total	40	100.0

Table 8.5   The Age of the Female Gardeners

Age Range	Number of women	Percentage
< 25	6	16.7
25 - 39	13	33.3
40 - 54	17	42.0
55+	4	8.0
Total	40	100.0

Source (for both tables): Field Survey, 1994/95.

Scales of Operation

The farm sizes of the 40 female farmers ranged from 0.5 ha or less (operated by the sole farmers), through 1 ha to 1.5 ha in the case of joint gardening. The large surface areas obtainable in respect of operators are not found in one block, but are made up of several farms at different locations.

Most of the women gardeners use locally-prepared seeds, instead of the improved seedlings from the UTC farms or imported ones, which are relatively costly. All the men on the other hand use at least one or more forms of improved seedlings on their farms. This results in low germination rates. Although the female farmers rely mostly on organic manure for improved soil nutrients, their accessibility to it is limited, because the men control the use of animal dungs, while the women also lack the basic skills of compost making - a viable source of organic manure. Their use of chemical fertilizers is generally low, because of exorbitant prices of fertilizers. Most of the men can afford to buy them in 50kg bags, while the majority of women buy them in 1 kg measures.

Crop types planted by the women show that they do not include exotic vegetables such as peas and celery. Rather, they tend to concentrate on the traditional vegetables, such as tomatoes, spinach and peppers, the handling of which they are conversant with, and those that can withstand drought. This is mainly because they encounter more difficulties in watering the farms. Some of them have not yet mastered the specialized skill needed for watering, nor can they afford to buy the rather costly motorized water pumps. Another reason is the general scarcity of water experienced by many gardeners in the southern zone where many of the women farmers operate. Other crop types planted by women gardeners are carrots, irish potatoes and eggplants.

Compared to other agricultural activities on the Jos Plateau, irrigation farming is operated mainly on a rather small-scale. The women are generally the smallest of the small-scale gardeners (cf. Omomoh, in this Volume). The levels of their various inputs in their farming activities are very small. According to our survey findings, cash investments in their farms ranged from 500 to 10,000 Naira each. The smallest operators among them invested only between 500 and 2,500 Naira each; the middle-range (moderate) ones invested 3,000 to 6,000 Naira each; while the relatively large-scale women gardeners invested from 6,500 to 10,000 Naira each. Such relatively large-scale women farmers were found among the joint owners of farms.

The extent of harvests by the women also vary according to the sizes of women's farm holdings. The harvest of tomatoes can range from 4 to 15 baskets in a single-owned farm and up to 10-30 baskets in jointly-owned farms. The harvest of carrots could be as much as 2 to 8 bags in a single owned farm, and about 9 to 20 bags in jointly-owned farms. Spinach is harvested at the same level as carrots except that it is measured in bundles. The harvest of irish potatoes could also range from 1 to 25 bags in jointly-owned farms. An average sized basket of tomatoes and a bag of carrot weighs about 60kg, while a bundle of spinach or a bag of irish potatoe weighs about 40kg and 100kg respectively. The smallest harvests from both types of farm holdings are usually of peppers and eggplants. Their harvests range from 1 to 10 bags in single-owned farms and about 10 to 25 bags in jointly-owned farms. The estimates given for the various harvests were for the farming season of 1994/95.

Access to Inputs

Accessibility of inputs such as land, capital (cash) and labour is highly tied to tradition and to a variety of market forces. The common ways of acquiring land for agricultural purposes in the study area are through:

a   getting allocation of portions of family land;
b   inheriting farm land from parents, husbands, wives or other relations;
c   free leasing or borrowing land from neighbours for specified cropping seasons;
d   receiving gifts of farm land from parents or other relations;
e   acquiring through outright purchase;
f   renting land; or
g   long-term leasing (for 35-99 years) from the local or state government.

The women in the study area can, at least in theory, get land through any of these ways. In practice, however, their access to farm land may be limited by several factors. For instance, in respect of dry-season farming, the suitable land is not enough to go round; so the highest bidders or those most effectively connected get them (Table 8.6). Predominantly, the women get gardening land through allocation of their family (marital or maternal) land.

The women in the study sample who had farm holdings got them mainly by inheritance. This applied mostly to widows or divorcees. But some of them were joint operators, either with their husbands, or with their grown-up children and other relatives, particularly their paternal brothers. The first type of holding is found among women who have been forced by circumstances such as divorce, separation or widowhood, to own farm plots of their own. Those separated from their husbands or the divorcees are given farm plots by their relatives. Some widows decide to use farms of their late husbands, in addition to getting some farm plots from their relatives. Also included in this category are women who won plots jointly with others, but at the same time acquire on their own additional farms to work on.

Table 8.6   The Form of Women's Farm Holdings

Type of and acquisition	No. of women	Percentage
1. Allocation of family land	24	58.4
2. Free leasing or borrowing	6	16.8
3. Renting	6	16.8
4. Outright purchase	-	0.0
5. Long term leasing	4	8.0
Total	40	100.0

Source: Field Survey, 1994/95.

Thus, in effect, many of the women have had access to gardening land. However, the true or flood-plain *fadama* areas have been virtually completely taken up. Thus, new entrants into market gardening may have to take over their late husband's shares or venture to the upslope irrigable farms. These latter demand relatively high capital inputs for 3-inch pumps and long conduit hoses to reach the distances involved to such farms. Such resources are not yet easily affordable by many of the women. This may limit the chances of new entrants into the sub-sector.

Cash, an important input in agriculture especially in irrigation farming, is not easily available to women, by getting loans from banks. The men control most of the farm produce and livestock kept at the homes. The stringent collateral conditions relating to securing bank loans also discriminate against the women. What women do to avail themselves of cash is to get involved in local revolving credit schemes or in the alternative local saving system popularly known as the adashe or asusu. There are also a few cases of women who get loans from their family members (not necessarily their husbands).

Accessibility of labour to women in the study area is not a problem except, perhaps, for the cost and the time of labour supply. Women use the services of men for activities like preparation of farm plots and basins, construction of water channels and, sometimes, for actual watering of the farms.

Whenever women approach prospective workers, the response they get is usually positive (for no one will reject helping a woman). But, the workers usually have to finish working on their own farms before going to work on the woman's farm. If a woman needs the work to be done urgently, she then has to pay thrice or more of the price normally charged for any work. Labour provided by their younger children is what they use to their best advantage, since it is always available whenever they need it.

Other farm inputs are generally not easily accessible to women farmers because most farm inputs are expensive and almost beyond their reach. As a result of this, the majority of the women, especially the sole operators use very minimal and generally low-cost farming inputs (Table 8.7).

Table 8.7   Farm Inputs Used

Soil nutrients, insecticides and pesticides	No. of women using	%	Seed form	No. of women using	%
Ash only	0	0	Locally prepared seeds	30	75
Chemical fertilizer only	0	0	Improved seeds	0	0
Organic manure only	17	42.5	Both local and improved seeds	10	25
Chemical fertilizers and organic manu.	13	32.5			
All types	10	25.0			
Total:	40	100.0		40	100

Source: Field Survey, 1994/95.

As we noted earlier, most of the women involved in irrigated farming are within the southern zone of the study area, which is particularly faced with the problem of water scarcity during peak dry months (Jan-March). Water which is a major farm input in irrigation is, therefore, a problem all women are faced with. They not only face the problem of water sourcing, but also that of getting water to the crops. This is because many of them do not own motorized water pumps to convey the water to their farms. These are very costly, a 2-inch pump today (1996) selling for over 30,000 Naira, while the 3-inch pump sells for about 45,000 Naira (US$ 375 and 560), respectively.

The women, therefore, resort to the use of less expensive, but laborious watering techniques such as by using buckets, cans or, at best, the shadoof system (Table 8.8). Where they can afford the price they, at times, hire the services of motorized pumps from those who own them. The implication of this is that watering which is done at specific periods of the day for effective and maximum utilization is delayed in the case of the women's farms.

Table 8.8 Methods of Watering Used by Women

Methods	No. of women using it	Percent
Buckets, basins, calabash etc.	26	66.4
Shadoof	7	16.8
Personal motorized pumps	0	0.0
Hired or borrowed motorized pumps	7	16.8
Total	40	100.0

Source: Field Survey, 1994/95.

These handicaps regarding accessibility of input, affect women's farms to various degrees. The solely-owned farms do not do well and the owners rarely have much to sell. Conversely, the jointly-owned farms do relatively better and at times fare as well as those owned by the men.

Entrepreneurship and Management System

Two management systems were encountered among the sample women in the study. They are referred to as the "sole management" and "joint management" systems (Table 8.9).

The sole management system is practiced by women who are the sole owners of their farms. In that case, they are the sole decision makers regarding their farms and the income accruing from the sale of the produce from such farms. One third of the women operate this management system while, ironically, farms under this system are also usually very small in size.

The joint management system is operated by women who own farms jointly with their relatives. Such women have some partial input in the decisions concerning the management of the farm or the sale of the farm produce. The degree of input in decision-making varies from one form of joint ownership to another. Where a farm is jointly owned together with a male child, the woman is the major decision maker. Her input in decision making is less if the joint ownership is with a brother or husband.

Table 8.9　Management Systems Used by Women on Farm Holdings

Management system	No. of Women	Percent
1. Sole	13	33.3
2. Jointly with husbands	17	42.0
3. Jointly with children or relatives	10	24.7
Total	40	100.0

Source: Field Survey, 1994/95.

Most of the women do not keep records of their gardening activities, and they depend on the effective recollection of events from their memories or those of their spouses or other relatives. Women who own farms jointly with their husbands feel they do not even need to keep track of events, since their input in decision making is minimal. This is because women in this group operate more or less as farm labourers. It is the women involved in other forms of farm holdings who are usually concerned about the recollection of happenings and returns or yields.

All the women encountered were literate but had never bothered to keep records in written form, because they felt they might get discouraged if they discovered at the end of each irrigation farming season that there were more expenses incurred than incomes from the farming operations.

Marketing Strategies, Experiences and Constraints

Many women are generally involved in the marketing of gardening crops either as wholesalers or retailers. More of the 40 female farmers also operate as marketers. As retailers, they visit nearby farms to buy vegetables for sale. They also buy from wholesalers in the mini and satellite markets. The wholesalers operate in the satellite markets, while the retailers operate in the mini markets. Many of the women said they operate in the mini markets because of the little capital, time and labour required to undertake the marketing. Of the 118 marketers surveyed, exactly half were women. About 47% of them operated as wholesalers while about 53% were retailers (Table 8.10).

Table 8.10 Level of Women's Marketing Operation

Market	No. of women marketers (traders)	% of total marketers	% of women who are retailers	% of women who are wholesalers
Radura/Foron Junction	17	28.8	0	100
Building Materials Market	3	5.0	0	100
Farin Gada market	23	39.1	86.6	13.4
Kwararafa market	16	27.1	25.0	75.0
Total	59	100.0	-	-

Source: Field Survey, 1994/95.

Even in the marketing of the products, men are still dominant, not so much in numbers, as in the amount of capital employed, and in the influence they exert. It is the men who transport vegetables to distant markets in neighboring states and who constitute the majority of the wholesalers in nearby markets. The male wholesalers have formed a formidable front in the market that determines not only the operation by the women, but also those of the male farmers and sellers. In all the four satellite markets visited in Jos no woman was a member of the Marketers' Associations' executive bodies.

Women who own farms usually sell off their products to their male counterparts on the farm in bulk or liaise with other men to bring vehicles to the farms and convey the vegetables to the satellite markets. As at the time of the study no woman encountered had taken any product to the markets in neighbouring states. This could be due to the fact that their farm sizes were usually small and could not produce large quantities of vegetables that could be profitably taken to the neighbouring states.

Case Studies

Some of the roles and working conditions of the females involved in gardening in Korot can be illustrated by the following three cases:

Case 1:

A 55 years old widow, a Birom and Christian, who had, by 1994/95, ten years experience as a market gardener. She has no formal education and lost her husband in 1987 until which date she had worked with him as joint owners of their four small gardening plots. Following the death of her husband, she inherited the farm plots and, at the time of the survey and documentation regarding the Korot subproject participants in 1995, she cultitvated only one, the smallest, of the plots. This was only about 0.4 ha which she said she could afford to cultivate that year with the limited resources and labour available to her. The relatively bigger plots of about 0.8-1.0 ha each were not irrigated that year but reserved for the less labour-demanding rain-fed farming. She undertakes some small informal tin mining to hire additional labour in view of her other financial responsibilities, including her children's education. Only occasionally does she hire adult male labour to assist, particularly in land preparation. As observed, the vegetables in her garden were mainly carrot, tomato, cabbage and garden eggs (eggplants). She does not own a water-pumping machine, but depends mainly on borrowing or sometimes renting one for her watering operations.

Considering the size of plot actually cultivated each season and the meager inputs employed, she falls within the group of very small of the small-scale gardeners. She expressed, however, the desire to increase the scale of her gardening if she could have access to more funds. She is grooming the second son to take over the farm eventually.

Case 2:

Two women who operate joint gardens with their respective husbands. They are Birom women of 28 and 35 years old, both Christians and married to two brothers. The older woman had about seven years experience as a market gardener while the younger had four years by 1994/95 season. Both women received full primary school education. While the older woman has four children, the younger has three all of who are still below or within school age.

The younger woman combines farming with some informal tin picking while the older one carries out some petty trading in Korot village. Their different garden plots measured only about 0.2 ha in each case, both located within the flood plane, while the vegetables in their plots were mainly carrot, tomato, cabbage and spinach.

Their cases are very interesting as they typify the joint operations by husbands and wives, as well as time management by such wives for market gardening in the region. According to the women and their husbands, the two brothers decided to give their wives use rights to portions of their own plots, as a way of helping the women to earn and use their own income for their personal needs. In both cases, the woman thus has a personal garden plot, and owns and operates a joint plot with her husband, while each husband has a separate personal plot as well. This means that each family operates at least three plots.

The women, therefore, work on their own separate plots; they work together with their husbands on the jointly-owned plots and also in their husbands' separate plots. Thus, they have to share their farming time between work in each of the three plots. Indeed, as reported, it is mandatory that they work on their husbands' and the jointly-owned plots in order to be allowed the time to work on their plots. Because of the very small scale of these gardening operations and the low capital input, family labour is used the most. Hence each of the women has to plan and manage her time judiciously to work in the joint plot, in the husband's and in her own plot. This poses some constraint on the women regarding devoting sufficient time to their own plots. As a compensation, however, they enjoy full control on the products of and income from their plots; those from the family plots are used for the family expenses and needs; while the husbands enjoy full control and use of those from their own plots.

Such cases are not many in the area and exist mainly among the Birom gardeners. The Hausa/Fulani and other northern Nigeria ethnic groups do not usually allow their wives to practice farming. Only widows among them seem to be forced by the loss of their husbands to take to farming but generally at very small-scale. Thus, in Korot village a Hausa woman, about 50 years old and a widow living all alone as a one-person household operates three small garden plots all rented, which she combines with food vending in the village. Another 55 years old Hausa widow, again a one-person household, operates two small garden plots one of which she inherited from her late husband while the second is rented. She owns a water pump, which she also rents out to other gardeners, particularly the women, as a supplementary income source. She combines farming with petty trading.

Case 3:

An elderly Kanuri widow, over 70 years old, and one-person household who was among the gardeners monitored in this study. The very small scale at which most of the women operate, the dependence on their individual labour and occasional help of free labour from neighbours for one-person households or on family labour where they exit, are typified by this and other cases. Similarly, this lady, because of very limited funds and other inputs, cultivates mainly lettuce, spinach and tomato, and uses mainly cow-dung burnt and mixed with ash as manure with little or no chemical fertilizers. And even for this she relies on picking whatever cow-dung she can see in and around her village in Bisichi. Again, as a necessary supplement to her income she does some informal tin scooping in the village.

She has five children of whom the elder son lives and work in Kaduna while two of her daughters are married out. Thus, she lives with her second son who is about 13 years old and third daughter, who is 15 years old, both being non-boarding secondary school students. They both also provide some of the family labour, in addition to the woman's, for gardening when they are not in school, and are maintained in school mainly from the proceeds of the gardening. According to the woman, when her two children are not available, she works alone on the farm as she has no money.

These cases illustrate not only the extent and justification for the participation of women in market gardening in the study area. They also explain why the typical size of the farms operated by women is small, and why women have limited access to resources.

Problems and Prospects

As observed in the study, problems that women face accounting for their low presence or near absence in irrigation farming include the following:

1   Irrigation farming is essentially market-oriented and requires substantial capital input. Because of the women's weak economic base, they remain handicapped in this regard. In addition, since the men also control the economy and the direction of capital flow, it is expected that men in this field will continue to be the leaders and women the followers.

2   Irrigation farming is a relatively skilled and new system of farming in Plateau State. Many women are not likely to venture into this new enterprise in the near future, unless genuine efforts are made to encourage them further.

3   As noted earlier, many of the female farmers are within their child-bearing ages (of about 25 to 40 years). The implication is that, in addition to their involvement in irrigation, most of the women also give birth to children, thus reducing their participation, general productivity and their overall involvement in farming activity.

4   The participation of women in irrigation farming can be enhanced through the provision of credit facilities for them at low interest rates for the purchase of farm inputs. There is also need for land reforms at the local level. The education of both men and women on the need to involve and utilize women in irrigation farming will, however, be helpful. The practical teaching and education of women about the various specialized knowledge and skills involved in farming will enhance their participation. Concerted effort should be made to encourage the women to become members of the farmers' associations, so that they can benefit from the advantages of membership.

References

Ajaegbu, H.I. (1994), *The Jos Project*, Annual Scientific Progress Report to NIRP, August 1993-January 1994.

Gellen, Karen (1994), 'Unleashing the Power of Women Farmers', *African Farmer*, No. 11.

Harsch, Ernest (1994), 'Getting Cash into Rural Hands', *African Farmer*, No. 10.

9 The Use of Satellite Imagery for Assessing Land Use and Water Potential in the Jos-Bukuru Area

LEO M. VAN DEN BERG, HENK KRAMER,
KRYSTOF SCHOENEICH AND EDWIN AGUIGWO

Introduction

As an integral part of the NIRP (Netherland-Israel Research & Development Programme) project on the Jos Plateau, satellite imagery was ordered and processed at the Winand Staring Centre in Wageningen, The Netherlands. The prime objective of this part of the project was to support and supplement the fieldwork that was done by the Jos team to map the irrigated farmland. Perhaps not all areas could be visited and the satellite image would show what was missed out or misrepresented. Two images were selected, one from 1988 (well before the project started) and one from 1995 (when the project was in full swing). This enabled us to describe the changes that took place over a seven-year period. Both images are from roughly the same time of the year: February-March, i.e., in the middle of the dry season. Since two different images were used, direct comparison of inter-imagery changes is difficult. The older imagery is from the American satellite LANDSAT, while the other is the French satellite SPOT. The first one is less costly but it does not provide an equally detailed picture as the second one, which was used for the second year. Essentially, the difference is a matter of scale and of information. The SPOT-XS images that were used have a higher resolution than LANDSAT-TM ones, but are less comprehensive in terms of the bands of reflected light. SPOT images from 1988 were not available. The second problem was relatively easy to solve by

163

using the bands from LANDSAT-TM that are also available in SPOT-XS. The first problem, however, was not satisfactorily resolved: SPOT-XS consists of pixels covering 20 x 20 metres on the ground, while those of LANDSAT-TM cover 30 x 30 metres.

A subsidiary goal of this part of the project was to find out which of the two types of imageries is better suited for the analysis of small-scale irrigated farming. Although the main concentrations of irrigated, hence moist, areas in dry surroundings are easy to distinguish, the small sizes of individual fields make monitoring by remote sensing techniques with either LANDSAT or SPOT extremely difficult. However, by combining field surveys creatively with the interpretation of satellite pictures,we expected to be able to make good use of LANDSAT, SPOT or both without suffering too much from this difficulty.

Results of the 1993 Survey of Irrigated and Irrigable Farmland of Greater Jos Area

The potential extent of irrigated farmland in an area of roughly 160 sq. km. around Jos-Bukuru (Figure 9.1), was mapped by two hydrological experts, using the relevant Federal Survey's topographical maps on scale 1:50,000, dating back from 1960 and 1961, and based on 1956 air photographs (fairly old but sufficiently accurate as far as the physical environment is concerned). The results were presented in the First Interim Report of the JOS team (Schoeneich and Aguigwo, 1993). In that report the concept of 'fadama' was stretched from its original meaning of irrigated river valleys to all irrigable land.

In all, three categories of irrigable land were distinguished: floodplain, upland and mineland 'fadama'.

- Out of a total of 4713 ha of irrigable land in the study area, the floodplains occupy only 7 percent (323 hectares). In order to irrigate this land gravity channels and small petrol pumps would do the job. The annual flooding of this land contributes to its fertility. Upland irrigable land (80 percent or 3796 hectares) is flat or gently sloping, presently used for rain-fed agriculture, but with sufficient water resources to warrant the installation of pumps and the construction of wells and uphill water reservoirs (weirs). Capital expenditure for this land category will be relatively high.

- Mineland 'fadama' is flat or gently sloping land near or inside former tin mining pits that are often filled with water. As the tin deposits are found in alluvial soils, the mineland 'fadama' tends to follow former, tertiary and present river courses. In a way, this category can, therefore, be considered as either a type of disturbed proper (floodplain) fadama, or disturbed watershed plain. With 594 ha this type constitutes 13 percent of the total irrigable land in the area. A small proportion (2 percent) of the latter is 'reclaimed mineland' the remaining being largely derelict spoils heaps and pits that need to be heavily manured first. With a fair amount of ingenuity and small petrol pumps that suck the water from the mining ponds or from shallow wells in dry mining pits, some of these areas are, and more can be, utilized at fairly low cost.

In this survey it is not only striking that only three floodplain areas were detected (Rafin Gora North, Gada Biyu and Korot with respectively 30, 203 and 90 ha), but also that no estimates were made of the areas actually under irrigation. The former is caused by the fact, that most floodplains in this area were disturbed by mining operations. The absence of data on the amounts of land actually under irrigation was the result of the 1993 fieldwork being done during the rainy season. The next section discusses the way in which satellite imagery could fill this gap. The 1993 survey focused on potentials: the amount of ground and surface water at each location and the extent of suitable soils within reach of this water at affordable cost. The quantity of irrigation water was calculated on the basis of the following assumptions (Schoeneich and Aguigwo, 1993, p.2):

- water demand is 1 cubic metre per square metre of irrigable land per dry season;
- rainfall is 1200 mm per year;
- base flow coefficient is 0.1;
- water saturated thickness of the soft overburden aquifer is on average 20 metre, while its effective porosity is 2.4 percent;
- average depth of mining ponds at the beginning of the dry season is 10 metres and evaporation from the open water surface is 2 metres;
- an average hand-dug well, sunk to a depth of 30 metres, can yield 30 cubic metres per day.

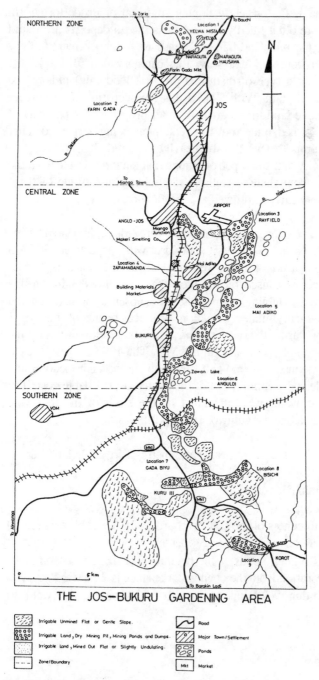

Figure 9.1   The Jos-Bukuru Gardening Area

Apart from polluted effluents from factories and households in the Jos-Bukuru area the water quality is good for irrigation. No results are available yet of laboratory tests of suspected irrigation water near sources of pollution, but this is likely to restrict the use of suitable land in the central zone for dry-season market gardening.

In total, the amount of agricultural water resources was estimated at 52.32 million c.m per year and the maximum potential demand from 4713 ha of irrigated land at 47.78 million c.m per year. Locally, shortages may arise, but in most instances transporting surplus water from nearby areas (Schoeneich and Aguigwo, 1993) can compensate these. This will require, obviously, fairly high capital investment, and may necessitate the involvement of the local authorities in the planned water projects.

Confronting the 1988 Satellite Imagery with the Fieldwork Results

In 1994 the Jos team members had an opportunity to compare their findings with a LANDSAT-TM imagery of 1988 (Schoeneich and Aguigwo, 1994). In line with experiences encountered elsewhere with the use of satellite images for small-scale landcover features (for instance with coffee farms in Costa Rica, see Barkhof, 1995) they considered this imagery very suitable for a rough estimate of the amount of (small-scale) irrigated farming. For this purpose the false-colour (red, green and blue for, respectively, bands 4, 5 and 3) data of LANDSAT were presented at a scale of approximately 1 : 64,000, which shows the individual pixels of 30 m x 30 m as small coloured squares. A bright red colour represents land cover with a high density of green leaves (large quantity of biomass). At this time of the year such situations occur only in irrigated areas and mango plantations. Other trees don't have much foliage, except for some in the urban areas where their juxtaposition with buildings and roads leads to a darker shade of red. It was hard to distinguish between the horticultural fields and the mango trees, but as both of these land uses tend to occur together this was not considered a major problem.

In all, 238 ha of irrigated land were counted, as little as 5 percent of the total irrigable land. The largest areas were found in derelict mineland: 164 ha (3 percent of the irrigable land in this category). Of the floodplain 34 ha were irrigated (11 percent), in 'upland fadama' 27 ha (1 percent) and in reclaimed mineland 13 ha (20 percent). In addition, some 79 ha were found to be irrigated although these had been excluded from the figure for 'irrigable land'. This exclusion was made for various reasons: 1. The land was very likely to be taken over by urban growth or belonged to institutions like the University of Jos and the Barikin Ladi Polytechnic; 2. The water used for irrigation was heavily polluted by domestic sewage; or 3. The land belonged to either large-scale commercial or hobby farmers.

From the estimates, it is clear that upland areas which are theoretically suitable for irrigation were not yet used in 1988. Both the capital required for investments and the know-how among the owners of this land (which is presently used for rain-fed agriculture), are absent. However, the study revealed that there was still much scope for expansion of the irrigated area in the river valleys. As long as this is the case, there is no need for investing in upland reclamation efforts.

The Problem of Matching Satellite Image with Topographical Map

Together with some problems of identifying the exact position of the pixels on the ground, the different shades of red were a matter of considerable confusion and debate among the members of the research team. At the time of fieldwork (February 1994 and 1995), a good match between topographical map and satellite imagery was not yet available. This was caused by the fact that in The Netherlands only a rough sketchmap (scale 1: 250,000) of main roads and irrigable land was available. Figure 9.1 is based on this sketchmap, but it now includes the main built-up areas as identified on the SPOT-XS of 1995. It was only after the 1995 fieldwork that the old 1:50,000 topographical map, that the Jos team had at its disposal, could be copied and used for matching with the satellite imagery.

After scanning the fairly detailed, though dating from the 1961 topographical map (the latest available!), it was possible, in principle, to show exactly where the individual pixels of SPOT or LANDSAT were located. For the village of Korot, one of the sample areas located in the southern edge of the area, this was done as follows: The relevant part of the topographical map was scanned and at least three points that were visible on the map and on the image were marked. These were either bridges or confluences of the various streams in the area. By matching the co-ordinates of these points, a visually correct merge of the imagery and the topography could be made. This matching was sufficient for the purpose, using the imagery as visual source for the field checks.

The attached colourplates show the result of this matching operation. In the process, topographic information that does not come out clearly on satellite images can be superimposed on the prints and some new features, not yet shown on the old (1961) topographical map, can be added. A remarkable feature which emerges from the comparison of the old map with the 1995 SPOT image is the disappearance of quite a number of the mining ponds during the perid of about three and a half decades which have passed since 1961. These were clearly demarcated on the old map. One cause of this disappearance is land reclamation -- in a few cases the heaps of mining debris were shoveled into the ponds to restore a fairly flat landscape as depicted by the SPOT image. Field observations led to the conclusion, however, that a substantial number of mining ponds were still there even though they did not come out on the SPOT image. This also applies to gravel roads, especially when they run through dry stretches of land. They are marked on the old map but are not visible on the satellite image at this time of the year. The probable reason is that they are too narrow, or that the reflection scores are not sufficiently different from the surroundings.

The Korot area, in the South-eastern corner (Figure 9.1, location 9), is chosen to illustrate how computer-processing of the data provided by the satellites helps us to estimate the amount of irrigated farmland. According to the 1993 field survey this area consists of 15 ha irrigable mineland, 90 ha irrigable floodplain and 590 ha irrigable upland. Visual interpretation of the 1988 imagery revealed that none of the mineland and upland areas were actually irrigated and of the floodplain only 16 ha (18 percent) were. In addition, 14 ha of irrigated land were found outside the 'irrigable land' in the original survey. This zone was around an abandoned mining dam and belonged to the Barakin Ladi Polytechnic.

The two smaller colourplates show the Korot area as it appears on processed imagery from LANDSAT and SPOT of 1988 and 1995, respectively. The information has been adjusted to scale of the topographical map. The problem of different resolutions (30 by 30 m for LANDSAT and 20 x 20 m for SPOT) was solved by considering the data as 'rough estimates only'. A direct comparison of the two images was not possible because of the different spectral bands that were used. From the LANDSAT-TM sensor, bands 3, 4 and 5 were used. These cover the red (R), near infrared (NI) and middle-infrared, respectively. From the SPOT-XS, bands 1, 2, 3 (green, red and near infrared) were used.

In both cases, however, a bright, red colour represents land with many green plants (leaves) and relatively high moisture content. From various ground checks it could be observed that for this time of the year such areas are either irrigated or covered with mango trees or tall grass that doesn't require irrigation. The stretches of tall grass in riverbeds in the dry season are very few and small in this area as compared with the irrigated land and mango groves. The latter two tend to occur together. Surrounding the bright, red pixels, which cannot represent anything else but irrigated fields, sometimes mixed with mango groves but always with a lot of biomass, there are pixels that are also red, but slightly darker. They represent less biomass for the pixels as a whole. During ground checks this was interpreted as either less lush vegetation cover on irrigated fields (young plants), or pixels only partly covering irrigated land. It is therefore considered safe to include the slightly darker pixels as small-scale irrigated fields.

To be able to estimate the vegetated (irrigated) area, a Normalized Difference Vegetation Index (NDVI) is calculated. The formula for the NDVI is NI-R/NI+R. This index will yield high values for vegetated areas because of their relatively high near-infrared reflectance and low visible reflectance. Non-vegetated areas like bare soil and rocks have a similar reflectance in near-infrared and red and consequently result in a vegetation index near zero. The NDVI values are visually compared with the satellite image and a threshold value between vegetated and non-vegetated is established. This is only a rough estimate for which the knowledge from the fieldwork is very important. When a threshold is set, all pixels with a higher value are selected and converted into hectares (1 SPOT XS pixel is 0.04 ha).

We tried three proposed sizes for estimating the vegetative area, for the 1988 imagery and an equal number for the 1995 one. They range from a more lenient definition to a very strict definition. After counting these pixels and converting the results to hectares the computer gives various 'rough estimates' of irrigated surface areas for Korot, which are shown under each diagram. As far as the ground checks allow us to do so, we take the middle proposal as containing the most likely spatial threshold of the market gardening zone. Two results, compared with the field observations, are as follow:

1. LANDSAT 1988: 32 ha   31 ha according to visual interpretation
   by Jos team
2. SPOT 1995:   44 ha   not yet available by field measurements
   by Jos team

There is reason to believe that these findings reveal the real seven year trends in Korot's irrigated areas. Provided that field measurements in the area would confirm the 1995 estimates, we may conclude that, in Korot, the surface area under small-scale irrigated market gardening has increased substantially since 1988. Korot was selected, indeed, because of its relatively high potential for growth. It is unlikely that the other locations have experienced a similar trend. Field checks in location 1 (in the Northern zone of Figure 9.1) led us to believe that in this case the area under cultivation has definitely not increased.

After confirming that our estimates of the irrigated areas for 'Korot' were fairly correct, it would be a small step to repeat the technique for the study area as a whole. To do that all at once, however, it is necessary that both the satellite image and the map with the areas of interest are geometrically correct. However, because the base map was outdated and the areas of interest were drawn on a small map (Figure 9.1), it was not possible to get a good match between the satellite image and the map as a whole. This means that the matching would have to be done separately for each location, which is quite possible but rather laborious. Once this work is done, the computer can produce similar figures for the other eight locations. This can, then, provide the necessary data for testing our hypothesis that the total area with market gardening has increased only slightly between 1988 and 1995.

Discussion and Conclusions

The most important lesson from this exercise is that satellite imagery is only suitable for rough estimates of the amount of land under irrigation. As it consists of measurement units (pixels) of at least 20m x 20m no edges of fields can be identified. The horticultural fields are far smaller than this and show great variations in terms of moisture content and biomass. This implies that even if a pixel as a whole has a very high score for biomass as compared to other pixels it is not uncommon to find several fields within it that contain hardly any biomass, either because a new crop has just been planted or because most of the old crops were just harvested. We should be aware of the fact that the pixel scores are averages for what could be extremely heterogeneous situations.

Combining the information obtained from satellite imagery of 1988 and 1995 with local knowledge about the situation regarding horticulture and derelict mineland at the time when the topographic map was produced (1960/1), we make the preliminary conclusion that there was an increase of the surface area of small-scale market gardening between 1988 and 1995, but that this was not spectacular.

In the small-scale sector the use of upland irrigation till now has been negligible. The bulk of (annually replenished) water resources is allowed to enter the aquifers and to feed the rivers in lower Nigeria. Once this sector would start to tap these resources on a large scale, water shortages downstream, in the dryer and hotter lowlands of Nigeria, are likely to increase, but from the data already presented it is quite clear that the total cultivated area can more than double its 1995 extent before this problem arises. Large-scale irrigation projects are more often situated away from the perennial streams. Since they use boreholes to tap the aquifers they are to be discouraged.

Because of its higher resolution, SPOT imagery proves slightly better for identification of small-scale irrigated areas. However, before satellite imagery can be applied more widely for the purposes of this study, more field checks are required. These include mapping the actual areal extent of irrigated land on the topographically reinforced imagery. This would help us to understand the meaning of various shades of red of the individual pixels for large-scale automated mapping projects. Consequently, the (rough) calculations of the surface cover can be substantially improved. Due to communication problems between Nigeria and The Netherlands it was not possible to carry out such timely and appropriate ground checks, but the material gathered so far can still be used for this purpose.

The benefits of applying remote sensing to large-scale arable farming has already been demonstrated. Our study shows, unfortunately, that it is not possible yet to use satellite imagery techniques to estimate yields of the main crops produced by the small-scale market gardeners.

References

Barkhof, M. (1995), *San Antonio Observed in Pixels: A Study to the Value of Remote Sensing and GIS for Land Use Classification and Detection of Changes in Land Use in San Antonio of Puriscal, Costa Rica*, Research Report, Waterloo, Canada: Faculty of Environmental Studies, University of Waterloo.

Schoeneich, K. and Aguigwo, E. (1993), *Map of Irrigable Land in Jos Metropolitan Area. Part 1: Maps and Part 2: Explanatory text*, First Interim Report, Jos: Population, Environment and Agency (PEDA).

Schoeneich, K. and Aguigwo, E. (1994), *Explanatory Text to the Map of Land Under Dry Season Irrigated Cultivation, 16 February 1988*. Second Interim Report, Jos: Population, Environment and Development Agency (PEDA).

Korot: matching Spot imagery with topographic map

1000   0   Meters

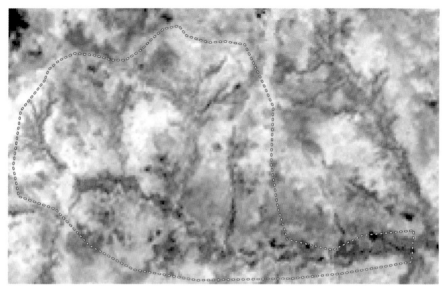

Korot: Landsat image, 16-2-1988

1000   0   Meters

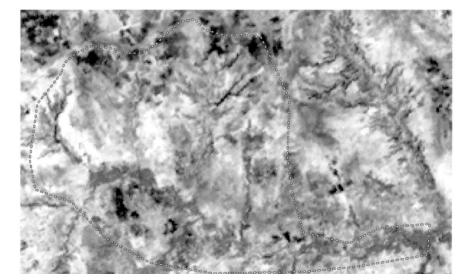

Korot: Spot image, 2-3-1995

1000   0   Meters

a. estimated vegetated area : 14 ha

Landsat TM image, only vegetated area is visible

b. estimated vegetated area : 32 ha

c. estimated vegetated area : 41 ha

Korot: 1988 estimates of areas under market gardening

a. estimated vegetated area : 27 ha

SPOT XS image, only vegetated area is visible

b. estimated vegetated area : 44 ha

c. estimated vegetated area : 62 ha

Korot: 1995 estimates of areas under market gardening

10 Small-Scale Gardening in the Jos Region, Nigeria: Partial Findings

HYACINTH I. AJAEGBU

Introduction

The Jos project was concerned with the study of food production and with prospects for income generation in the face of accelerated urban growth. It started in August 1993, and is expected to last for three years. At this stage (June 1996) we begin to summarize what we have actually found. A sub-project gardening improvement experiment in one of the study areas is, however, continuing in the field. So also are extension services and advocacy activities in respect of the gardeners in all our nine study locations.

Since the study began three years ago, we have summarized some of our findings in three successive annual scientific reports. In the first of these reports, we presented the results of our surveys on the extent and characteristics of the study area, the *fadama* areas, the irrigated market gardening zones and the potential irrigable farm lands. We also discussed the irrigation water balance situation in the different market-gardening zones in the study area. The study area itself stretches for about 30 km north-south and some 15 km east-west at its widest points (in the southern zone) and covers altogether an area of about 160 sq. km.

According to the information that we obtained from the preliminary analyses of the field-survey data, the study area contained nine locations that had some fifty *fadama* and irrigation farming sites. Of these, we studied about 20 percent. This area had 370 dry-season gardeners, of whom 39 percent were included in the study. We also included about 27 percent of some 430 rainy-season farmers, i.e., those who practiced rain-fed agriculture. We estimated that during the 1993/94 rainy-season and dry-season there were altogether, about 2,300 and 2,000 operators, respectively, in the project study area. In about 70 percent of the cases, however, the dry-season gardener and rainy-season farmer was the same person.

The preponderance of the settlers and migrant dry-season gardeners, as well as the gradual but increasing entry of the indigenous people of the area into the dry-season gardening sub-sector were also revealed. So also were their age and sex characteristics and ethnic composition.

By the 1994 reporting period, further analyses of the data from the surveys and monitoring components of the activities revealed more information on the gardeners and the nature of their gardening operations. Thus, in that annual report we discussed the gardeners' marital and household characteristics, the main features of their farming activities, their marketing processes and practices, the main constraints facing them, and the main features of comparison between the dry-season gardeners in the Jos-Bukuru area and those operating in the Kaduna urban area.

Thus, by the 1995 reporting period we had analysed the major local and other solutions to the constraints facing the gardeners. We had also arrived at possible options considered feasible regarding the small-scale nature of the gardeners' operations and their relevant indigenous local knowledge and technology. Hence, we formulated and started a pilot gardening improvement sub-project in Korot (Loc. 9) (see Ajaegbu, 1995b).

A project workshop held in June 1995, at the Wageningen DLO-Winand Staring Center in The Netherlands, provided an arena for us to summarize and present our findings on several more aspects of the study, as follows:

a   project components and study area;
b   market gardening activities in Nigeria: the case of the Jos urban area;
c   profile of selected market gardeners in Jos-Bukuru area;
d   irrigated market gardening in Kaduna urban area;
e   irrigation water and *fadama* farming practices in the Jos-Bukuru area;
f   small-scale irrigation farming techniques and vegetable marketing in Jos area;
g   constraints to sustainable dry-season gardening in the Jos-Bukuru urban area;
h   complexity of land tenure in dry-season gardening in the Jos-Bukuru urban area;
i   small-scale market gardening, land tenure and the urban fringe: the Jos-

Bukuru case in international perspective;
j   mapping the *fadama* area;
    i   estimating the areal extent of irrigable and irrigated farm land in the Jos-Bukuru urban area, through ground surveys and topographic maps;
    ii   landsat and SPOT images as mapping tools for *fadama* farming in Jos-Bukuru urban area;
k   development of farmers' associations on the Jos Plateau, Nigeria;
l   the pilot market-gardening improvement sub-project: formulating and implementation process.

Two other papers emanated from this study and were presented at an international symposium on Environmental Changes and Environmental Problems in Nigeria that was held at the German Cultural Center, Goethe Institute, in Lagos, Nigeria, during 22-24 February, 1995. The papers were presented by K. Schoeneich, on groundwater and watersupply on the Jos Plateau, and by H.I. Ajaegbu on environmental problems on the Jos Plateau.

The training component has yielded the following M.Sc. dissertations, while a Ph.D. candidate is yet to complete his thesis. The M.Sc. dissertations completed in 1993/94 were by F.Y. Ganga on urban farming in Jos, and by E.V. Nyam, on labor participation in agriculture in Jos South LGA. Those completed in 1994/95 were by E.O. Omomoh on labor utilization in the dry-season farming in the Greater Jos Area, by Adamu Hena on concentration of trace-elements in surface water in Jos, and by M.A. Izang on the role of middlemen in marketing vegetables in Jos.

The workshop sponsored by the project team in June, 1995, gave us the opportunity to start to look back to the very beginning to ask ourselves what we had actually found. This was in the context of the study problem and objectives we had set out for the project. We discuss, henceforth, some of the answers so far.

Suggested Model: Market Gardening, Urban Growth, and Sustainable Income Generation

The factors and pattern of the operation of the small-scale gardening practices, as well as the efforts to achieve sustainability in the Jos area are multi-faceted, while the linkage process and interrelationships are complex (Figure 10.1) The gardeners occupy a crucial position as the principal actors regarding the gardening practices and production. They use the resources (physical, human and technological), while urban growth and external influences present several positive and negative effects. In the operation, several constraints are encountered, arising from many of the components including the gardeners themselves. The constraints call for purposive intervention packages in order to enhance achieving sustainability, indicated essentially by sustainable gardening improvements, ecological and resource use, income generation human development.

As regards urban growth influences, there are both positive and negative effects on gardening, and vice-versa. Thus, market gardening has been stimulated in the study area by, and has been responding to, urban growth and demand for vegetables and fruits both locally in the Jos metropolitan area and in other urban centres in the southern parts of Nigeria (Figure 10.1 and List of Factors and Effects). The small-scale gardeners have been responding to the stimulus of rising demand.

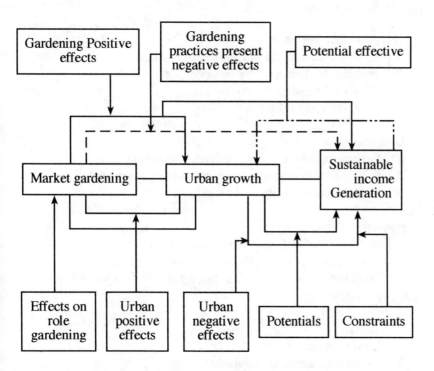

**Figure 10.1   Model of Market Gardening, Urban Growth and
Sustainable Income Generation: Jos Region**

List of Factors and Effects

A. Gardening positive effects
    1   Meeting local and distant market demand
    2   Influencing and responding to urban consumer preferences
    3   Contributing to solving urban food needs
    4   Providing employment for urban poor and middle class
    5   Providing opportunity for treating urban waste refuse and
         enhancing urban environmental quality.

B   Gardening negative effects
    1   Land use conflicts, competition or squatting
    2   Water pollution, e.g., chemical fertilizers, insecticides, etc.
    3   Polluted vegetables in a few gardening sites
    4   Lack of enough fertilizers
    5   Soil over used.

C   Urban positive effects
    1   Provides stimulus for gardening through demand
    2   Provides ready market for products
    3   Source of middlemen who handle,
         transport and market the products.

D   Urban negative effects
    1   Encroachments on *fadama* and other gardening land
    2   Pollution of gardening land, water, air and crops in places
    3   Exploitative activities of the middlemen.

E   Potentials
    1   Assured local and external market demand
    2   Considerable physical resources
    3   Possibilities for improvement through facilitation intervention
         packages.

F   Constraints
    1   Land insecurity
    2   Urban and industrial pollutants
    3   Unfavourable marketing and pricing systems
    4   Diseconomies of small-scale and, in some places, of distance

5   Unorganized, undeveloped communal cooperation and approach to common problems.

Some of the gardeners sell the crops directly in the local markets, but most use the service of middlemen. However, there are a number of gardeners who take their products all the way to Onitsha, Enugu, Makurdi or other southern cities.

The gardeners influence consumer preferences in the cities through the types, quantities and quality of vegetables and fruits that they produce each season. The farmers have also evolved gardening practices such as relay-cropping and multi-cropping aimed at providing different varieties of products for the market at various months of the year.

The available physical resources (gardening land, soil fertility, irrigation water) are generally adequate, although there are some local variations and constraints particularly regarding water availability. These resources ensure that the gardeners will be able to produce for the increasing demand that is experienced each year. Unmet demand is, however, quite high and increasing.

The gardeners are responding to the demand by intensifying the land use in the river flood plain *fadamas*, the reclaimed and the unreclaimed mined-out land *fadamas*. They are also extensifying through expanding their gardens onto upslope irrigated farms, away from the traditional *fadama* plains. They have adopted new fruits and vegetable breeds which are early maturing, high yielding or pest/disease resistant.

These and more examples show the favourable aspects of urban growth in the relationship, as the cities provide the stimulus to which the gardeners are actively responding, in a stimulus-response situation. The other side of the coin, however, presents various constraints posed by the urban growth process within the study area for the gardeners, particularly the small-scale farmers as well as for the migrant and some of the settler farmers. In this regard, for instance, there have been considerable encroachments by urban land uses on the market-gardening land (*fadamas* and adjoining upslope areas) particularly within the northern gardening zone.

This is extending into the central zone around the expanding urbanized district of Bukuru-town. Furthermore, urban industrial wastes and refuse (solid, plastic or sewerage, etc) are increasing. They, thus, constitute pollutants to the soil, water, air and crops in parts of the northern zone, close to the polluting industrial establishments, or to refuse disposal locations.

The southern gardening zone and most of the central zone (the areas outside Bukuru town) are still free from the encroachments or the urban-generated pollutants. Yet, all the small-scale gardeners in all the zones face the problem of the urban middlemen and their pricing system that leads to relatively low prices and low returns to the gardeners. In some cases, the gardeners become very indebted to the middlemen, resulting in small incomes and the lack of sufficient capital to invest in gardening activities.

The relatively greater distances from the gardening areas of the southern zone to the urban centers (20-40 km) as opposed to the other zones (less than 15 km), pose some problems for the former (Ajaegbu, 1995a). This problem is particularly severe for the small-scale at which many of the gardeners operate and produce. It is also affected by the spatial preferences of the middlemen who dominate the marketing system. The nature of production and marketing works, thus, to the disadvantage of the producers, particularly in the southern zone. These farmers have, so far, been unable to escape from the cycle of small-scale farming and poverty.

This scenario discussed so far affects the sustainability of the gardening activities of the small producers as well as their income and welfare improvements. On the one hand, the potentials of physical resources and market demand and the handling, bulking, transporting, packaging and marketing provided by the middlemen, are among several factors working in favor of sustainability of the sector in the area. On the other hand, the constraints of land insecurity, pollution, exploitative middlemen, etc. are proving enormous and intractable for most of the small-scale gardeners.

On balance, many of the constraints have continued unsolved partly because the gardeners have so far operated largely as incapable lone-rangers and poor business managers. Hence, the need for greater cooperation between them, for a concerted communal approach to tackling the constraints, and for some reorientation and training regarding managing their gardening activities and marketing their products.

This aspect of the study highlighted the herculean task of solving the identified problems and removing the constraints facing the gardeners. The small-scale nature of the gardening operations has given rise to a vicious cycle of diseconomies leading to resigned, non-commercial oriented, attitudes to gardening. The gardeners need to break-off from the web in order to attain growth, development and sustainability in their operations. As shown in figure 10.1, however, many more factors are involved in attaining sustainable gardening in the area. All of them need to be addressed.

Patterns and Determinants of Variation Among Small-Scale Gardeners

The investigations also revealed the considerable variations that exist between the gardeners under study. A hypothetical trend line shows the relative positions of the different categories of small-scale gardeners in the study area (Figure 10.2). Thus, there are the relatively small group (the smallest of the small-scale gardeners), the relatively moderate, and the group of relatively large garden operators.

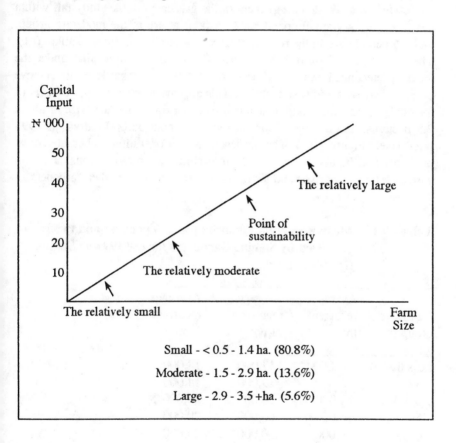

Figure 10.2   Observed Relationship between Farm Size and Recurrent Capital, as Reported by the Sample Gardeners, 1992/93 Season

As revealed, some of the gardeners have succeeded in advancing beyond the others (on the continuum). The relatively very small-scale gardeners generally operate (cultivate) altogether less than 1.5 hectares of gardening plots and have capital or turn-over of below twenty thousand naira per gardening season. For the relatively moderate gardeners the numbers are between 1.5 and 2.9 hectares and from fifteen to thirty thousand naira. The corresponding sizes of the other operations are 3 ha and above and between thirty and fifty thousand naira in respect of the relatively large and successful ones. While 80.8 percent of the gardeners in the study fall within the group of very small operators, 13.6 percent are in the moderate group, and 5.6 percent are in the relatively large, successful category (Table 10.1). There seems to be a threshold, or critical size of operation, that under the local agrotechnical system, affects the ability of the gardener to achieve economic success and sustainability. This appears to be at the upper level of the moderate income group, which is marked by operating farm size of about 2.5 hectares, and average recurrent input of about 35,000 nairas, at 1993 price level (Figure 10.2). The gardeners whose operational characteristics, practices and inputs are above the threshold may provide, thus, a useful yardstick for comparison and for possible targeting by the other gardeners.

Table 10.1   Mean Recurrent Financial Input, Turnover and Profit Reported by Sample Gardeners for the 1992/93 Season (in 1993 Naira)

Farm size group (ha)	Average recurrent input	Average recurrent turnover	Average recurrent profit
Less than 0.5	6,000	17,000	18,000
0.5-0.9	8,000	19,000	14,000
1.0-1.4	13,000	28,000	22,000
1.5-1.9	16,000	60,000	20,000
2.0-2.4	9,000	30,000	23,000
2.5-2.9	7,000	5,000	2,000
3.0-3.4	16,000	56,000	34,000
3.5 +	46,000	no answer	no answer

Source: Field survey, 1993/94.

Figure 10.2 also shows the approximate point of sustainability. It should be noted that many of the gardeners who are below this point are also those unwilling or unable to state, or even guess, their total recurrent financial input, their turnover, or their profits. They generally play down the implication of their monetary status, their spending or their earning, though they insist they are poor. Hence, the financial information from them tends to be fairly unreliable in comparison with that obtained from the higher income groups.

The figure also indicates that with better, more favourable conditions and opportunities, many of the gardeners can advance, while the relatively successful ones can still advance even further. It is not clear, however, from the findings so far whether there is a possible point of 'diminishing return' for these small-scale gardeners and what that point can be; or, whether the situation is just a matter of removing the constraints and then ensuring growth and sustainability in their operations. It is, of course, possible that external factors, such as market conditions in the local or more distant consuming centers (in the country and ultimately overseas) may still pose some limits.

Another question is whether there is a critical number of gardeners, and combinations of different categories of the farmers, that may successfully and sustainably operate within the available present and potential market-gardening areas and resources (land, water, etc.). Again, the shrinking per farmer land and water resources, and the insecure tenure that arises with increasing urban growth may affect the issue over time, thus influencing changes in the critical numbers as circumstances of resources, technologies and management practices, etc. change. This may necessitate helping displaced growers to find new land.

Finally, can there be a point of sustainability in the operations of these small-scale gardeners? It may be expected that such a point may be derived based on, say, $X1$ = given size of farm holding/cultivated and other inputs; plus $X2$ = amount of products yield and proportions sold directly to the markets or through the middlemen, etc, plus $X3$ = income from gardening each season, capital invested, amounts saved, etc.

The Farmers' Constraints and the Way They are Confronted

One other finding is that the farmers' perceptions of their constraints are complex and need to be addressed accordingly in order to achieve some of the objectives of the project in general and the sub-project in particular.

Their ranking of fifteen of the identified constraints (see Job, 1995) shows the greatest concern for the short-term rather than the long-term issues; for the very day-to-day as against the more fundamental and more lasting concerns. This is revealed in Table 10.2).

Table 10.2   Ranking the Farmers' Constraints according to Number Reporting Each Type (Quartile Ranges)

Upper Quartile	1	Fertilizers
88 - 25%	2	Fuel scarcity
(in each case)	3	Finance and low investment
	4	Implements and equipment maintenance
	5	Weeds, pests and diseases
	6	Water shortage
Middle rank orders	7	Herbicides
19.1- 4.1%	8	Labor
(in each case)	9	Seeds and seedlings
	10	Poor marketing system
	11	Transportation
Lower Quartile	12	Water pollution
3.4 - 0.5%	13	Low yield
(in each case)	14	Preservation of produce
	15	Land insecurity

Apart from finance and low investment (the small-scale character) rated third, some of the very crucial constraints were perceived and rated rather low. They include water shortage (6th), poor marketing system (9th), water pollution (12th) and land insecurity (15th). Most of the farmers could not perceive, mention or rate highly the constraints arising from, say, their own low farming (business) management levels or their little concern for costs and profits (and the balance between them). Nor were they concerned with the effects of their lack of record keeping or their generally low educational levels. In some cases, they regard farming activities generally, including market gardening, as just a way of life rather than a profit-oriented venture.

Many cannot read simple instructions in English, Hausa language or in other local languages.

This rather low level of perception and assessment of their constraints has also affected their approaches to and capacity for solving them. Thus, for instance, there is not much long-term planning in their gardening activities. They rather tend to operate, as it were, within each gardening season or, even on the basis of one phase of the three or so cropping cycles within the season (in a relay rotation system), at a time. Planning for, mobilizing and storing resources (inputs) and marketing strategies for two or more seasons (years) at a stretch are hardly undertaken.

There is a widespread sense of resignation to their fate, say, regarding the exploitative role of the middlemen in the marketing and pricing systems operated, or in the face of irrigation water pollution by industrial waste water, urban encroachment on gardening land, or the acute shortage of water for irrigation during peak dry months, in the locations that these constraints occur. This is mainly because the small-scale gardeners in general; and the very small ones among them in particular find themselves as individuals incapable of solving the constraints.

During discussions with them, however, they appreciated the possibilities that could be explored through a communal approach, although they still considered some constraints, including the dominance of the middlemen, as intractable even with their common efforts as the middlemen are very much organized and their association is very powerful.

Therefore, the sub-project aims to, among other things, explore the ways of mobilizing the participating gardeners to distinguish the constraints they can tackle as individual farmers (or on individual basis) from those that require concerted communal effort. In the remaining period of the present project's life the Korot local farmers' association is being sensitized, and the local resources are being harnessed towards alleviating some of the constraints. The gardeners are also being trained regarding forward planning, record-keeping and concern for costs and benefits (profits) in their farming operations.

Farmers' Associations and Communal Cooperation

Farmers' associations have gone through a very checkered history in the study area. As discussed by Igoche (1995) such associations were first founded at different locations in the Jos area between 1965 and 1985.

Indeed, as regards eight out of nine project study locations, the associations were actually started in the 1960s, in one location; during the 1970s in three locations; and during the 1980s in four other locations. In the ninth location it was founded only in 1994, in the course of our project.

However, because of several problems and dashed expectations, most of them became non-functional (dormant) or disbanded. Efforts were made through the auspices of this project to resuscitate all of them during the 1993/94 season, as well as strengthen them through establishing in 1994 a central farmers' association and meetings linking the associations in the nine study locations (Figure 10.3).

And, in 1995 the Plateau State branch of the Nigerian *Fadama* Farmers' Association was established, to which the various local associations filed their registration applications. The sub-project activities afforded us added opportunity to work with and strengthen one of these associations (the Sabon Gida, Korot Farmers' Club), even further.

The investigations into their histories during the last reporting year, in particular, showed very varying levels in the performances and relative successes of the nine associations. A few have been relatively successful in mobilizing their members, in increasing their membership, in securing short-term inputs, especially fertilizers and seeds or seedlings from the Plateau Agricultural Development Program (PADP) or the markets for their members, and in harnessing some local funds from the members for the associations' activities. The most prominent example has been the Yelwa Farmers Association (dry-and rainy-season farmers' branches of the same association) in location one.

The ethnic mix of indigence and non-indigence had a profound impact on the association's prospects. The mixture of indigenous and settler gardeners (the migrant farmers are members only when they are actually in the area during gardening seasons), and the grouping of gardeners from widely-varying age groups. These socio-cultural characteristics have posed several constraints. some of the problems were suspicion, lack of trust and inadequate enthusiasm of group action.

In virtually all the locations and associations, the males were predominant. In only one location (Bisichi) there was a female who functioned as a chairperson (of Bisichi Dry-Season Farmers' Association).

Leadership commitment and willingness to democratize and allow popular participation by and equal benefits to all members, irrespective of age, sex or ethnic origin, etc. have also been crucial in the relative success or failure of the local associations.

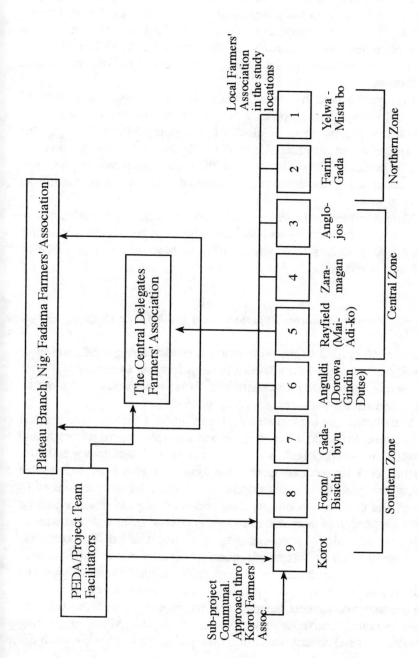

Figure 10.3 Fadama Farmers' Associations in the Study Area

Indeed, partly because of the fear of leadership actions and commitment to working for the good of the group members rather than just for the leaders, the delegates to the central farmers' association have continued to express reluctance to take over completely its affairs from the PEDA Project Team. Figure 10.3 illustrates the relationship between PEDA and the various associations.

Finally, the need has been revealed for developing and facilitating horizontal linkages and cooperation between all the associations in the nine locations. Similarly, there is need for adequate linkages between the associations within each zone. This will enable the gardeners in the northern zone, in particular, and also those in the central locations to pool their resources to tackle, say, urban encroachment on land or water pollution from industrial wastes.

The sub-project activities in Korot gardening location, discussed below, are aimed at experimenting on how intractable these and similar constraints to effective gardeners' associations are and how they can possibly be eliminated or reduced.

The Sub-Project In Korot: Experience and Preliminary Findings

Well over 60 percent of the project field activities during 1995, and more than 80 percent of the field activities between July and December that year, were devoted to the sub-project activities. Effort was made to carry out all the planned activity packages (see Ajaegbu, 1995b).

In particular, we implemented the organizing and training, land and soil improvement, irrigation water sourcing and management, the advocacy and extension service packages. We carried out several facilitatory activities with the local farmers' association members as a group, as well as the participating gardeners as individuals. There were, for instance, series of one-day training sessions on preparing and using organic manures and on proper application of inorganic fertilizers; control of pests with and without pesticides; maintaining water-pumping machines; and on the objectives, responsibilities and advantages of farmers' associations for self-help actions.

Furthermore, week-end courses, spanning through chosen Friday and Saturday periods, were also organized focusing on small (farm) business attitudes and management, simple farm record-keeping and the value of farmer-propelled marketing and pricing strategies. Moreover, during countless trips and contact hours, the participating gardeners were given on-farm advice and demonstrations. The emphases included increasing their yields through better land preparation and soil treatment practices; more use of compost and farm-yard manure as supplements (or, in cases and circumstances, substitutes) to chemical fertilizers; more care in the irrigation practices to conserve the available water (low water use/water-saving practices); and, on raising the quality of the fruits and vegetables produced.

Among the various findings in the sub-project component to date, the following are highlighted here. The first is the generally high level of willingness and participation by the farmers in the organization, the communal actions and in the training activities including the on-farm advice and practical work. This is true of the participating gardeners from the indigenous (Plateau ethnic) groups and the settlers (the non-indigenous groups). It is also true of the few women members and the relatively younger and older farmers alike. Thus, it is expected that the enthusiasm that was raised by the project, even among the gardeners who are not registered in the association or participating in the experiment, will prove useful in attaining the objectives of the sub-project.

The second finding is, however, that the farmers have some reservations (in some cases very strong ones) regarding their ability to oppose the middlemen's marketing and pricing machinations, or in mobilizing local resources to construct earth dams and small reservoirs across the river. This explains the considerable reluctance to do something about such constraints. Thus, there are issues or constraints that the gardeners perceive they cannot overcome or are beyond their control. Here again, their perception of the constraints, their assessment of their ability to do something or to succeed or fail and their ultimate attitude to the constraints (action or resignation) are crucial in the context of this sub-project as well as regarding the overall objectives of the project (sustainable gardening and income generation).

The third finding derives from the inability of the Korot farmers' association, and the participating gardeners in particular, to successfully implement the irrigation water sourcing plan-of-work mapped out and pursued. It concerns especially the following points:

- Apparent inability of the different ethnic groups in the village to actually work together, out of distrust.
- Inability of the local (ward) head, who is also the chairman of the local farmers' association and our main contact person, to perform due to lack of dynamism.
- Misplaced expectations by the people who were hoping for what PEDA

and the Project Team were to give to them rather than what they could do for and by themselves, inspite of our explanations.

- Self-centered motives by the leaders, and suspicion of the leaders by the younger farmers in the community. The leadership apparently side-tracked many people in the hope that benefits could accrue to themselves. They, therefore, did not want the strong, efficient association in which all would participate in a democratic system. Thus, they did not inform many of the members about discussions and work schedules.
- Because the local farmers' association could not in the circumstance function effectively, the PEDA Team decided that it had to be more directly involved in summoning association's meetings and in organizing and supervising the communal activities;
- The need for continuous sensitization and mobilization sessions with the gardeners in general meetings, as well as for the different age groups, sexes and ethnic groups separately.

Thus, the individual on-farm activities and the self-development training for the gardeners have been very enthusiastically received and pursued by all. On the contrary, the general constraints that require or involve communal effort and resources were not dealt with successfully. This situation has, therefore, posed the question of how to mobilize for effective communal effort and cooperation among the gardeners in the sub-project. How can leadership efficiency and mutual trust be enhanced? These are among the issues being pursued further in the execution of the sub-project activities.

Conclusions

Discussions and brainstorming on the findings and conclusions of this study project, as well as practical and actionable recommendations from it are continuing. This present workshop is one such occasion, as we are in the process of writing the final report of the study.

References

Ajaegbu, H.I. (1995a), *Market-Gardening Activities in Nigeria: The Case Of The Jos Urban Area,* Paper presented at the project workshop on small-Scale

Market Gardening Around Jos, Nigeria, DLO-Staring Centre, Wageningen, 27-28 June.

Ajaegbu, H.I. (1995b), *The Pilot Market-Gardening Improvement Sub-Project: Formulating and Implementation Process*, Paper presented at the project workshop on Small-Scale Market Gardening Around Jos, Nigeria, DLO-Staring Centre, Wageningen, 27-28 June.

Igoche, A.O. (1995), *Development of Farmers' Associations on the Jos Plateau, Nigeria*, Paper presented at the project workshop on Small-Scale Market Gardening Around Jos, Nigeria, DLO-Staring Centre, Wageningen, 27-28 June.

Job, Christie D. (1995), *Constraints to Sustainable Dry-Season Market Gardening in the Jos-Bukuru Urban Area*, Paper presented at the project workshop on Small-Scale Market Gardening Around Jos, Nigeria, DLO-Staring Centre, Wageningen, 27-28 June.

11 On-Farm Demonstration, Training and Advice: Gardening Improvement Activities in Korot, Nigeria

SUNNY O.S. OKWUDIRE

Introduction

It is widely accepted among agricultural researchers that on-farm conditions and farmers' practices must be closely studied and respected. It is also argued that farmers need to play very active roles in agricultural research and experimentation (Chambers, 1994). It is expected that the participation of the farmers in on-farm adaptive research will result in sustainable development processes more attuned to the farmers' actual needs and their indigenous knowledge. This paper is based on work conducted among small-scale market gardeners in Jos-Bukuru area, in which these principles were applied.

Both Drinkwater (1992) and Farrington (1988) emphasized the need for partnership between application of indigenous knowledge and science for sustainable development. However, they stressed the significance of taking into account the dynamic nature and the strategic purpose of the farmers' practices. Pratt and Boyden (1985) stressed, similarly, that on-farm demonstration and training, as well as the accompanying advice, constitute strong instruments for applied research and extension to small-scale farmers.

In line with the basic objectives of the project on 'market gardening, urban growth and sustainable income generation' and the pilot sub-project we embarked on several on-farm training, advice and demonstration activities. The purpose was to improve the income and welfare of the Jos-

Bukuru gardeners by involving them in the development process. This was to ensure that processes, activities and results of the programme would be useful to the people.

As part of the on-going implementation of the sub-project programme, intensive effort has been made to facilitate some of the gardeners in Korot to develop, improve and apply modern or alternative gardening practices and technology in their farms. Several on-farm demonstration and advice sessions were carried out to enhance their efficiency. They were most intensively implemented during the August 1995 to March 1996 gardening season.

The following aspects of the identified constraints have so far been addressed through on-farm demonstrations, training and advice on:

a soil impoverishment and land degradation;
b water shortage;
c inefficient farm management systems including lack of record keeping;
d pest invasion.

On-farm Demonstration: Soil Improvement and Composting

This package is aimed at addressing the issues of soil impoverishment and land degradation. The problem was identified as a clear result of inadequate or improper soil management practices. An added contributing factor was the 'soil-mining' cropping system adopted by the people throughout the year, i.e., continuous cropping through both rain-fed and irrigated agriculture. 'Soil mining' is defined as season-by-season removal of soil nutrients due to intensive cropping without any replenishment programme. Other contributing factors included poor soil amendment, inadequate supply and high cost of fertilizers, as well as low organic matter return to the soil. Our intention was to encourage informal discussions on various agrotechnical subjects, and to offer advice on simple principles of sustainable soil fertility management. After several deliberations, field visits, and the evaluation of all potential methods that are based on a number of low-cost soil improvement options, we discovered that there was an abundance of compostable material in the area. Therefore, we agreed on a programme that enabled us to process and utilize the available materials. A soil improvement package focused on composting was thereafter developed to broaden the farmers' knowledge on the principles, processes and methods of compost manure production and use. The package was designed to train the farmers and demonstrate to them practical aspects of composting in selected fields. The participating farmers were then divided into two groups on the basis of the location of their fields, i.e., in the eastern, or in the western, bank of the Korot stream. Each group was then provided with a demonstration compost pit on its side of the stream.

The participating farmers, in their respective groups, were taught the way to use the package during one day of informal training. This included discussions and demonstrations on the principles, processes and methods, as well as other aspects of composting. During this on-the-site informal training, the discussions were on the introduction processes of decomposition and all other factors influencing different aspects of compost manure production. There was no need to redefine the concept of composting as the farmers already had the basic knowledge of it. They defined it as the process of gathering different materials in heaps, and letting them rot over time, in order to use them as 'native fertilizer'.

Therefore, we started by enumerating all the potentially compostable materials, earlier identified in the field. These include:

1   a variety of crop residue;
2   grasses and weeds;
3   leaves and other litter from the trees;
4   municipal and household refuse (sorted for relevance);
5   dry cow dung that is gathered in the bush, as well as other animal waste products.

We defined decomposition and decay as a process of disintegration of organic materials (compost materials) as a result of microbial activities over time, under conditions of ample temperature and moisture that exist in a compost heap or pit. Since it was necessary to explain the factors affecting these processes, we discussed in some length the following topics:

a   Carbon-nitrogen quotient of various organic materials listed by the farmers above. They were made to understand that succulent plant materials, which include fresh crop remains and leaves and litter from trees, decompose faster than other sources of dry organic matter. This is because the relatively high nitrogen to carbon ratios attracts the decomposers to them. Therefore, the larger the carbon-nitrogen ratio, the longer the composting period, and the lower the quality of the end product. Also, we discussed the importance of sorting the materials before composting and the   possibility of performing the pre-composting treatment, such as physical breaking of lumpy materials.

b   The significance of the moisture content of the materials was reviewed. The discussion focused on dry matter and fresh materials including cow dung, in relation to the rate of decomposition. We agreed that the rate of decomposition of dry material is too slow.   Fresh materials decompose faster, and are considered, thus, better compost materials.

c   The role played by the temperature and moisture regimes of the compost heap or pit was also reviewed. These are very important factors influencing the rate of decomposition. Ample temperature and moisture are required by the decomposes to operate at optimal levels throughout the composting period. Therefore, constant wetting and turning, as a means of moisture and temperature control, were explained.

d   The two common methods of composting, i.e.,   heap and pit, were reviewed in the light of their advantages and disadvantages. The discussion focused mainly their suitability in a given environment. For instance, on a steep slope pit composting should be recommended, while heap composting should be adopted on a site that has a shallow water table. The quality of the compost materials produced in either way has to be maintained by avoiding leaching out the nutrients as a result of excess wetting. Covering the heaps or pits with a thin layer of soil is another conservation means.

The farmers were given indicators or signs showing that the compost is ready for use. These include, absence of the pungent smell, change in the colour from black to brown, change in physical condition. For example, well rotten compost is less sticky, and very friable. When these are observed, the farmer exposes the compost to more aeration and cooling in a last heap or pit. There was no need for elaborate talk on the use, because they were all used to broadcasting compost in thin layers in the field.

At last, we marked out the plots into three areas and pegged out the space for each of the three shallow pits. Two of them had dimensions of 0.6 metres deep, 7 m long and 7 m wide, while the third measured 0.6 by 5 by 5 metres respectively. The pits were dug up by some of the farmers using diggers and spades, while others were engaged in gathering compost materials. One pit was then filled by laying the materials in homogeneous strata of 10cm (for each of the compost materials). Small tree branches pruned from the local cultivated trees and from the surrounding forest trees formed the first layer. Successive layers were made of the vegetable crop residue, dry maize stover, dry cow dung, and, finally, other grass weeds. The heap in the pit was compressed, leveled, and chopped with a spade. The heap was then wetted with water and a thin layer of solid cow dung was sprayed on it. Thereafter, the heap was covered with leaves and maize stalks.

Follow-up monitoring visits to supervise the turning of the heaps showed that individual farmers and groups of two or three farmers each had established 20 heaps. Table 11.1 shows the distribution of the participating farmers among the three groups.

Table 11.1   Grouping of Farmers for Composting Experiments

Group identity	Group size	No. of heaps	No. of farmers
A	1	12	12
B	2	5	10
C	3	3	9
Total		20	31

Source: Field survey, August 1995 to March 1996.

At the time of these on-farm demonstration activities we had registered some 31 participants on the sub-project. All of them were involved in adopting the use of compost. The groups were mainly formed by farmers whose plots were sited in close proximity to one another and those living in the same neighbourhoods, such as in the case of two groups who established their own pits in the village area. For the improvement of gardening soils composting is treated as either an alternative or a complement to inorganic fertilizers. It is, hoped, therefore, that when the benefits of the established compost heaps are enjoyed by these farmers, more people will be attracted to get involved in this soil improvement programme.

On-farm Water Sourcing Activities

The problems of inadequate irrigation water supply and inefficient water management practices are among the most pressing constraints faced by the market gardeners in Korot and other locations. These problems have in recent times impeded any meaningful development and expansion of the areas under irrigated farming. Cultivation is extremely difficult after the middle of the dry season when the Korot River, its tributary streams, and the mined-out pond reserves, dry out. Irrigation water is a key input which must be available throughout the farming season for market gardening to be sustainable. The farmers, therefore, must be sure of water for irrigation. There was, thus, the need to address this problem and to work out both short-term and long-term solutions to the seasonal water shortages experienced by the Korot farmers.

Part of the sub-project attempted, therefore, to assist the participating farmers to develop several irrigation water reservoirs and other sources of water on a trial basis, which could last at least for one farming season. A sustainable, long-term, solution could be derived from the experiences gained by the initial work. An irrigation water reservoir was made by constructing a dam across a water course under specific conditions. These included:

a   topographic, soil, and geologic conditions suitable for such
    development;
b   insufficient irrigation water during part of the irrigation season;
c   storage from surface run-off stream flows and sub-surface reserves
    that could build up reserves during the rainy season (USDA, 1969).

An integrated programme meant to trap surface flow and explore ground water reserves was designed to address the irrigation problem faced by the entire farming community. This involved several field visits to identify and evaluate potential water sources and the possibilities of constructing some earth embankments, earth dams and farm ponds. It was also aimed to expand and stabilize hand-dug wells, if possible, within the *fadama* areas. This was followed by several indoor discussions and planning sessions to initiate three community-owned and managed earth dams across the Korot River. During these planning sessions, three main activities were agreed upon as follows:

1   construction of community-owned and managed irrigation reservoirs from two earth dams across the Korot River, one on the up-stream, the other on the down-stream stretch and a third across one of the river's main tributaries;

2   reconstruction, expansion and stabilization of existing mining ponds in the area;

3   construction of hand-dug wells at identified and agreed sites.

On-farm activities took the form of informal training talks on the specifications, materials and labour requirement of each of the proposed sites. Site-specific, on-the-spot assessments and discussions lasted three Saturdays. During this period the entire gardening zone was covered. Thereafter, another indoor discussion session was held, during which we agreed on a work plan for activity one above.

Dates were fixed for the farmers, in each of the earth dam catchment areas, to gather construction materials such as stones, tree branches, maize stover and grasses for the three sites. Three different dates and days were proposed and accepted in August and September. Similarly, dates and times were agreed upon for the actual construction work. Unfortunately, all the effort and time put into this activity failed to produce many tangible results. Nonetheless, it revealed some hidden intricate characteristics of the community, including lack of unity of purpose at the community level. These were not identified early enough to allow the execution of the work plan within the period.

Lessons from this phase enabled us to base further work on smaller groups of farmers. Thus, groups of different sizes were identified, based on age sets, religious sects and good neighbourliness. There exists a relatively high level of trust and cooperation between such group members. In addition, the groups have hitherto been working together to handle their individual and group challenges. Hence, great success was recorded in phases two and three of the component. Thirty registered participating farmers were involved in one water-sourcing activity or the other after the remobilization exercises.

During the regular monitoring visits, individuals and small groups were assisted in developing previously identified potential additions to water sources close to their farm plots. A group of three elderly settler farmers was able to construct one earth embankment for their use. Mr. Pam Tok and his two relations reconstructed a nearby mined pond using stones and cement. The association's chairman and his two sons constructed a diversion channel and reservoir, among others, working in the stream locations.

Similarly, at the down-stream locations, the secretary of the association and his brother constructed an embankment and a diversion trench to their farms. Another farmer, together with his brother and cousin working in close proximity, developed one hand-dug well, an embankment and a feeder trench for their farms located downstream. Two families (husbands and wives) were assisted in developing two paddocks, while Mr. Gwom prepared an embankment and paddock for himself. Table 11.2 shows the sizes and numbers of small groups participating in the water-sourcing activities of the sub-project.

Table 11.2   Sizes and Frequencies of Water-Sourcing: Small Groups' Experiment

Group	Group size	Frequency	No. of farmers
A	1	1	1
B	2	5	10
C	3	5	15
D	4	1	4
Total		12	30

Source: Field Survey August 1995 - March 1996.

Table 11.2 indicates the level of cooperation among the people. It is worthy to note that the one-man group is a Birom farmer whose plot is located in between migrant farmers' plots. The migrants were working farms on land rented from his uncles. The team of four is made up of two Birom farmers, one settler farmer and a migrant farmer. This group developed diversion terraces from a mined pond close to their farm plots. The most frequent experiment peer group (B) is very common to the younger farmers, settlers or migrants. Further remobilization and sensitization of the farmers to execute the water component are continuing.

On-farm Training and Advice on Record Keeping

During the data-gathering surveys and monitoring aspects of the main project, the column of our questionnaire meant to capture information on the farmers' inputs and output was hardly completed because such data could not be provided by the farmers. This problem has made it very difficult for them to assess the progress of their business, forecast yield and income, or to plan ahead.

In general, most farmers shy away from any discussions regarding the economics of their business. It is not surprising to hear a farmer with over seven years' experience in the market-gardening subsector saying he did not know the quantity of fertilizer, fuel or seeds he had used so far in the current or previous season. In fact, there is no record to give an idea of the planting dates to meet specific market demand, or to make extra profit from a particular crop. The importance of record keeping has been discussed at the apex level (Farmers' Associations Delegates Meeting) in all our quarterly farmers' forum meetings in PEDA's office. Reports from various Farmers' Association Leaders and responses from a few selected farmers in all locations show that the farmers avoid record keeping because they will feel disappointed and discouraged to continue in the case of nonprofit.

The record-keeping programme of the sub-project is meant to educate the farmers about the benefits of records in the overall farm business. We designed on-farm training, advice and assistance for the participating farmers in the following subjects: (a) farm diary and labour records, (b) simple cash accounts, (c) input record and (d) produce account.

Farm Diary and Labour Record

A farm diary gives an inventory of the day-to-day operations performed, or to be performed, in the farm by a number of people over a given period. It also shows the labour use and cost per day. A labour analysis sheet gives a summary of the amount of labour in the farm and the actual working hours put in. These were explained to the farmers regarding each plot and each crop, during October 1995 (see Table 11.3).

The table explains the way a farmer's working hours are distributed in the early season October. The farm diary (a) records all the farm operations performed by the farmer and his peer group, as well as the time spent on

such activities; while (b) the labour analysis sheet gives a breakdown of the
time according to the cultivated crops or plots worked by him.

**Table 11.3   A Sample Farm Diary: Labour Use Record of a Farmer
for October 1995**

(A) Farm Diary				(B) Labour Analysis		
Date	Work done	No. of People	Time (hrs)	Time spent (Plot/Crop) on		
				spinach	tomato	cabbage
6/10/95	Clearing of farm	2	6	2	2	2
7/10/95	Irrigation	2	3	1	1	1
8/10/95	Tilling the field	4	9	3	3	3
10/10/95	Planting	2	4	0.5	2	1.5
10/10/95	Irrigation	2	3	1	1	1
15/10/95	Irrigation	2	3	1	1	1
19/10/95	Irrigation	2	3	1	1	1
23/10/95	Weeding	4	6	2	2	2
24/10/95	Fertilizer	2	1.5	0.5	0.5	0.5
24/10/95	Irrigation	2	3	1	1	1
29/10/95	Irrigation	2	3	1	1	1
Total		28	44.5	14	15.5	15

Cash Accounts

This records the expenditure and the revenue of the farmers, gives the
summary of all money spent on inputs and on the farm operations, as well
as the revenues realized from the sale of produce in the whole season,
month-by-month. We designed and illustrated a model cash account record
during one of the training and discussion sessions. The entries were made on
the spot using information supplied by a participating farmer, based on his
September 1995 experiences (Table 11. 4).

As the illustrations and discussions on record keeping went on, the
farmers were always reminded to make prompt entries to the relevant record
sheet at the end of the day, using pencils. They were also reminded to keep

receipts of items purchased during the season. At the end of each session, they were left with a sample copy of the record discussed.

Table 11.4   A Model Cash Account of a Farmer, September 1995

Date	Income	Amount (Naira)	Date	Expenditure	Amount (Naira)
2/9/95	Balance b/f	3,000.00			
			3/9/95	Purchase tomato seed	200.00
			3/9/95	Purcha. cabbage seed	300.00
			6/9/95	Clearing operation	100.00
			7/9/95	Purchase fuel/oil	125.00
			8/9/95	Wages for labour	150.00
			9/9/95	Purchased fuel	100.00
11/9/95	Sales of green maize	900.00			
			12/9/95	Purchased fertilizer	2000.00
			15/9/95	Purchased fuel/oil	125.00
8/9/95	Sale of green maize	600.00			
			19/9/95	Purchased fuel	100.00
			23/9/95	Purchased fuel	100.00
			23/9/95	Wages for labour	200.00
			27/9/95	Purchased fuel/oil	125.00
				To Balance c/d	875.00
		4 500.00			4,500.00

The table shows a detailed cash flow record of the farmer for the month of September, starting with cash at hand (otherwise called opening balance or b/f = brought forward). In this table, the balance carried down (b/d) is the difference between the cash received (income) and the expenditure made. This balance, brought down (b/d) is the amount left to be carried forward to the next month's (i.e., opening balance as b/f brought forward).

Purchased Input Records and produce Accounts

The accounts in respect of all types of inputs used during the season were contained in this part of the farmers' record book. The most frequently used inputs purchased by the farmers formed the basis for the demonstrating the nature of a typical farmer's input record sheet for October 1995 (Table 11.5). The data was compiled as an illustration during training sessions.

Table 11.5   Model Input Record Sheet of a Contact Farmer, for October 1995

Input	Type	Quantity	Total Cost (Naira)
Fertilizer (50kg)	SSP (single super phosphate)	2 bags	1,000.00
	NPK (Nitrogen phosphorus potassium compound)	2 bags	1,300.00
	Urea	1 bag	800.00
Fuel (litres)	Petrol (gasoline)	40 (L)	2,000.00
	Engine oil	4 (L)	800.00
Seeds (grams)	Tomato	80 (g)	200.00
	Green peas	300 (g)	300.00
	Green beans	250 (g)	200.00
	Pepper	50 (g)	150.00
	Carrot	60 (g)	400 00
	Cabbage	60 (g)	300.00
Manure	Cow-dung	1 truck	800.00
	Chicken dropping	1 truck	1,500.00
	Municipal garbage	4 trucks	1,600.00
Pesticide (litre)	Karate E.C.	0.25 (L)	450.00
	Actelic E.C.	0.25 (L)	400.00

Source: Field Survey 1995.

Information contained in this sample is meant to help the farmers to fix prices for their produce. Entries for transportation and other running costs may also be created.

The farmers were also instructed to keep a produce account book. This portion of the farm record presents the summary of information regarding the cash value of all produce from the farm, whether sold, stored or eaten at the time of harvesting, on a month-by-month basis. Table 11.6 shows a model produce account for July-Sept. 1995, based on information supplied by one of the farmers who was engaged in rain-fed farming as well as in gardening. In this case the items are either sold by the farmer on the day of harvest the day after.

Table 11.6   Model Produce Account, July-Sept. 1995

Date	Crop harvested	Quantity	Date	Action	Value (Naira)
7/7/95	Spinach	5 bundles	7/7/95	Sold	350.00
11/7/95	Carrot	3 bags	12/7/95	Sold	800.00
14/7/95	Lettuce	9 baskets	14/7/95	Sold	540.00
	Green beans	1 bag (15kg)		Sold	120.00
	Spinach	6 bundles		Sold	420.00
27/7/95	Egg plant	2 bags (30kg)		Sold	380.00
	Green beans	2 bags (20kg)		Sold	400.00
	Spinach	8 bundles		Sold	600.00
	Lettuce	4 baskets	28/7/95	Sold	320.00
2/8/95	Green maize	500 cobs	2/8/95	Sold	1,750.00
	Egg plant	6 bags (30kg)		Sold	1,020.00
	Lettuce	4 baskets		Sold	260.00
	Beet root	4 baskets		Sold	380.00
	Spring onion	2 bundles		Sold	180.00
9/8/95	Green maize	1000 cobs	9/8/95	Sold	3,000.00
17/8/95	Egg plant	5 bags (30kg)	18/8/95	Sold	700.00
	Beet root	2 baskets		Sold	200.00
	Spring onion	2 bundles		Sold	190.00
1/9/95	Carrot	3 bags (40kg)	1/9/95	Sold	1,200.00
	Pepper	1.5 bags (15kg)		Sold	600.00
	Cabbage	1 bag(38kg)		Sold	800.00
13/9/95	Maize grain	1 bag (50kg)	14/9/95	Sold	430.00
	Dwarf beans	1 bag(25kg)		Sold	1,470.00
21/9/95	Irish potatoes	5 bags (50kg)	22/9/95	Sold	1,500.00
Total:					17,310.00

Source: Field Survey 1995.

As the illustrations and discussions on record keeping went on, the farmers were always reminded to make prompt entries to the relevant record sheet at the end of the day, using pencil. They were also reminded to keep receipts of items purchased during the season. At the end of each session, they were left with a sample copy of the record discussed.

During the several surveys and monitoring activities of the project, cases of yield losses, which were suffered on various crops due to pests, were reported. The losses varied from crop to crop, from pest to pest, and between locations and seasons (Okwudire, 1994). The escalating cost of pesticides, which has made them less affordable to farmers, was also reported in other developing countries during the period discussed here, e.g., in Kenya (Kaaya,1993). This makes most farmers resort to a 'no-action' approach when faced with pest problems (Barfield and Stimac, 1990; Amoako-Atta, 1991). Besides, Haskell (1987) pointed out that craving for high priced chemical insecticides is a clear waste of time and money, because they do not fit into the traditional farming system and the farmers cannot use them effectively.

On-farm Demonstration and Training: Integrated Pest Management

This component of the improvement sub-project focussed on the problem through teaching, demonstration and training of the farmers to develop skills required to cope with the occurrence of pests in the area. After a review of field situations and available natural materials, we discussed the use of garlic and soap in an integrated harmonious manner to achieve the quickest desirable result. A low-cost pest management method for the poor resource market gardeners in the Jos area was devised from the mixture.

Neem-Soap Insecticide

Research findings on the insecticidal properties of some plants including neem, tobacco and garlic, have been popularized by the Henry Double Day Research Association, (HDDRA), International Centre for Insect Physiology and Ecology (ICIPE) and by the Technical Centre for Agricultural and Rural Cooperation (CTA) In recent times, pesticides are no longer exclusively factory made with the growing awareness that many insecticides are natural products of plants that can be extracted by the simple method described here.

Neem is a very common plant known to most people here as a multi-purpose tree. Its leaves and seeds have been used by farmers for storing grains. Soap detergents are also useful pest-control materials, especially when used well. A combination of the insecticidal but non-injurious properties of these, therefore, gives a broad-spectrum insecticide, which the farmer can prepare and use to control an array of crop pests, such as aphids, caterpillars, beetles and other suckling, boring insects and nematodes. Neem insecticide contains azadirectin, a complex insecticide equivalent of aziphos-metryl+ (Kidd and James, 1991). Neem powder can be used for soil dressing against soil pathogens.

A demonstration of the extraction and use of neem-soap insecticide was carried out during one of the training periods. Three handfuls equivalent of 150g neem seeds were crushed and pounded. This was infused in hot water for 15 minutes (alternatively overnight) stirred well and the concentrate was filtered into a CP15 knapsack sprayer. A little soap marsh (10g) was added and stirred well. The concentrate was further diluted by topping with water to 20 litre mark on the sprayer. The preparation was then used to spray an insect infested cabbage plot. The result was effective enough to impress the farmers to start gathering neem seeds for their individual use.

Garlic-Soap Insecticide

Garlic is quite cheap in the Jos area. It is grown by some gardeners. For this demonstration, 40 units of garlic, 5 soap, and 2 detergents were used to prepare an emulsifiable insecticide concentrate which kills green fly aphids and caterpillars instantly on contact.

Preparation procedure:

1   Chop 100 garlic cloves and pour into two teaspoon-full of kerosene. Leave for 2 hours,
2   Add 10g soap and 5g detergent, and mix,
3   Add 0.5 litre of water, and stir well,
4   Filter through cloth (fine sieve was used), and add 10 litres of water to dilute the solution,
5   Turn into CP15 knapsack sprayer, ready for use.

The demonstration ended with one participating farmer taking the knapsack and spraying a pest-infested egg plant/pepper plot in the field.

At the end of the two demonstrations, the farmers expressed satisfaction with the methods illustrated to them. They were told that they should try to grow more tobacco and other crops, which they could also use, more so when the pests co-evolve. The need to carry out integrated, unified pest management in the area to further boost the sustainability of the new adopted methods was stressed.

Conclusions

A Strategic Expansion Campaign (SEC) methodology is applied here. The emphasis is on the practical application of problem-solving strategies. Planning, training and demonstration are tailored to the identified constraints, which have deterred the development of market gardening in Korot and Jos areas.

Using this participatory problem identification, analysis and solution process, and based on the farmers' Knowledge, Attitude and Practice (KAP) regarding causes and effects, the pilot improvement sub-project tries to help the farmers. The constraints identified are approached and solutions to them sought through the joint efforts of the project team members and the farmers. In this way, the farmers' concerns and needs form the main focus of our demonstrations and recommendations.

Therefore, one can tentatively conclude that the success recorded in this aspect of the project has been due to its orientation and approach. This has enabled us to evolve intervention packages to ensure sustainable solutions to the farmers' problems. Such solutions have, as stated earlier, been generally based on their indigenous knowledge, values, beliefs and practices, without which not much success can possibly be recorded. The dam construction project showed, however, that cooperation among a larger number of farmers with different backgrounds and interests is far more difficult to achieve than having 2 or 3 people team up.

References

Amoako-Atta, B. (1991), *Role of community knowledge in developing integrated pest management in Africa*, Nairobi: ICIPE Science Press.

Barfield, C.S. and Stimac, J.L. (1990), 'Pest management: An entomological perspective', *Bioscience*, No. 30 pp., 683-689.

Chambers, R. (1994), *Beyond farmers' first, Intermediate.* London: Technology Publications.

Drinkwater, M.J. (1992), Methodology evolution within ARPT (Adaptive Research and Planning Teams): The use of farmers' research group and RRA international surveys within the central Copperbelt province, Revised version of a paper presented at the Methodology review session of the ARPT, Biannual Review Meeting, Mongu, Zambia, 13-16 April.

Farrington, J. (ed.) (1988), 'Farmer participation in agricultural research', *Experimental Agriculture*, No. 24.

Haskell, P.T. (1987), 'Integrated pest control and small farmers' crop protection in developing countries', *Outlook on Agriculture*. Vol. 9, pp. 121-126.

Ham, Kidd, M. and James, D.R. (1991), *Pesticide index,* Cambridge, U.K.: The Royal Society of Chemistry.

HDRA (Henry Doubleday Research Association) (1995), *Neems,* Coventry: Ryton Dumsmore Press.

Kaaya, G.P. (1993), *Biological control: an environmentally-safe alternative to the use of chemical pesticides.* Nairobi: ICIPE (International Centre for Insect Physionlogy and Ecology), Science Press.

Okwudire, S.O. (1994), *The rising need for an integrated pest management for dry season irrigated market gardening in Jos-Bukuru Area of Nigeria. A field situation report,* Jos: PEDA (Population, Environment and Development Agency).

Pear, P. and Shermann, B. (1990), *How to control farm and vegetable pests,* Coventry: Henry Doubleday Research Association, Ryton Dumsmore Press.

Pratt, B. and Boyden, J. (eds) (1985), *The Field Directors' Handbook: an Oxfam Manual for Development Workers,* 4th ed., London: Oxford University Press.

USDA (1969), *Technical guide for soil and water conservation in Northern States of Nigeria.* Washington: USDA (United States Department of Agriculture).

PART III
ACCESS TO RESOURCES
AND INPUTS:
CAPITAL, TECHNOLOGY
AND INFRASTRUCTURE

12 Accelerating Technology Transfer by Means of ATTA (Advanced Technologies in Traditional Agriculture)

DAN RYMON AND URI OR

Introduction

The main lesson to be learned is that accelerating technology transfer to a farming community - as opposed to a step-by-step approach - is a viable option; this without the prior development of a complete infrastructure comprising all of the required 'software' and 'hardware.' The ATTA approach (Advanced Technologies in Traditional Agriculture) may, therefore, offer an economically and socially acceptable way to overcome shortages of relatively high-value food crops in the growing metropolitan centers of developing countries.

Development and Technology Transfer

Development processes and ways to optimize them have been the focus of much research and pragmatic thinking. The development objectives of decision makers are often not clearly defined. The global struggle against migration from rural to urban areas has not been successful, and as a consequence it is obviously essential to supply food to these growing urban centers. Accordingly, this paper adopts the approach that one of the aims of development is to increase agricultural production in order to supply these growing food requirements. The transformation of a traditional farm sector into a commercial one requires critical changes in a number of production factors, such as land distribution, social structure, technological level, as

211

well as in various other structural components.   Since it is generally assumed to be impossible to change all of these at the same time, decision makers are faced with the question of which of them to address first and how to proceed thereafter.

- The formulation of answers to the following questions might serve as a practical starting point for development action:
- Assuming the economic well-being of the inhabitants as the first priority, what should be changed first: land titles, social structure, technology, or some other structural feature ?
- Should the advanced technology be introduced all at once or step by step, and if the latter how can this process be accelerated?
- What are the features of a 'mature' technology?
- What role should the public sector play in accelerating the development process ?

The Jordan Valley Case Study

The case study covers close to two decades of development - from the end of the 1960's until the mid-1980's.   During that relatively short period the traditional agriculture of the region underwent a dramatic change as a direct result of the introduction of a new agricultural technology based on drip fertigation.   Increased yields, and the corresponding increase in farmers' incomes, have resulted in capital accumulation and further development. In this sense technology has played a key role in upgrading the lifestyle of the local population.

The questions formulated above will be analysed here on the basis of the data collected within the framework of the case study.   A parallel study, using a simulation model, was conducted by Regev et al. (1989).

Background to Develoment

The study area is located to the west of the Jordan Valley, on a strip 20 km wide and 100 km long, situated along the Jordan River to the north of the Dead Sea. The area lies 250-400 metre below sea level, with the Samarian mountains   700-900 m above sea level to the west. The valley is a desert area with hot, dry summers and a short rainy season between December and

February. Mean annual rainfall is 140-170 mm; Mean temperatures ranges from 17°C (winter) to above 30°C (summer), and evaporation increases from 7 mm/day in winter to 14 mm/day in summer.

Traditional agriculture, producing mainly winter vegetables, has been practiced in the Lower Fari'a (known as Jiftlik) Valley, a western tributary of the Jordan, since the early twentieth century. A survey conducted in the late 1960's by the Dutch consulting firm NEDECO (1967) reported the production of over 33 irrigated crops (23 vegetables, four types of fruit trees, and six fodder and grain crops) and five unirrigated ones. Land use amounted mostly to one crop per year, and yields were at reasonable levels for a traditional technology (yields per ha were 16.5 ton tomatoes, 11.6 ton cucumbers, 12.7 eggplants, 8.3 potatoes). Seeds were obtained mostly from the previous year's yield. Other production aspects, such as flood irrigation, poor plant nutrition (local manure). No crop rotation was practiced. This was also in accordance with the traditional system.

A number of springs on the mountain slopes serve as the source of water, which entered an earth canal and later a concrete one. Under the local historical rights, water was allocated on a time basis (5 to 8 day cycle) and could be used by one of four consumers (zones) at a time (Zamonski, 1977). Efficiency of irrigation - mostly by furrows or flood - is estimated at less than 30 percent (Or, 1988). At the time of the survey the population consisted of approximately 4,000 Bedouin families, two-thirds of them traditional farmers (previously nomads). Average annual income per capita was less than US$200.

The social structure was based on a semi-feudal system, with collabouration between landlords and farmers. Each party contributed to the crop production. The landlord provided land and water ownership rights, access to credit and connection to the marketing agencies either directly (by selling in the market by himself) or indirectly. The farmer provided mainly labour. Labour requirements were relatively intense and, unless hired labour was added, placed a limit on the size of the family's cultivated area. In addition, the farmer has commonly provided a small warehouse for inputs and a packinghouse as part of his contribution to the partnership.

Develoment Approach and Methodology

The overall objective was to replace the traditional technology by an appropriate modern one, as a package of techniques. This is the first major step in development. Accordingly, the following 'hardware' components were introduced (the term 'hardware' is used here to include the physical components of the technology as listed hereunder):

a   earth-built water ponds to enable provision of the water supply according to crop needs, independently of the traditional allocation based on water rights;
b   drip irrigation system including all of its peripheral components;
c   seeds (usually hybrid varieties) and seedlings;
d   plastic sheeting (used for mulching, low tunnels, etc.);
e   Chemicals (fertilizers, insecticides, fungicides, etc.).

The initial investments, including purchase of the required inputs, were made possible by loans from an NGO (Non-Governmental Organization) i.e., the Mennonite Church, and the ongoing accelerated diffusion of the technology was a result of the economic success of the project.

The 'software' components introduced were those considered optimal for the Valley, on the basis of their previous record of operation in the Israeli agriculture under similar conditions. The term 'software' includes technology's components such as know-how organizations and institutions.

Social Structure

The Valley population has enjoyed a stable social structure for decades. The collabouration between landlords and farmers was not altered during the period of adoption of the new technology. The life style of the adult population has not been significantly affected. The new generation, however, is deriving the benefit of a higher standard of living, both on the personal level (health and education) and professionally (training and experience).

The landlord provides access to credit and marketing, though his personal and direct involvement in traditional credit and marketing institutions. The supply of credit facilitates the flow of inputs, while the marketing involvement reduces the price fluctuations to which the farmer is exposed. The latter is thus able to operate with minimal risk, so that his task becomes merely to achieve high yields of good quality produce.

In developing countries it is frequently found that 'transformation implies ... a removal of obstacles hindering the flow of inputs,' and 'the privileged, both traditional and 'modern', are bound to oppose the transformation... likely to jeopardize their position.' (Sadan, 1985). Here, because of the stability of the social community, this did not apply. Instead, both collaborating parties derived benefit from the transformation, and had good reasons to accelerate it.

Infrastructure and Agricultural Technology

The existing infrastructure in the Jordan Valley at the start of the period was capable of supporting the projected changes. Relatively speaking, this is the situation in most if not all the vicinities of the big cities. Development of agricultural services such as outlets for the sale of inputs and supply of spare parts for farm machinery were adequate. Investments in the regional infrastructure were the responsibility of the authorities, while on-farm investments were left to the two parties comprising the farming sector.

Agricultural technology may be defined as the overall combination of complementary techniques employed in the production of goods of market value. Another outlook views technology as composed of 'software' and 'hardware'. As an example, fertilization is one such technique, while vegetable growing in all its stages is carried out by means of an agricultural technology. Adoption of the advanced agricultural technology by the Valley farmers led to a notable change in cropping patterns. There is now a greater dependence on intensive cash crops (vegetables), fewer types of crops are grown and land use has almost doubled (see Table 12.1).

The changeover from the traditional to an advanced agricultural technology is reflected both in the inputs purchased and in the distribution of the irrigated areas (see Table 12.2). Lack of flexibility in the supply of production factors such as land, water and labour persuaded the farmers to opt for the new technology. In order to implement it, they had to purchase inputs (e.g., tractors, seeds, plastic materials and fertilizers). Over the development period there has been a change of less than 50 percent in the total land area utilized and in the amount of labour employed, and no change in the total quantity of water used. In contrast, the purchase of commercial inputs over the same period has increased by approximately eightfold (see Table 12.3). Two important points are illustrated by the data:

1   By 1985, more efficient use of the same quantity of water enabled farmers to irrigate almost ten times the area irrigated at the beginning of the development process.

2   The rate of increase of the irrigated land is 16% annually, despite the fact that the total amount of water does not change.

Table 12.1   Jordan Valley - Cropping Patterns, 1965-1985*

Crop	1965 %	1985 %
Barley, wheat (rainfed)	41.5	--
Vegetables	51.8	162.6
Plantations (banana, citrus)	7.1	17.4
Total - cropping intensity	100.4	180.0

*   Percent of arable land. The meaning of 180% is that a second crop was obtained from 80% of the land.

Sources: Quart. Agric. Statistics, Central Bureau of Statistics, Israel and
    NEDECO (1967).

Table 12.2   Expansion of Irrigation and Uptake of Advanced Technology in the Jordan Valley 1970-1985 (ha)

Year	Irrigated Area Annual Growth		Area by Type of Irrigation		
			Furrow/flood	Drip	
	ha	%	ha	ha	%
1970	430	-	425	5	1.2
1975	1550	72	1375	175	12.3
1980	2290	30	350	1940	84.7
1985	4170	36	390	3780	90.6

Source: Quart. Agric. Statistics, Central Bureau of Statistics, Israel.

There was a rapid move from flood and furrow irrigation (more than 90% of the irrigated land in the early 1970s) to drip fertigation (more than 90% of a much larger irrigated area in the middle of the 1980s).

Table 12.3 Purchase of Agricultural Inputs in Judea and Samaria Region, 1970-1986

Year	Tractors No.	Annual Growth (%)	Seed, Chemicals, and Plastic Materials NIS '000 (of 1987)	Annual Growth (%)
1970	460	-	236	-
1975	1049	46	476	40
1978	1673	31	653	27
1982	2606	31	1095	34
1986	3763	29	1687	3

Source: Quart. Agric. Statistics, Central Bureau of Statistics, Israel.

Table 12.4 Jordan Valley - Increase in Yields, 1965-1982 (Ton/ha)

Crop	Flood	Irrigation Method Furrow	Drip
	1965	1975	1982
Tomato	16.5	20.0	60.0*
Cucumber	11.6	--	25.0
Eggplant	12.8	20.0	70.0
Onion	5.2	15.0	35.0
Hot Pepper	2.8	10.0	15.0
Watermelon	--	--	80.0

* Yields per ha, estimated by Matar and Azzeh (1978), are 15 tons under furrow irrigation and 81 tons under drip irrigation.

Sources: NEDECO (1967); Regev (1983).

The adoption process since 1975, when the technique was proven in the field, is calculated to perform at an annual rate of 40.7%. It is important to point out that the introduction of new irrigation methods is accompanied by employing a whole series of complementary inputs. In parallel with the drip fertigation system in the Valley came the introduction of high quality seeds, farm machinery, plasticulture (soil bedding, low tunnels), solar soil sterilization, plant protection chemicals, etc.

Agronomic and Economic Results

The results achieved by the farmer of the Valley were similar to yields obtained in Israel under similar conditions. The quality of the produce has been greatly improved, thus explaining its acceptability in the markets of the Arab oil countries and Europe. Yields are presented in Table 12.4. In general, they increased by three to five times per her.

No direct calculation was made of the growth in farmers' incomes after completion of the first development phase, say, in the mid 1980s. On the basis of the tenfold increase in the quantities marketed (Table 12.5), as well as quality considerations, one can estimate the increase in farmers income.

Table 12.5   Jordan Valley - Production of Vegetables 1971-1984 ('000 Tons)

Crop	1971	1980	1984
Tomato	4.6	45.2	66.9
Cucumber	6.8	22.2	25.9
Eggplant	6.5	17.3	18.2
Melon	1.2	19.6	80.6
Total	19.1	104.3	191.6

Source: Quart. Agric. Statistics, Central Bureau of Statistics, Israel.

This evaluation is supported by Matar and Azzeh (1978), who estimated the growth in yields and income during the development process (1978) at five- to sixfold (yields) and more than ninefold (net income per hectare). Further support comes from Tamari and Giacaman (1980). It seems that covering all capital recovery is less than 3% of the revenue, and that the advanced farmers income is three to four times that of a corresponding traditional neighbour (see Table 12.6).

The opinion is sometimes expressed that the introduction of a modern technology might lead to unemployment. This is probably a myth, and is certainly contradicted by the present case study.

Table 12.6 Estimated Crop Budget, in US$/ha

Cost of Inputs	Tomato (tradi-tional)	Crop Enterprise Cucumber+ Tomato (Advanced)	Tomato+ Melon (Advanced)
Land Preparation	100	250	250
Seed / seedlings	30	800	700
Fertilizer	240	550	550
Chemicals	120	440	350
Plastic Sheeting	-	800	800
Irrigation	-	120	80
Packing material	80	300	120
Interest	80	330	280
Sub-total	820	3,550	3,130
Capital recovery (irrigation system)		668	668
Grand Total	820	4,218	3,798
Revenues			
Quantity (ton)			
Tomato	20	60	60
Cucumber	-	25	-
Melon	-	-	60
Prices ($/ton)			
Tomato	200	300	300
Cucumber	-	300	-
Melon	-	-	400
Total Revenue ($)	4,000	25,000	42,000
Land and water lease charges (50%)*	2,000	12,275	21,000
Net Revenue	2,400	12,750	21,000
No. of man-days	280	650	700
Return per man-day	7.1	19.6	30.0

* Including credit and marketing, earnings of the landlord.
Source: Tamari, S., Giacaman, R. (1980).

For example, the labour requirements per hectare of tomatoes estimated by Zamonski (1977) are greater for drip irrigation (430 man-days) than for furrow irrigation (280 man-days), mainly because of the higher yields and the additional labour required to harvest them and prepare them for the market. The technological change has enabled farmers to be freer and, due to the change in labour composition, to make more efficient use of family members as a labour force.

Another myth concerns the level of investment, which is generally thought to preclude the adoption of advanced technologies such as drip fertigation systems by poor farmers or under the usual budgetary conditions of development agencies. Observations by Bergman (1983) and estimates by Rymon and Fishelson (1988), for cotton grown in Israel, indicate an entirely different situation: Drip irrigation was found to be cheap in terms of capital per unit of revenue. Shortage of labour is not generally a problem in the Jordan Valley (or, indeed, in other developing regions). The study of cotton growing is unique in that the investment in the different technologies is considered not only in terms of its initial expense, but reveals the necessity of two 'corrections':

a   the investment is calculated per unit of product (e.g., ton of tomatoes) and not in relation to another production factor (e.g., hectare);
b   other factors are incorporated in order to distinguish between the outcomes of the various technologies (e.g., labour requirements, land utilization, plant protection associated with each technology, quality of the produce, etc.).

In the Valley, for example, the appropriate tactics of introduction - together with the other relevant factors - made the drip fertigation system the most suitable technology. Use of the data presented by Matar and Azzeh (1978) in a simulated calculation shows that adoption of the complete agricultural technology is correlated with an increased income level and a rapid capital accumulation Three to four years are sufficient for capital recovery. This period is shorter than the technology's operative life span and the farmer can, therefore, invest from his own savings once the desired performance has been demonstrated reliably.

Lessons from the Case Study: Accelerating Technology Transfer by Means of 'ATTA' Approach

Within the constraints of this case study, the results indicate a clear-cut answer to the first of the four questions posed at the beginning of this paper. Technological change proved to be a remarkable successful means of initiating development, and the resulting rapid increase in farmers' incomes is without precedent to the best of our knowledge worldwide. Obviously, the introduction of an advanced technology must necessarily involve certain problems; however, any problems encountered at the time were minor and in looking back more than a decade later they appear to have been insignificant. The answer to the second question is similarly clear: The introduction of the new technology as a complete package proved to be a highly successful strategy, and seems preferable to the stepwise approach often considered necessary because of limiting factors such as poor technical background of farmers, required investment, etc. Even with traditional farmers, the package approach appears to be better than one which introduces the components of a technology gradually, or starts by improving farmers' skills and/or existing regional infrastructure.

An important feature of the radical agricultural changes that takes place during the accelerated adoption of an advanced technology is the way in which these changes occur. In the present case this was as follows:

a   on each plot or farm the success was immediate, with most of the
     increase in yields being achieved within one or two seasons;
b   the yields remained stable at a high level over the next few years, after
     which improvements were marginal;
c   in fields where the advanced technology was adopted later, farmers
     experienced major yield increase similar to that of their neighbours.

It should be noted that the 'ATTA' approach involves a change in the traditional attitude toward the operation of the extension system. The common procedure in which the introduction of a new technology is closely supervised by extension officers makes critical demands on their effectiveness and credibility, which in turn determine the success or failure of the technology transfer.

In the present case, because of the stability of the farming community, and its well-established connections with the markets, the main focus of credibility was shifted from the extension officers to the technology itself.

As a result of the findings of the Jordan Valley case study, a new approach to accelerating technology transfer and to development was formulated, based on the rapid introduction of 'ATTA'. The main features are its operation within a stable social system and towards a well-defined market, and the rapid introduction of an appropriate technology with full participation of the farmers and suitable government involvement. It should be noted here that our concept of technology transfer, in contrast to other definitions, emphasizes the target users, i.e., the farmers, irrespective of the technology's source.

A stable social structure is an important factor. In assessing the sociocultural elements that may affect the introduction of an advanced technology, special attention should be paid to the following:

a   rights to use production factors such as land and water;
b   customary division of labour and responsibility between age, sex and social groups;
c   forms of cooperation within and between farm families;
d   Sense of ownership.

A well-defined market implies the existence of a group of products to which a particular production technology is suited. In areas of increasing urban population, it is most likely that cash crops are likely to be in high demand. Alternatively, the demands of a particular market (i.e., an export market) can be identified by means of mission-oriented marketing research. It is assumed that in most cases both the marketing system and the organizational channels exist, although they may not be favourably disposed towards new supplies of traditional producers.

The appropriate technology for single-stage accelerated absorption, as described by Or (1988), has several unique features which may be said to characterize it as a 'mature' technology:

• a complete package;
• fully tested and proven in the field;
• full compatibility between its component parts;
• minimal after-sales service requirement;
• simple to operate and ease of adaptation in the field;
• a relatively long effective life span.

The existing regional infrastructure of the Jordan Valley was not a barrier to the rapid development. Other developing regions close to major metropolitan centres can also be expected to possess and adequate infrastructure, at least in relative terms:satisfactory roads, sufficient outlets for physical inputs, e.g., seeds, fertilizers and chemicals, and a close link to credit institutions.   The farmer in this case study did not experience problems such as those described by Sadan (1985), where 'because credit is irregular, the cost of utilizing fertilizers to the peasant is far higher than the social opportunity-cost.'

At the outset, participation requires initiative on the part of the farmers, and their involvement will increase as their confidence builds up:

- Awareness of current farm practices and understanding the farmers' views and problems with regard to the proposed scheme.
- Evaluation of the farmers attitudes to the proposed system prior to the introduction of the advanced technology.
- Facilitating the process of adoption of the advanced technology by suiting it to the experience and capabilities of the farmer.
- Promoting farmers' cooperation and active participation in the planning of each step of the development of their region.

In general, the desirable situation is one in which the public sector conducts the development process in such a way that farmers feel themselves an integral part of it, as if the development is entirely their own.

As a final question, one might ask where and under what circumstances the conclusions of this case study and the ATTA developed from its lessons can be successfully implemented. It is not difficult to identify regions in which the basic social and economic features are similar to those found in the Jordan Valley population prior to its accelerated adoption of the advanced technology.

Post Script (updating to 1995)

The political events in the Middle East, especially the Intifada, has weakened the direct contacts between the Israelis and their co-partners, the Palestinians who took part in the Case Study. During the last decade the farmers in the area continued purchasing most of their inputs in Israel and as before, exporting their agricultural products to the markets of Israel, Jordan and Europe. The major change in the area has to do with the water conducting system. The existing system of open channels and pools was replaced by covered pipes - most of the places are getting its water via pipes which flow by gravitation from the sources uphill.

Below is a data presentation for the years 1991-94.

The irrigated fields which in 1985 comprised 4,170 hectares, have increased slightly, to 4,420 hectares in 1993. Of this, 1,420 hectares were in the autonomous territory of Jericho and 3,000 in the other areas. In the year of 1994 there was a reduction (to 2,690 hectares), in the size of irrigated fields in the areas located outside Jericho, which is explained by the fact that a large number of former agricultural workers preferred to be employed in Israel in the construction industry. This was considered as more profitable than agriculture. Another change which can be seen mostly in Jericho, is a move to crops in greenhouses, among them highly elaborated greenhouses for vegetables and flowers. The reason for this change is that the lands in the Jericho area are fully owned by the growers. In the rest of the Jordan Valley, on the other hand, most of the land is held by the farmers under short-term tenancy agreements. The movement from low tunnel into elaborated greenhouses is therefore, slow. The tenancy systems have not changed in the past decades and the situation is still fairly similar to that encountered in 1985.

Table 12.7   Agricultural Production (in thousand tons) since 1990 Compared with Production Before 1984

Crops	1984	1991	1992	1993	1994
Tomatoes	66.9	52.0	48.2	58.0	27.8
Cucumbers	25.9	28.5	48.5	50.4	40.5
Eggplants	18.2	17.4	14.9	14.8	16.0
Marrow	-	16.6	20.0	20.5	19.4
Cabbages	-	15.1	15.6	15.0	9.7
Melons	80.6	5.6	13.6	10.1	1.7
Other	-	26.9	30.5	32.6	30.5
Total	191.6	162.1	191.4	201.5	145.6

The data for 1994 do not include the area of Jericho which had previously accounted for about one third of the total cultivated areas. If it were included it can be assumed that it would have contributed an addition of about 70 thousand tons. The total production would reach, thus, the amount to 215-220 thousand tons.

Between the years of 1990 and 1991and during the Intifada, there was a drop in cultivated fields which had an influence over the whole production. However, since 1992-3 the relative stability of the political situation has had a positive influence on the level of production.

Acknowledgment

The authors would like to thank their colleagues S. Barghouti, G. Fishelson, E. Sadan, J. Sagiv, Y .Sarig and J. Shalhevet and two anonymous referees of this journal, for helpful comments. The project was assisted by a contribution of the Agricultural Research Organization (3263-E, 1991 series). This is a revised version of an article published in the *Journal of Sustainable Agriculture*, Vol. 2, no. 1, 1991. It is printed here with the permission of the Haworth Press, Inc. © All rights reserved.

References

Bergman, H. (1983), 'Economic Considerations in Choosing Irrigation Systems'. *Proceedings of the 3rd International Conference on Irrigation*, 3-6 October 1983, Tel-Aviv: AGRI-TECH , pp.47-57.
Matar, I. and Azzeh Y. (1978), *Typical Farm Budgets for the Years 1977 and 1978*, Jerusalem: Unpublished report.
NEDECO (1967), *Agro-Economic Conditions. Appendix E to a consulting work on the Jordan Valley*, Submitted to the Government of Jordan, Amman, December 1967.
Or, U. (1988), *Drip Irrigation Development in the Arab Sector of the Jordan Valley as a Model for Developing Countries*, Master Thesis, Hebrew University of Jerusalem, Faculty of Agriculture, Rehovot.
Regev, A., Jaber, A., Spector, R. and Yaron, D. (1989), *Economic Evaluation of the Transition from a Traditional to a Modernized Irrigation Project*, Rehovot: Hebrew University of Jerusalem, Faculty of Agriculture.
Regev, Nava (1983), *The Arab Sector in the Jordan Valley, 1975-1982*, Haifa: World Zionist Movement: Settlement Division, Northern Region, Israel (in Hebrew).
Rymon, D. and Fishelson, G. (1988), 'Economic Analysis of Cotton Irrigation Technologies'. in: D. Rymon (ed), *Optimal Yield Management*, London: Gower, pp. 221-34.
Sadan, E. (1985), 'Settlement, Rehabilitation and Reform: Dilemmas in Agricultural Development Projects in Latin America'. *Journal of Rural Cooperation*, vol. 13, pp. 135-51.
Tamari, S. and Giacaman, R (1980), *ZBEIDAT: The social impact of drip irrigation on a Palestinian peasant community in the Jordan Valley*, Birzeit: Birzeit University,, Part I (The Agrarian System).
Zamonski, Edna (1977), 'The Arabs in the Jordan Valley - Settlements and agriculture', in: A. Shmueli, D. Grossman, and R. Zeevi (eds), *Judea and*

Samaria: Studies in Settlement Geography, Jerusalem: Canaan, vol. 2, pp. 605-29 (in Hebrew).

13 Katheka Revisited: Urban Agriculture, Participation and the Challenge of Intensified Resource Utilization

RICHARD FORD

Introduction

This paper is presented as a preliminary offering, based on recent field work in three rural Kenyan communities: Katheka, Mbusyani, and Gilgil. Each lies within a 90 minute drive of Nairobi. The field work reviewed activity in each of the communities, based on earlier analyses and action plans (1987, 1988, and 1992 respectively) which were designed to strengthen capacities of community institutions to carry out effective natural resource management and production.

The methodology drew, in part, on conventional data gathering instruments, including questionnaires. The field team also relied heavily on group discussions and interactive data analysis, using techniques derived from Participatory Rural Appraisal (PRA).[1]

The paper selects the community of Katheka for detailed analysis. Situated in a harsh ecological setting, the previously small population supported itself largely through pastoralism. Population increases in the last few decades, combined with severe drought, have reduced livestock numbers and increased dependence on agriculture. Yet the current agricultural practices evolve from skills acquired in zones where rainfall was more abundant. The findings suggest that explicit attention to commercial crops well-suited to rainfed, dryland agricultural conditions would be more appropriate than Katheka's current agricultural practices. The author assumes that Katheka represents many peri-urban communities in contemporary Africa and that similar stresses of agricultural expectations in very

227

dry conditions are causing hardship and ecological stress in these communities as well.

The recommendations, therefore, though pointed primarily at Katheka, have applicability to many communities. It is suggested that farmer-based trials of a multitude of dryland food and commodity crops be initiated to provide Katheka residents with:

- agricultural harvests more suited to their dryland environment;
- more reliable annual yields, even in times of poor rains; and
- a more constant livelihood that will enable households to increase productivity of their semi-arid farmsteads.

The field work has brought insight into pressures which peri-urban communities are experiencing in Kenya and has led to four working hypotheses and five recommendations for further action research and experimental implementation.

Working Hypotheses:

- **Rising Urban Demand.** As Africa's urban populations increase, demand for food and especially products for local urban and small town markets from the immediate peri-urban area will increase. These demands will create new economic opportunities but will also impose new stress on already marginal eco-systems;

- **High Potential Lands Proximate to Urban Areas Already Full.** Given the particular history of Kenyan agriculture, the areas of abundant and mostly reliable rainfall adjacent to urban areas are already in full utilization;

- **Dryland, Rainfed Crops as Primary Food and Market Products Have Not Received Serious Consideration.** Given: (a) that the three peri-urban communities investigated in this field work are all dryland areas; (b) that investment capital is indeed scarce for these communities while need for cash income is overwhelming; and (c) that there is a high priority for action and strong previous achievement in these communities, an important response is development of crops that are within their technical, capital, and marketing reach; Israel already experienced with many such crops. Given the history of Israeli agriculture, there is already experience and expertise with many dryland, rainfed, market crops including (for example) Marula, Desert Apple, White Sapote, Black Sapote, Sapodilla, Monkey Orange, Angel, Mmilo, Prickly Pear, Pitaya, Kei Apple, Argan, Pulmelo, Jojoba, Yehib, Mongongo and others.[2] However, the particular combination of linking dryland and rainfed market crops with the social and economic aspirations of peri-urban communities, in collaboration with African institutions, has only been lightly tested. My recommendations, therefore, come from this recent and field-based experience and seek to link community priorities, African institutional strengths, Israeli dryland experience, and methods that mobilize community institutions.

Recommendations

As a result of the investigation, five recommendations are put forward. They include:

- **Field Tests** Focus attention on village-based field testing (not on research station plots) of dryland, rainfed food and commodity crops with potential cash value;

- **Experimental Villages** Work with a select number of experimental, dryland villages that meet the following criteria:

  ... have demonstrated achievement of community-based institutions;
  ··· have taken a decision, as a village, to become a field trial and experimental community;
  ··· have indicated willingness to engage in community-wide action (e.g. bench terracing, tree nurseries, road improvement, cut-off drains) that may be needed to open and support experimental activities;

- **Conduct Field Trials** Introduce dryland cereal, tree, bush, browse, and horticultural crops that may have commercial value in the community's ecological and economic setting;

- **Organize Community Action Plan** Develop, with the community's groups, an action plan for this experimentation, along with indicators which the community has selected, to determine whether the experiments are achieving the community's expectations. Include in the plan a means to monitor and record these variables as well as a means to change how the experimental crops are being tested;

- **Marketing**   Develop a marketing and possibly a small-scale food processing strategy (e.g. drying mangoes, pressing oil seeds) that will test the market potentials and viability of the new crops.

Background to Field Work Sites

In June, 1996, a team of two Clark and three Egerton University researchers, two Kenya Government staff (Ministry of Research and Ministry of Water Development) and one NGO researcher spent a total of three weeks in three communities.[3] These included the sublocations[4] of Gilgil which lies about 80 kms north of Nairobi on the road to Nakuru; Katheka which is about 90 kms east of Nairobi in Matungulu Division (Machakos) and Mbusyani, near Katheka in Kangundo Division, also Machakos.

All three lie in Kenya's semiarid zone.   They experience unreliable rainfall on a regular basis. Charts which villagers constructed in Gilgil demonstrate the uncertainty of rainfall, linked to unreliable food production. These charts follow as Figures 13.1 and 13.2.   Village charts prepared for Mbusyani and Katheka demonstrate similar fluctuations in rainfall and food between 300 and 500 mms.

In the case of Gilgil, it is a new settlement area, dating back only to the late 1970s and 1980s.   Most land holdings consist of five acre tracts.   The area is so dry that many land owners have never occupied their farms, holding them for speculation or perhaps in the hope that one day water will come.

Katheka and Mbusyani are older communities, with first settlement coming at the turn of the century.   Land holdings are irregular in size, generally less than five acres though a few recent arrivals have acquired ten to fifteen acre tracts.   These newcomers hope to produce horticulture for export to the urban areas though they have not yet solved their water problem.

In the case of Gilgil, any surplus produce -- tomatoes, cabbages, beans, onions -- is generally sent to markets in Nakuru -- a 30 minute drive to the north.   Katheka and Mbusyani export some items -- pawpaws, mangoes -- to the local market towns of Tala and Kangundo.   Longer terms plans call for production for Nairobi and perhaps for export to Europe as well.

While tracking developments in all three communities is of interest, time limitations suggest that a close review of one of the three will provide insight into patterns for all three.

Explanations

- 1992-1996 Poor rain and poor harvests
- The dotted line for 1992 indicates time when original community,action plan was set in place

Figure 13.1   Trend Lines for Gilgil: 1992 and 1996 - Rainfall

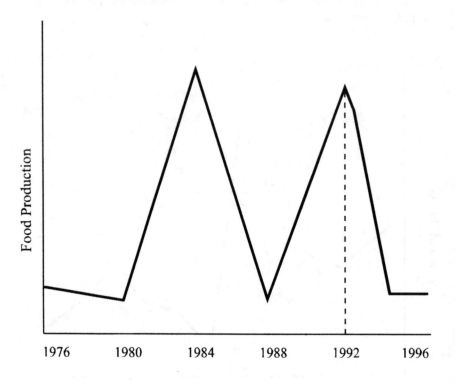

Explanations

- 1992-1996 Poor rain and poor harvests
- The dotted line for 1992 indicates time when
  original community,action plan was set in place

Figure 13.2   Trend Lines for Gilgil: 1992 and 1996 - Food Production

The Case of Katheka

Katheka sublocation lies in a difficult environment. The climate is harsh, soils porous and rocky, vegetation sparse, and livelihood frugal. It includes three villages of about 1,500 people each or a total estimate for 1996 of about 5,000. The official census figure for 1979 was 2,285. Located thirteen kilometers from the market town of Tala, down a rutted, dusty road, Katheka has neither electricity nor piped water. In 1987, no resident owned an automobile or, for that matter, even a motorbike. While there are occasional good years in which rainfall may exceed 1,000 mm, for most years precipitation is considerably less. Even so, like many communities in semi-arid areas, Katheka receives sufficient rainfall to carry out agricultural activity if the crops planted are varieties appropriate for dryland areas and water is properly harvested and managed. They have had good success with pigeon peas, mangoes, cassava, and in previous years, oil seeds. They have achieved moderately good results with Katamani maize, a special hybrid variety developed in Machakos for dryland conditions.

The sublocation is approximately 11 sq. km. in area. The terrain is rugged; elevation varies from 1240 to 1500 meters in the space of less than two kilometers. Nearby, the Kanzalu Hills rise to 1700 meters and the small mountain, Ol Donyo Sabuk, less than 10 kilometers away, reaches 2145 meters.

Soils are rocky and hard to work. Tools wear out quickly. Plowing with oxen is always a challenge. Sparse vegetation offers little protection when torrential rains and surging streams carry away massive amounts of soil. The Ministry of Agriculture classifies the sublocation as Agroecological Zones Three (marginal coffee) and Four (oil seeds and sorghum/millet).

As one travels south toward Tala, precipitation increases and land use changes considerably. Whereas Katheka supports only marginal coffee, estimated at two to three kilos harvest per bush per year, as close as Kinyui (4 kms south), harvests are two or three times better. In the high potential areas of neighbouring Kiambu and Murang'a Districts (50 to 75 kms west) harvests range as high as 15 kilos per bush. In Katheka, coffee grows only reluctantly; as a cash crop it makes no one rich.

Economy and Land Use

For decades, Katheka has been looked upon as an isolated and even forgotten sublocation. Although it enjoyed a brief period of prosperity in the 1930s when it was temporarily designated as a market centre, most of its history has been one of neglect and inactivity. One hundred years ago, no one lived there on a permanent basis. Rather the residents were nomadic pastoralists who practiced little or no agriculture.

In the 1890s, major changes began among the Akamba who were then, as now, the principal inhabitants. First, an extended drought and a disastrous rinderpest epidemic crippled the Akamba's herds. Then, as the British-built Mombasa to Uganda railway passed through the southern part of Machakos, European settlers began to arrive. Though no settler staked out land in Katheka itself, coffee and sisal plantations appeared within a few kilometers along the Kalala and Athi Rivers.

The immediate effect, rather than to alienate land and displace people, was to attract settlers from nearby Kangundo and Machakos Town, about 45 kms away. As demand for plantation labour increased, so did Akamba settlement in and around Katheka. For example, one patriarch of Katheka who recently passed away, Andrew Maundu, came with his family before World War I and settled. Although as an adult he lived mostly in worker housing on the coffee plantations across the river, he always kept his large family and sizeable herds in Katheka. Other workers did the same.

As settlement gradually increased, so did pressures on the land. Herders kept their cattle and goats in the area for longer periods of time; total livestock numbers increased. By the 1920s, overgrazing and expanding agriculture were creating problems. Further, the Akamba's traditional land use and grazing control systems were wholly unable to deal with these new pressures as the British had removed authority from traditional leaders. Previously a Council of Elders had governed each community and would take whatever action was necessary in land disputes or cattle grazing jurisdictions, but the Colonial Office replaced the Councils with appointed Chiefs whose task it was to carry out the Colonial will.

By the late 1920s, overgrazing had become a severe problem. As the vegetation disappeared, gullies began to appear on the steep hillslopes. Katheka's former Assistant Chief, William Mutua, grew up in the sublocation. Now an honoured elder in the community, he remembers his father describing major gullies of ten meters depth as common occurrences by the 1930s.

Colonial Interventions

Colonial officials became justifiably concerned. Yet rather than treat the underlying problem, land alienation, the British treated the symptom, overstocking and gully erosion. Colonial officers ordered villagers to halt soil loss through coerced gang-labour and to reduce their holdings in livestock. Villager response was two-fold: refusal to do either soil conservation or destocking; and active involvement in political mobilization. Anti-conservation became the rallying cry for organizing an anti-colonial offensive which, by the late 1930s, led to major protests, boycotts of Colonial orders, and a 10,000 person march on the Governor's office in Nairobi. Eventual imprisonment of the anti-conservation leadership followed.

World War II brought a temporary truce to the coercion while soil loss continued, unabated. When the war was over, the British conservation campaign began again. It reached a high point in the early 1950s, precisely on the eve of the Mau Mau Emergency. In 1951, livestock quotas were determined for each shamba (farm) in Katheka. In the case of Maundu, his allowable livestock quota was 15; his cattle holdings, 500. Colonial officers took his 'surplus' cattle to nearby Mwala where they died of disease. For farmers such as Maundu, the act was a personal tragedy and disaster. For the village as a whole, it marked an irreversible change in land use from pastoralism with bits of agriculture to primarily agricultural.

Present Agriculture

Land use today is essentially agricultural. Of the 57 households surveyed in Katheka in 1987, seventy percent owned at least one cow and 85 percent at least one goat. Severe drought and increasingly difficult economic times in the late 1980s and 1990s have further reduced Katheka's livestock to the point that those who own even one cow are the exception. So great are the cattle reductions that when Katheka's cattle dip began to leak some months ago, no one bothered to repair it.

Looking at livestock ownership before the drought of 1984-85 reveals how closely the community lives with and is limited by its environment. Drought losses or drought induced sales reduced cattle ownership from pre-drought averages of 5.36 per household to 2.7 in 1987 and goat averages from 12.66 to 6. The 1996 numbers are even smaller. Illustrated another way, before the drought, 15 households owned 20 or more goats and afterward, only two families had 20 goats or more.

Thus, in the last two decades, Katheka's farmers have turned increasingly to crop production for their own food as well as modest cash sales. In good rainfall years, 85 percent of those interviewed were self-sufficient in food. Cropping patterns show uniformity in several things grown such as maize, beans, and pigeon peas which are found on virtually every shamba. Bananas (75 percent of those interviewed) and coffee (60 percent of households) are somewhat less universal but still appeared on a majority of shambas. Papaya, mangoes, vegetables, oranges, and cotton appeared with less regularity.

Problems of Production

The rocky soil and uncertain climate make production of traditional food crops an unreliable source of cash. For example, during routine drought years many families in the sublocation buy much of their food and during the severe droughts of 1984-85 and the early 1990s, 90 percent of the households could not grow sufficient food to feed themselves.

Further testimony to the sublocation's weak economic condition comes in the number of household possessions. Of the 57 sample households in 1987, only 33 owned radios, 15 wheelbarrows, 14 bicycles, and only 8 possessed ox carts. Preliminary reviews of the questionnaires from June 1996 suggest the level of household possessions to be even lower. Given the figures on livestock ownership and the difficult agricultural environment, a picture of hard toil and struggle in daily life emerges.

In addition, there is little employment and there are few income-generating opportunities in Katheka. A consequence is significant male out-migration to nearby coffee plantations for seasonal employment and to Machakos Town and Nairobi for long-term employment.

Data from the 1987 study suggest as many as 70 percent of the households receive remittances from outside the community. Yet the data also indicate that these funds, for the most part, provide only small support to help meet daily needs. For example, only 13 of the 57 received more than Kshs 500/ (US $ 30) per year. Rarely are they sufficient for making significant investments to enhance the productivity of the land. The situation for 1996 appears to be essentially the same, if not worse, except for the newcomers who have brought capital with them..

Land holdings, though small, provide at least a foundation to support agricultural production. Of the 57 interviewed in 1987, the median-sized shamba was between 3 and 4.9 acres. According to the Assistant Chief, all land is in private hands. Present land use practice in Katheka presses on the limits of the natural resource potential. It is clear that the land cannot support the current population, even at subsistence levels, using current technologies under present ecological conditions. Yet the population continues to grow and pressure on the land is escalating. These trends are unquestionably intensifying in the 1990s.

Nature of Needs and Priorities

In the 1987 survey, residents universally noted that their greatest need was for improved access to water. They also identified priority for soil erosion control, tree planting, improved health, greatly reduced sand scooping,[5] improved facilities for education, and income generation activities. As a result of these rankings, a brief community action plan was adopted, with water as the first priority and control of soil erosion the second. Drawing on their own resources and also working jointly with outside agents, residents of Katheka installed a hand pump and accelerated their work on bench terracing, in part through a contribution of hand tools from a friend of the community. The trend lines noted in Figure 13.3, recorded by villagers at a group meeting in 1996, note the perception of the community concerning how well they have done in bringing their priorities of 1987 under control.

These trend presentations note that:

- rainfall continues to be erratic,
- income levels are extremely low,
- soil erosion control has been highly effective though fading in the last few years as low rainfall imposes exceptional economic pressures on the people,
- education is gradually improving, and
- sand scooping is greatly reduced.

These group discussions and questionnaires in 1996 have revealed other changes, including:

1 *Soil Erosion Stabilized* The major effort in bench terracing over the last ten years has brought much of the village's soil erosion under control. There is still one very large gully on the northern slope of the Kanzalu Hills and a second that seems actually to be expanding in Kavumbu and Misikwani. Even with these two gullies, the overall situation in soil loss is greatly reduced from the 1980s. This seems to have been accomplished largely by the *mwethya* (self-help) groups, working in cooperation with landowners and providing inspiration to the entire community. Whether the new pressures on the mwethya, noted below, will curtail the struggle against soil erosion remains to be seen. For the moment, however, it is clear that Katheka is succeeding in its fight against soil erosion.

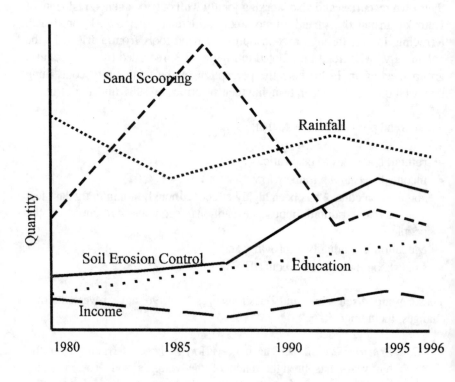

**Figure 13.3   Trend Lines for Katheka: 1996, Important Trends
(Men's Groups)**

2   *Fuelwood Supply Dwindling* Fuelwood has always been a problem in
     this sparsely wooded area. One recent change promises to make the

problem even more severe. A large farm across the Kalala River has been idle for many years and has offered a good source for collection of fuelwood for many of Katheka's families. The farm has recently been subdivided and plots sold to individuals, mostly from Nairobi, who plan to grow commercial vegetables. They will draw water from the Kalala River. This change will remove many acres of land from Katheka's fuelwood gatherers and place even greater pressure on the small stocks of cooking fuel. The more affluent families have already begun to purchase fuels such as kerosene and charcoal. While those with available cash will survive, many of Katheka's residents have very little cash income and, therefore, may encounter great difficulty in meeting fuelwood needs.

3   *Status of Mwethya Groups Weakening* While still an important element in the fabric of Katheka society, the mwethya groups are clearly reduced in activity and impact from earlier levels. The change is partly because of the poor rains over the last two years which have increased demands on women's time for collecting fuelwood and carrying water. Yet the pressures seem to be deeper than the drought. Older women say that the younger women do not seem to have the time or the loyalty to the mwethya groups in ways that their generation had. Others suggest that there are organizational and leadership problems, as even the older women have less time for community and civic projects and must spend more time tending to the needs of their families.

4   *Churches and Schools Growing in Numbers and Membership/Enrollment/.* As the village grows, so do its churches and schools. The Salvation Army which previously had a church only in Miseleni has now opened a second congregation in Katheka Centre. A very large Pentecostal Church is near completion in Katheka Centre. The existing Coptic, ABC, and AIC churches are growing and the Catholic parish has greatly expanded. Its membership was a few hundred in 1987 and is now approaching 1,000 members. This is remarkable for a community as small as Katheka. The school situation is similar. While the older ABC primary school in Katheka Centre has lost a few student enrollments, this is because a new primary school has opened in Kithayoni, to the north of Katheka Centre. The secondary school is also adding classrooms and hopes soon to open a laboratory. A new village polytechnic has also opened in Katheka Centre.

5   *Health Facilities Improving* Katheka's health facility, previously only a center for family planning, has recently been renovated and services expanded. There is now a nurse living in the village, offering regular clinic hours. During the first three days of operation, the nurse treated 13 cases of malaria, 8 cases of internal and stomach disorders (including bilharzia), and 5 cases of surface wounds. Patients pay a small fee which defrays part of the cost of treatment. The Government provides the nurse's salary and medicine. The community pays the health assistant.

6   *Livelihood Structures Changing* In the 1980s, a number of families derived much of their livelihood from external sources, especially remittances from family members working away from the village. The two largest sources of these remittances were from males working in either the army or the police. Given changes in national politics, the Akamba are less represented in these units than previously and, as a result, remittances from outside of the community are less available. In addition, some of the young men in the community who previously would have obtained employment in the army or police are now at home and unemployed.

7   *Livestock Decreasing* In 1987, livestock had reduced considerably because of the impact of the 1984 drought. By 1996, livestock numbers were even fewer. Of the 28 households interviewed in 1996, only 3 had any cattle at all.

8   *Reduced Income* In 1996, family income was indeed small. Declining remittances, reduced agricultural production, declining livestock, and persistent drought spelled problems for the poor of Katheka. While income generating activities were under discussion and while water projects for drinking and irrigation were getting started, the fact of life for 1996 was that if relief food did not come soon, there would be major problems of malnutrition, ill health, reduced production, and greatly reduced income as the drought persisted.

9   *Extension Services Declining* In 1987, while extension services were sometimes unavailable, they were certainly mentioned as an important element in Katheka's development activities. In 1996, extension was scarcely available. The restructuring of location and sublocation boundaries, combined with heavy reductions in government staffing and

budgets, has meant that extension is scarcely available in the sublocations. The Community Development Officer (CDA) appeared in only one of the institutional diagrams. In the mid-1980s, extension officers appeared as need demanded. In the mid 1990s, they are scarcely available. While the cutbacks in government staffing are carried out in the name of structural adjustment reforms designed to improve economic performance, it is important to realize that the reductions do have an adverse impact on services available to people in communities such as Katheka.

10 *Hand Pump Continuing to Work Effectively* While water for the entire community continues to be a problem, a hand pump installed in Kavumbu in 1988 continues to work effectively, even in the driest years. Routine maintenance is handled by a local water committee; funds for replacement parts are raised by the committee. The well is a source of clean water for many households including water vendors who come several kilometers in ox carts to collect water for delivery to many distant points.

11 *Grandparents Caring for Young* One alarming development, not identified in 1987, is the incidence of young children becoming permanent members of grandparent households. In one particularly disturbing family setting, a 64 year old widow headed a 14 member household. The other 13 members were under the age of 18. And of those 13, 8 were below the age of 4. The grandmother explained that all of the children were her grandchildren and that the parents were away working or looking for work. She indicated that very little money came from her children to support the grandchildren and that what she had to eat and to feed her household came from her three acre shamba.

These changes in the last ten years create an ominous prospect for Katheka's next decade. They suggest a downward spiral in the economic well-being of the community, blended with rising population, dwindling availability of natural resources, and a deepening dependence on a livelihood system that cannot be sustained. While the energy and organizing that has helped Katheka to gain control over soil erosion and to expand churches, schools, and the dispensary are to be commended, it must not be overlooked that these improvements have not altered the basic economic dilemmas of the community. While the gains have created a foundation upon which to build, it is only a first step toward building community self-sufficiency that leads to better resource utilizationse.

Conclutions follow, based on the findings of the field exercises and pointed toward the recommendations that appear above.

Conclusions

Within the context of available knowledge and resources, Katheka has done extremely well However, the community cannot now control its livelihood system and is among the first to receive drought relief food from the Government or donor agencies, once the rains fail. These conclusions therefore note that:

1   Responses to Katheka's livelihood challenges are limited by available knowledge, technology, and capital. While the knowledge level of traditional crops and produce is quite high, while the energy level for known technologies such as bench terracing is very high, the capacity to adapt to changing crop and market conditions is limited.

2   The situation in Katheka is much the same as in Mbusyani and Gilgil, though details, ethnicity, ecological conditions, and community

3   There are hundreds of semi-arid Kathekas in Kenya and probably thousands in Africa.

4   At present, for young people in Katheka, the only meaningful livelihood choices

5   In the midst of the current malaise in which Katheka finds itself, there are dozens if not hundreds of choices in land use, livelihood systems, andresources management that are available to them. Most residents, as in hundreds of similar communities, have modest land holdings, but they are mostly unproductive because the conventional wisdom of the colonial and later independence extension services promulgated high value cash crops - coffee, tea, green beans, cut flowers. These are crops that require good rainfall or sophisticated irrigation - neither of which are available to the farmers of Katheka.

6   Alternatives are known, including examples such as those offered above (from the experiments of researchers of Ben Gurion University).

7   Yet, technology alone will not solve the problems of Katheka. Also needed are strong community institutions. For example, it is clear that the accomplishments in bench terracing did not come about because individual farmers took action. Rather, they occurred because groups organized, identified goals, and in the traditional spirit of community cooperation, worked at solutions. This paper therefore concludes that a major new effort to work with small, commercial, income generating farmers in the drylands will assist poor and small farmers, such as those in Katheka, who are quickly running out of options. That many, if not most of these farmers are women adds even more urgency to the recommendations, given the additional vulnerability that women face, raising a household and, in many cases in Katheka, bearing responsibility for the family livelihood system as well.

Notes

1   Participatory Rural Appraisal or PRA is a field-based methodology which helps community groups gather and analyse their own data and build community actions plans on the results of the analysis. It was first introuced in the late 1980s and has spread to many agencies and institutions across Asia, Africa, and Latin America in the interim.

2   This list complied while on a field visit to the Negev with Professor Yossi Mizrahi of Ben-Gurion University.

3   The team included Dr. Francis Lelo, Njeri Muhia, and Stella Muthoka from Egerton University; Professors Barbara Thomas-Slayer and Richard Ford from Clark University; Nicholas Mageto from the Ministry of Research; and Charity Kabutha, formerly of the National Environment Secretariat, Ministry of Environment and Natural Resources.

4   In Kenya, a sublocation in an administrative unit, unually consisting of a village though sometimes combining two or three villages. It is headed by an Assistant Chief.

5   Sand scooping is the practice of lorries from Nairobi driving to riverbeds in the community and digging sand for transport to Nairobi. Removing sand reduces the ability of the riverbed to retain water and therefore greatly reduces water availability for use of community residents. The financial gain for the lorry drivers somes at the expense of Katheka's residents, especially women, whose task is to gather water.

Suggested Bibliography

Chambers, R. (1997), *Whose Reality Counts? Putting the First Last*, Bath.: International Technology Publications.

Edwards, M. and Hulme, D. (eds) (1996), *Beyond the Magic Bullet: NGO Performance and Accountability in the Post-Cold War World*, West Hartford, Conn.: Kumarian Press.

Ford, R. et al. (1996), *Negotiating Conservation: Reflections on Linking Conservation and Development in Madagascar*, Worcester, Mass.: Clark University, Program for International Development, and SAF (Sampan 'Asa Momba ny Fampandrosoana) (a Malagasy NGO).

Ford, R., Lelo, F. et al. (1996), *Conserving Resources and Increasing Production: Using Participatory Tools to Monitor and Evaluate Community-Based Resource Management Practices*, Njoro, Kenya and Worcester, Mass.: Egerton University and Clark University, Program for International Development.

Krishna, A., Uphoff, N. and Esman, M. (1997), *Reasons for Hope: Instructive Experiences in Rural Development*, West Hartford, Conn.: Kumarian Press.

National Environmental Secretariat, Egerton University, Clark University, and Centre for International Development and Environment of the World Resources Institute (1989), *PRA Handbook*. Worcester, Mass.: Clark University, Program for International Development.

Oduor-Naoh, E., Asamba, I., Ford, R., Lelo, F. (1992), *Implementing PRA: A Handbook for Facilitating Participatory Rural Appraisal*, Worcester, Mass.: Clark University, Program for International Development.

Program for International Development, Clark University and National Environment Secretariat, Ministry of Environment and Natural Resources, Kenya (1989), *Introduction to PRA.*, Worcester, Mass.: Clark University, Program for International Development

Razakamarinara N., Rasamison, F., Rakotoarison, B., Rakotoniaina, O., Sodikoff, G.M., Toto, E.N., Ford, R., and Wood, S. (1995), *Using Village Logbooks for Monitoring and Evaluation: A Guide to Community Based Project Management*, Worcester, Mass.: Clark University, Program for International Development.

Reveley, P.S., Rajaona, J., Rasamison, F., Ramambasoa, H., Rabarison, H., Razakamanarina, N. and Razafindrakotohasina, N. (1993), *Analyse Participative en vue de la Reduction de Pression sur une Aire Protegee, Andasibe, Madagascar*, Worcester, Mass.: Clark University, Program for International Development.

Thomas-Slayter, B., Esser, A.E., and Shields, M.D. (1993), *Tools of Gender Analysis: A Guide for Field Methods for Bringing Gender into Sustainable Resource Management*, Worcester, Mass.: Clark University, Program for International Development.

Thomas-Slayter, B., Polestica, R, Esser, A.., Taylor, O., Mutua, E. and Tototo Home Industries (1995), *A Manual for Socio-Economic and Gender Analysis: Responding to the Development Challenge,* Worcester, Mass.: Clark University, Program for International Development.

Wanjama, L., Mbuthi, N., and Thomas-Slayter, B. (1996), *Adapting to Resource Constraints in Gikarangu: New Livelihood Strategies for Women and Men in Rural Kenya,* Worcester, Mass.: Clark University, Program for International Development.

14 Credit for Small-Scale Producers: African Options

MENAKHEM BEN-YAMI

Introduction: Why African Rural Producers are Economically Handicapped?

African small-scale rural producers are socially and economically handicapped in comparison with their colleagues who live in more developed countries. Apart from inferior living conditions, education, health, and social security systems, they often lack equitable access at reasonable terms to:

1   Facilities, such as basic infrastructure (roads, bridges, boat shelters for fisherfolk) access to markets, storage, electric power, fuel distribution system, etc.;
2   Professional and public services (e.g., agrotechnical and veterinary extension, transport and communication);
3   Equipment (e.g., modern tools and vehicles, engines, and power tools);
4   Formal and equitably accessible credit at normal banking rates;
5   Resources (e.g., water, land), and supplies (especially in remote areas).

Thus, they encounter higher production costs and, in remote areas, a lower share in consumers' price compared with those located near the near cities.

The Traditional Credit System

Credit is needed for basic investments, however small as e.g., tools, for working capital, and often for survival till the harvest time. Usually, rural folk can borrow from their produce dealers, money-lenders, and equipment and goods' suppliers, that is through the informal, traditional credit system. This is an easily accessible system that usually keeps the rural producers alive and at work, but at what a price!

The cost of the traditional credit, which in most places is the only one available to African farmers and fishermen, is very high, because (1) as a rule, rural producers are obliged to sell their produce to their creditors, usually at a predetermined price almost always lower than the market price; and (2) loans given in kind are in the form of equipment, fertilizers, fuel, home supplies, etc., that are usually priced higher than the regular market prices, (Ben-Yami and Anderson, 1985).

The cost of traditional credit can be illustrated by the following actual case calculated at the 1988 exchange rates and prevailing prices in Nigeria. The example demonstrates also the benefits the rural producers, in this case fisherfolk, may derive from an access to formal credit (IFAD, 1988).

The Case of the Nigerian Credit Seeker

A fisherman obtained a loan of 2,000 Naira from a fish dealer, and gradually repaid it in kind out of his catch during six months. Let us try to calculate the actual interest rate charged by such traditional money lender.

If the fisherman could have sold that part of his catch on the free market at prices prevailing during that time, he would have earned 2,857 Naira. Thus, he paid, in fact, 857 Naira interest on the loan of 2,000 Naira. The loan, however, was repaid in monthly instalments. Therefore, during the six months that he was indebted the average sum due to the creditor was only 1,167 Naira, approximately. Accordingly, the actual annual interest rate paid by the fisherman was:

$$100 \times (857 \times 2): 1,167 =\sim 147\%/\text{year}.$$

For the same loan (2,000 Naira for 6 months, repaid in monthly instalments), at a formal interest rate of 15%, the interest the fisherman would have had to pay would have been:

$$1,167 \times 0.15: 2 = 87.5 \text{ Naira},$$

To this sum he would have had to pay commission, say, some 12.5 Naira service costs, bringing the total to 100 Naira. The extra cost of the traditional credit for a 2,000 Naira loan for six months in 6 instalments, as compared with formal credit was, therefore:

857 - 100 = ~757 Naira.

Thus, in this particular case, the traditional credit was about 8.5 times more costly than a formal credit would have been. It is, however, not easy to replace the well-established traditional system with a formal banking one. The former has many advantages:

1   Relations between the debtors and the creditors are informal and direct.
2   Borrowers deal with familiar people rather than with institutions.
3   No bureaucracy, no paperwork and, virtually no collaterals are involved.
4   Repayment is flexible if things go wrong.
5   Traditional lenders often assume a patron role so that the rural producers have somebody to turn to for help if extra money is urgently needed.
6   Often the money lender is a member of the close relative or a member of the extended family.
7   Social norms, often with deep roots in local culture and often accompanied by certain contract ceremonies, ensure loan recovery, making the traditional system more reliable than any formal one.

While money lenders of the traditional credit system may come from various sectors of the society, and from ethnic groups which differ from that of the producers, it is important to emphasize that there is a basic difference between outside dealers and local traders in agro-produce on the one hand and fish-mammies on the other. The latter are all members of the producers' communities and may be their own wives, mothers, sisters, or other relatives. While the latter are usually poor, hard-working people, and are in many cases women, (Librero, 1987), the former are full-scale merchants and money-lenders of either gender, with plenty of cash at their disposal, who frequently command their own means of transport and other facilities along the marketing channel.

In addition, small-scale dealers or money lenders in fish and agro-produce are usually organized in 'market unions'. These associations give them some protection as well as privileges. The benefits include assistance in tracking down borrowers in default of their payment (Udom, 1991).

Formal Credit

The first stumbling block in the way of formal credit to rural societies in

Africa is the attitude of bank executives and employees. Banks - a medieval European invention - have developed under conditions of a Western capitalist market system to serve the 'haves' rather than the 'have-not'. Most African banking students and trainees indoctrinated within western banking rules, procedures, traditions and conservative way of thinking, have been very successful in running their banks, but were unable to serve the poorer sections of the populations in general, and rural communities, in particular. Therefore, any rural credit scheme based on formal banking credit requires a serious change of mind on the part of the bank personnel involved, including rewriting procedures and attending special courses and training seminars for the banks' executive and field staff (IFAD, 1988, 1990).

To make credit schemes work, all procedures must be simple and relatively fast. All contacts with the bank must be carried out within the villages, and by well-motivated itinerant staff who are regularly and easily accessible to the potential and actual borrowers. Rural credit schemes should be intended to carry the credit line mainly to the poorer sectors of the community, that is to people who have no personal collateral, securities, or wealthy guarantors. Additionally, since farmers and fisherfolk, women and men alike, may, from time to time, need very small short-term loans, special village credit schemes, operated by the community's own tribal or democratic institutions can be formed. They should be financially and operationally assisted by the credit-providing bank or a special project.

But, no credit scheme based on regular banking would be sustainable without a considerable improvement in the approach of the small producer to loans repayment. This is for two reasons: (i) general lack of social norms and cultural-traditional deterrents with respect to repayment of loans to 'anonymous' lenders such as banks and government sponsored schemes; (ii) the tendency of many loan-distributive projects to express little motivation for repayment. Their beneficiaries have become accustomed to consider any formal loan to be a grant from the government or from another donor (Oboh, 1981; Udom, 1991). This has become a common approach rendering all such loans irrecoverable.

Hence, the importance of channeling the credit through existing traditional community institutions, tribal and family groups, or thrift societies that may offer collective responsibility and conform to the social norm of loan repayment. Where such groups do not exist, new institutions such as mutual guaranty societies, may be introduced, but this involves a lengthy participatory process (Ben-Yami, 1964).

The Option of Traditional Saving Associations

In many West African communities there are traditional associations in the form of savings and credit groups or clubs, known, in many places, as *osusu* or *esusu*, though they come also under other local names. While their character varies from tribe to tribe and from place to place, they may play an important role in channeling formal credit to rural folks. The osusus are rather small groups of a few tens of members (the number of 20-30 is mentioned most often) who usually come from a similar background. They may be members of one age group, that is, people who grew up together and know each other from childhood; they may be of the same occupation, for example, marine fishermen, or inland water fishermen, or women farmers. They may be migrants coming from the same 'homevillage' etc. Normally the membership will be of one tribe, i.e., of people who speak the same language and have a similar socio-economic status (Ekpoudom, 1987). In a large village, there may be tens of osusu groups.

The primary objective of osusus is to give some stability to the financial position of their members and to help them during periods of need. An osusu society is usually managed by a small committee comprising a President and a Secretary who keep the record, if any. Membership is not necessarily equitable. As a rule, each member must periodically deposit a payment in the group's fund, according to the number of shares he (or she - where women clubs exist) holds in the group. Obviously, the number of shares one can afford and is willing to hold determine his/her hierarchical position and social status in the group. Thus, the biggest share holder would normally be also the osusu's president. In Nigeria (1988), such sum may vary from a few tens of Naira in a poor village to hundreds of Naira among, for example, the relatively well to-do marine fishermen, fishing 'bonga' sardines in large and fast canoes.

According to one system, every member is entitled, in turn, to a loan from the fund. Usually, though not necessarily, it is used for buying equipment. Interest is charged. Even if the member declines to accept the loan, he/she is obliged to pay all the interest. However, when his next turn comes, he can obtain a double sum, etc. Towards the Christmas festive season, when work ceases for a period of a month or so, and many of migrant farmers or fishers go 'home' to the place of their origin, a part or all of the cash may be disbursed among the members. Some osusus issue money to their members in cases such as family events that require sudden expense, such as births, weddings, funerals, etc. (Udom, 1991).

Although in strictly financial terms, the osusu is not very productive (some of them do not even demand interest), it seems that the osusu societies function relatively well, and that a social norm embedded in the local culture creates sufficient pressure to ensure their effective performance. Also, their contribution to the procurement of equipment (in particular engines by fishermen) is substantial, though in no way adequate. Here is an example: An osusu group having, e.g., 25 members and 30 shares, with a bi-weekly payment of 100 Naira a share, may collect during a year's time: 30 shares x 100 Naira x 26 fortnights = 78,000 Naira, or 2,600 Naira per share.

In 1988, the year this survey was executed, this would have given every single-share holder the theoretical opportunity to buy an outboard motor every three years. However, this could be done if he/she was not making any withdrawals in between. Obviously the position of the multi-share holder is much better in this respect. In less well off groups, with a bi-weekly payment of, say, 50 Naira only, if the same formula is applied, a single share would produce half the above amount during the same period. A single-share holder may have, thus, a theoretical opportunity to buy an outboard engine every six years. This means, in practical terms, that he will never be able to do so. Although, in their present state, most of osusus are unable to provide adequate and equitable credit facilities to their members, if drawn into formal rural credit schemes that provide outside (bank or project) financing, they can play an essential role as the identification and disbursement mechanism of the loans as mutual guarantee groups.

With the osusu institution taking care of many aspects that otherwise would fall within the domain of the traditional credit systems, the chances of an innovative credit scheme to compete successfully with the traditional system are greatly improved. Another condition for success is an extension service providing technical advice on equipment (choice, operation, and maintenance) and information on appropriate prices, as well as monitoring the way loans are spent, and assuring that they are being spent as intended. A well-proven procedure is that after the borrower chooses the materials or equipment he/she is given the loan for, the money is paid directly by the lender to the supplier indicated by the borrower.

Rural Credit and Inflation

Inflation, especially if spiraling, requires that the credit scheme, to protect the real value of its basic credit capital maintains a linkage between the loan capital and/or interest rates and the inflated currency real value (using, say, price indices, and/or foreign exchange rates).

Spiraling inflation bears inherent disadvantages for any formal rural credit scheme. This must be kept in mind while designing such schemes:

1   A rise in interest rates may lag behind the reduction in the currency value. This has caused, in countries that had experienced spiraling inflation, numerous forms of malpractices, e.g., using loans for 'investment' in black market credit rather than for the intended legitimate purpose.

2   When the inflation eventually slacks off, the borrower may continue being charged the now unjustified high interests, which may lead to impoverishment and bankruptcy of the small borrowers.

Summary

While traditional credit has long been a mainstay of rural production, its economic costs depress rural producers. Formal credit schemes, much cheaper for the producers, may succeed if they are operated at the village level, if procedures are brought to minimum, if flexibility is introduced, and if they rely on existing traditional intra-community institutions and intra-group social norms.

References and Further Readings

Abasiatai, M.B. (ed.) (1987), *Akwa Ibom and Cross River States, The Land, the People, and Their Culture,* Calabar: Wusen Press Ltd.

Ben-Yami, M. (1964), *Report on the Fisheries in Ethiopia,* Jerusalem: Ministry of Foreign Affairs, Dept. for International Cooperation.

Ben-Yami, M. and Anderson, A. M. (1985), *Community Fishery Centres, Guidelines for Establishment and Operation.* Rome: Food and Agriculture Organization of the U.N.

FAO (1988), *Women in Fishing Communities.* Rome: FAO.

Hamlisch R. (1979) Credit for Aquaculture, in *Advances in Aquaculture.* Fishing News Books (for FAO), pp. 77-84.

IFAD (1988), *Nigeria: Artisanal Fisheries Development Project,* Appraisal Report, Main Text and Working Papers. Rome: International Fund for Agricultural Development.

IFAD (Prepared by M. Ben-Yami) (1990), Artisanal Fisheries Development Project in the Cross River, Rivers and Akwa Ibom States: Guide for the Implementation of the Project Rome: International Fund for Agricultural

Development.

Librero A.R. (1987), 'Womens' roles in institutions and credit', in C.E. Nash, C.R. Engle and D. Crossetti (eds), *Women in Aquaculture*. Rome: FAO, ADCP/REP/87/27, pp. 83-90.

Merrikin P.A. (1989), Credit in Fisheries: A Select Annotated Bibliography, *FAO Fishery Circu*, No. 816.

Oboh, D.O. (1981), 'Problems of loan repayment under the agricultural credit scheme', in M.O. Ojo, C.C. Edordu and J.A. Akingbade (eds), *Agricultural Credit and Finance in Nigeria: Problems and Prospects, Seminar Proceedings*. Abuja: Central Bank of Nigeria, pp.180-184.

Tietze, U. (1987), *Bank Credit for Artisanal Fisherfolk in Orisa, India*, Madras: BOBP/REP32, FAO/SIDA Programme for the Development of Small-Scale Fisheries in the Bay of Bengal.

Udom, D.S. (1991), Informal Savings and Credit Groups in the IFAD-assisted Artisanal Fishery Project Area. Lecture Paper, Training Course for FDU Extensionists. October 1991, Awka, Ibom State, Nigeria.

PART IV
THEORETICAL ISSUES, APPROACHES TO DEVELOPMENT AND POLICY CONSIDERATIONS

15 Drought Mitigation Policies: Waste Water Use, Energy and Food Provision in Urban and Peri-Urban Africa

HENDRICK J. BRUINS

Drought and Urban Farming

Severe droughts are recurring phenomena in many parts of Africa (Garcia and Escudero, 1982; Glantz, 1987; Downing, Gitu and Kamau, 1989). Their impact on different segments of society varies with respective vulnerability and the success or failure of coping mechanisms at both the household and national level. The mechanisms include social and economic networks, food reserves, water reserves, financial reserves, food imports, food distribution, food availability, marketing and prices.

A straightforward relationship between drought and famine is generally too simplistic. Close examination reveals that the causes for famines and food crises (Akong'a and Downing, 1988; Bohle et al., 1991, 1993; Cannon, 1991; Downing, 1993) cannot merely be explained in environmental terms only. Drought, however, may still be the major actor on the crowded stage to cause or trigger famine. Without diminishing all the other complex socio-economic and political factors, it may be said that famine in the Sahel during the late sixties and seventies would have been considerably less severe without the occurrence of drought. Indeed, the phenomenon of drought itself may be regarded as the most complex and one of the least understood of natural hazards (Wilhite, 1993).The response by governments to the impact of drought is usually organized in an ad-hoc manner. However, proactive planning for drought (Wilhite and Easterling, 1987; Wilhite, 1993; Bruins, 1993, 1996; Bruins and Lithwick, 1998) on a

257

national, local and household level, is far better than ad hoc crisis management.

In a monograph about urban farming in Africa, particularly related to Kampala (Uganda), the relative role of drought in contributing to the deteriorating economy was emphasized by Maxwell and Zziwa (1992) in the following manner:

> The 1980s have been referred to repeatedly as a decade of crisis for African development. None of the factors underlying this 'crisis' are new: declining terms of trade, declining per capita production of food crops, increasing foreign indebtedness, environmental degradation and continued high rates of migration by the young from rural to urban areas. But combined with two catastrophic droughts through much of sub-Saharan Africa and the conflicts and political turmoil of the decade, the 1980s have witnessed the collapse of much of the formal, modern sector of Africa's economy, with a resulting decline in the standard of living for both urban and rural people. The droughts in particular provided the media with the necessary imagery to depict Africa as a continent in crisis.

At the macro-level Maxwell and Zziwa (1992) mention the fundamental problem of annual urban growth rates of up to 8 percent, almost twice as fast as the population increase in general, and the inability of urban economies to absorb the increase. They suspect urban living standards to have suffered greater losses than rural economies in relative terms. Poor people in the cities are constantly faced with the problem of how to survive at the household or micro-level amidst economic decline and the lack of job opportunities:

> Rather than return to the countryside, much of this urban population has resorted to any means at their disposal to survive in the city... The various survival mechanisms of the urban poor have come to be called the 'informal sector', so named by the International Labour Organization's investigation of employment conditions in African economies in the 1970s' (Maxwell and Zziwa, 1992).

Urban agricultural production is often included in the informal sector, because cultivation and livestock rearing within urban sectors were generally forbidden during the colonial period. This hostile attitude by the authorities toward urban farming has usually continued after independence.

Nevertheless, urban agriculture has been an integral part of African cities from the beginning of their development, as pointed out by Rakodi (1988). This fits also well with the perception of urban migrants, who view the city as their farm (Aronson, 1978), as it becomes part of their extended geographic sphere, while the rural home often remains 'home', despite their living in the city.

Three fundamental observations concerning urban agriculture are noted by Maxwell and Zziwa (1992):

• Urban agriculture is an important component of household survival strategies for the urban poor.
• Urban agriculture has provided livelihoods and food to an increasing number of urban and peri-urban residents.
• Urban and peri-urban agriculture has a potential to provide productive jobs for the urban unemployed, while contributing significantly to the food provision of Africa's cities.

Drought, Urban Wastewater and Solar Energy

The combined effect of increasing population size and shrinking land availability demands increased food production per capita. This can only be achieved through a more intensive management of resources in all aspects of food production. Urban and peri-urban agriculture, to be encouraged and guided by the authorities, should be included in such an approach (Mbiba, in this volume). Agriculture requires water, which may come from direct rainfall (rainfed farming), or irrigated farming from a variety of sources such as rivers and streams, piped water and treated wastewater, wells, or rainwater harvesting (Bruins et al., 1986). The occurrence of severe droughts will undoubtedly cause a decline in the level of food production under rainfed agriculture. To maintain food availability and consumption at a secure level the resultant decline in locally produced food has to be obtained from existing reserves or from imports.

One of the characteristic aspects of urban development is the widespread availability of piped water, sewage systems and the resultant production of urban wastewater. Because water is, in the short run, even more critical than food for human survival, governments have usually planned to maintain the piped water supplies to cities from secure water resources that can be used even during times of drought. Therefore, the output of urban wastewater also continues during meteorological droughts. The rather stable production of this wastewater should be perceived by planners as a real asset not to be wasted!

Four reasons can be given for the importance of urban wastewater treatment and purification in Africa:

- Urban wastewater needs to be contained and purified for reasons of public health.
- Raw urban sewage should not be permitted to flow freely on the surface, polluting streams, surface water and groundwater resources.
- Treated wastewater can be used successfully and safely in urban and peri-urban farming, at or near its urban source, to produce food without the need for chemical fertilizers.
- Drought mitigation by proactive action: Urban wastewater will be available even during periods of drought, enabling urban and peri-urban food production to continue.

Since urban sewage treatment requires government planning and supervision, and in view of possible health hazards, it seems reasonable to suggest agricultural extension, legislation, and supervision concerning the agricultural use of the treated wastewater by individual farmers. However, a detailed world bank report about wastewater irrigation in developing countries (Shuval et al., 1986), came to the conclusion that public health positions have often been overly conservative. The report recommends the use of low-cost stabilization ponds, considered to be a robust method of wastewater treatment well suited to the needs of developing countries. 'In fact, as we have already pointed out, 20-day stabilization ponds can remove almost all bacteria and viruses and can produce an effluent suitable for unrestricted irrigation of vegetables' (Shuval et al., 1986).

Solar energy is a potential source of energy (Campbell-Howe and Wilkins-Crowder, 1966) that can be used independently by an individual urban farmer to power water pumps for irrigation. The cost of photovoltaic power is steadily decreasing (Oppenheim, 1996), although its use by the urban poor would probably require initial investment capital from external sources and additional extension services.

Centralized development of urban wastewater treatment facilities by the authorities is certainly most desirable. However, solar energy could enable small-scale water disinfection from small streams, which might be polluted and small-scale toilet and wastewater treatment facilities (Cobb 1996) for use by small communities in self-help projects. For example, in one solar water disinfection system, water from a stream, pond or community water supply flows into a tank with a capacity of 200 liters. Cold water at the bottom flows into a low-pressure solar hot water heater, in which the water is heated to 70 degrees C and is thus pasteurized. Grey water and brown wastewater (from kitchen and toilet) can be pasteurized with a similar system of solar heating in a composting toilet, such as the so-called SOLatrine, as described by Cobb (1996).

Solar disinfection of drinking water (Anderson and Collier 1996) can also make an important contribution to family and community health in areas where safe potable water is not available. Such solar systems can be set up on a small scale through private initiative by individual families or small communities. Infected drinking water causes death to an estimated 15 to 20 million children per year through diarrheal diseases. Anderson and Collier (1996) emphasize that heat is one of the most effective methods to disinfect drinking water. There is no need to boil water for 10 minutes, tests have shown that all waterborne enteric pathogens are instantly inactivated at temperatures above 90 degrees C. The system designed and tested by Anderson and Collier (1996) uses a parabolic trough solar concentrator to heat water in a receiver. A standard automotive thermostat at the end of the receiver ensures that water will not exit the system until it has reached the required temperature. A system of ca. 55 m of aperture, costing about US$3,300, would produce some 6,000 liters of disinfected water daily.

A much cheaper system to pasteurize drinking water and prepare food for a single person or family is the solar cooker. A new design by Solar Cookers International, the solar panel cooker costs only US$10 and is also produced in Nairobi, Kenya. As of January 1997, more than 3,000 families had learned to use these solar cookers in the large refugee camp at Kakuma in northwestern Kenya.

Participatory Development

The informal private sector of urban and peri-urban farming should not be taken over by the government, although the treatment of urban wastewater and its subsequent use in urban agriculture does require government planning, investment and extension services. Participatory development of urban and peri-urban farming may enable proper integration between central planning of wastewater treatment and its use by private farmers. Special legislation for the use of land for farming purposes, in or near the cities, should be made as flexible as possible. Municipalities in The Netherlands, for example, provide certain municipal zones, divided in small plots, for farm use by interested individuals. Temporary permits are given and a small yearly fee has to be paid. The users, however, do not acquire title to the land. Yearly extension of such permits in urban and semi-urban Africa could be made conditional on observing proper use of wastewater and on observing public health regulations.

Possible development relationships of constituent elements in urban and peri-urban food production are displayed in the accompanying flow-chart (Figure 15.1).

Food Reserves, Food Security and Food Provision

Drought usually causes a straightforward environmentally deterministic decline in food production based on rainfed farming. However, drought does not need to cause famine conditions. The latter depends on complex socio-economic and political factors that cannot be explained by a simplistic deterministic approach. Food production, based on irrigated farming that depends on a relatively secure water supply, such as treated urban wastewater, can continue during droughts. Nevertheless, the decline in food production from the rainfed sector needs to be compensated from other sources. National food reserves would enable additional supply on the macro (national) level. Such food stocks give national food security even if food availability on the world market is critically low. However, sufficient food reserves on the national level do not guarantee food security on the micro, or household, level, and cannot compensate for the decline in food production as a result of drought. For example, the urban poor may be unable to pay for the supplies from national food stocks if the food prices are too high in relation to their purchasing power. Thus vulnerability to famine differs in a given society according to economic status. Bloody food riots have occurred in Africa, Asia and Latin America as a result of increased food prices. This has repeatedly resulted from the International Monetary Fund demand to remove subsidies in the name of economic realism (Garcia and Spitz, 1986).

Moreover, national food reserves are of little value if the food is not equitably distributed throughout the country and made available to the population at affordable prices. This underscores the relevance of food reserves at the micro or household level. However, a price strategy may be virtually impossible for the poorest of the urban poor. Local, national and international welfare policy may be the only remedy for offsetting famine conditions among the poor groups, in such cases, and when famine, triggered by a drought, gradually worsens the food supply condition and endangers food availability.

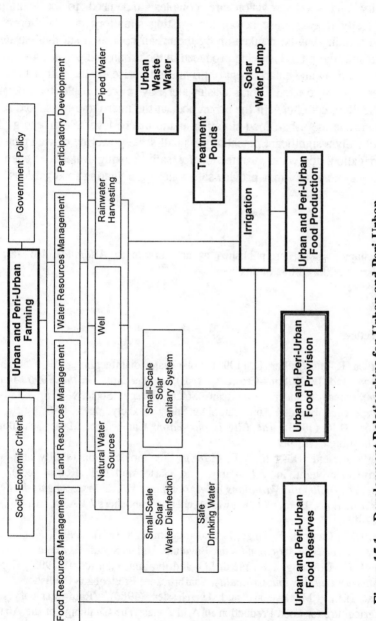

Figure 15.1   Development Relationships for Urban and Peri-Urban Farming and Food Provision

Conclusions

The relationships between drought, food production, food reserves, food security and food provision are complex and need to be examined specifically in each case before the existing situations can be improved. Urban farming has been taken up by the urban poor as a survival strategy. As a result, more food is being produced in the urban and peri-urban sphere. Encouragement and enlargement of private enterprise, by the authorities, and proper use of treated urban wastewater, by more people by adequate organization, could benefit the urban poor at the micro and household level, and improve the urban food situation at the macro level. Solar energy has undoubtedly a significant potential for small-scale powering of water pumps for irrigation, for water disinfection for safe drinking water and even for sanitary systems that may provide safe water for irrigating food gardens.

Note

This chapter was pre-published as an article in *Aridlands*, No. 42, by Permission of the editors of this book.

References

Anderson, R. and Collier, K. (1996) 'Solar water disinfection', in R. Campbell-Howe and B. Wilkins-Crowder (eds), *Proceedings of the 1996 Annual conference*, Boulder: American Solar Energy Society, pp. 184-88. *Conference*, Boulder: American Solar Energy Society, pp. 184-88.

Aronson, D.R. (1978), *The City is our Farm*. Cambridge, Mass: Schenkman Publishing Company.

Akong'a, J.J. and Downing, T.E. (1988), Smallholder vulnerability and response to drought. in M.L. Parry, T.R. Carter and N.T. Konijn (eds), *The Impact of Climatic Variations on Agriculture. Vol. 2: Assessments in Semi-Arid Regions*, Dordrecht: Kluwer Academic Publishers / IIASA / UNEP, pp. 221-47.

Bohle, H.G., Cannon, T., Hugo, G. and Ibrahim, F.N. (eds), (1991), *Famine and Food Security in Africa and Asia*. Bayreuth: University of Bayreuth.

Bohle, H.G., Downing, T.E., Field, J.O. and Ibrahim, F.N. (eds), (1993), *Coping with Vulnerability and Criticality*, Saarbrücken: Breitenbach Publishers.

Bruins, H.J., M. Evenari and U. Nessler (1986), 'Rainwater-harvesting Agriculture for Food Production in Arid Zones: The Challenge of the African famine', *Applied Geography*, vol. 6, 13-32.

Bruins, H.J., (1993) 'Drought risk and water management in Israel: Planning for the future', in D.A. Wilhite (ed), *Drought Assessment, Management and Planning: Theory and Case Studies,* Dordrecht: Kluwer Academic Publishers, pp. 133-55.

Bruins, H.J. (1996), 'A rationale for drought contingency planning in Israel', in Y. Gradus and G. Lipshitz (eds), *The Mosaic of Israeli Geography,* Beersheva: Ben-Gurion University of the Negev Press, pp. 345-53.

Bruins, H.J. and Lithwick, H. (1998), 'Proactive planning and interactive management in arid frontier development', in H.J. Bruins, and H. Lithwick (eds), *The Arid Frontier - Interactive Management of Environment and Development,* Dordrecht: Kluwer Academic Publishers..

Campbell-Howe, R and Wilkins-Crowder, B. (eds), (1996), *Proceedings of the 1996 Annual Conference,* Boulder: American Solar Energy Society.

Cannon, T. (1991), 'Hunger and Famine: Using a Food System's Model to Analyse Vulnerability', in H.G. Bohle, T. Cannon, G. Hugo and F.N. Ibrahim (eds), *Famine and Food Security in Africa and Asia,* Bayreuth: University of Bayreuth, pp. 291-12.

Cobb, J.C. (1996) 'Solar sanitary system (SOL-SAN)', in R. Campbell-Howe and B. Wilkins-Crowder (eds) *Proceedings of the 1996 Annual Conference,* Boulder: American Solar Energy Society, pp. 167-172.

Downing, T.E. (1993), 'Concepts of Vulnerability to Hunger and Applications for Monitoring Famine in Africa', in H.G. Bohle, T. Cannon, G. Hugo and F.N. Ibrahim (eds), *Coping with Vulnerability and Criticality.* Saarbrücken: Breitenbach Publishers, pp. 205-25.

Downing, T.E., Gitu, W and Kamau, C. (1989), *Coping with Drought in Kenya: National and Local Strategies.* Boulder: Lynne Rienner.

Garcia, R.V. and Escudero, J.C. (1982) *Drought and Man. Vol. 2: The Constant Catastrophe: Malnutrition, Famines, and Drought,* Oxford: Pergamon Press.

Garcia, R.V. and Spitz, P. (1986), *Drought and Man. Vol. 3: The Roots of Catastrophe,* Oxford: Pergamon Press.

Glantz, M H. (ed.) (1987), *Drought and Hunger in Africa,* Cambridge: Cambridge University Press.

Maxwell, D. and Zziwa, S. (1992), *Urban Farming in Africa: The Case of Kampala, Uganda,* Nairobi: ACTS (African Centre for Technology Studies) Press.

Mbiba, B. (1997), 'Urban agriculture in Southern and Eastern Africa: Policy questions and challenges'. In this volume.

Oppenheim, J. (1996), 'Photovoltaic economics: Cost-effective for some choosing least-cost power in the marketplace', in R. Campbell-Howe and B. Wilkins-Crowder (eds), *Proceedings of the 1996 Annual Conference.* Boulder, American Solar Energy Society, pp. 321-26.

Rakodi, C. (1988), 'Urban agriculture: Research questions and Zambian evidence', *Journal of Modern African Studies,* vol. 26, pp. 495-515.

Shuval, H.I., Adin, A., Fattal, B., Rawitz, E. and Yekutiel, P. (1986), *Wastewater Irrigation in Developing Countries: Health Effects and Technical Solutions,* Washington, D.C.: The World Bank, World Bank Technical Paper 51.

Wilhite, D.A. (ed), (1993), *Drought Assessment, Management and Planning: Theory and Case Studies,* Dordrecht: Kluwer Academic Publishers.

Wilhite. D.A. and Easterling, W.E. (1987), *Planning for Drought: Toward a Reduction of Societal Vulnerability,* Boulder: Westview Press.

16 Conceptual Evaluation of Urban and Peri-Urban Production and Marketing of Fruits and Vegetables in Developing Countries

DIETER MARTIN HÖRMANN

Introduction

When examining agricultural sub-sectors, the term 'Structure-Conduct-Performance approach' (SCP) is often used. The term originates in industrial organisation theory, and has been developed much further in the course of time.

This contribution shows the basics of this development of the SCP approach, whereby particular attention is paid to one concept orientated to behavioural sciences. It presents an SCP approach, developed as a model to examine urban and peri-urban horticultural production. It compares the key advantages and disadvantages of the theoretical concept, and discusses empirical observations as examples for specific criteria of this approach.

In order to evaluate the urban and peri-urban horticultural production according to its contribution to development, the author of this study also uses a comprehensive catalogue of criteria (Hörmann, 1994, p. 69 ff.) in addition to the SCP approach. This catalogue includes a set of important development criteria concerning the physical flow of goods, the quality of provision for the population, monetary aspects, both employment and structural effects and also the environmental compatability of the production, which, apart from a few examples, cannot be dealt with here.

The empirical experience of the author of this paper originates predominantly from East and South African countries, in particular from Ethiopia (Hörmann, and Shawel, 1985), Tanzania (Hörmann, 1993; Yachkaschi, 1996), Kenya and Zimbabwe.

The Theoretical Concept

The Sub-Sector Analysis and the Theoretical Framework of Orientation: the Vertical Production and Marketing System

The *sub-sector analysis* is one of the system analysis approaches to the examination of economic activities. This analysis particularly stresses the interdependent relationships between economic units involved in the production and distribution processes, which are important for the comprehension of the dynamics of changes and developments and the interdependent grouping of further organisations, resources, and institutions, which are involved in the production and distribution (Marion, 1986, p. 52).

In his essay entitled 'On the Concept of Sub-sector Studies', Shaffer says: 'The uniqueness of sub-sector studies is not in the methodology or approach but in the scope and comprehensiveness of the research' (Shaffer, 1973, p. 333). This illustrates the difference between the sub-sector approach and older methods, such as the Commodity Approach (Goldberg, 1974). With reference to Shaffer's essay, Holtzman (1982, p. 23) makes a precise comment:

> Rather than focusing horizontally on producers or traders, which are the conventional units of analysis in traditional production or marketing research, the sub-sector approach forces the analyst to examine the vertical set of activities (input supply, production, marketing, trading, retailing, consumption) that facilitate productive transformation and exchange at each stage of the value-adding process.

In other words, in its horizontal and vertical orientation to comprehensive studies, the sub-sector approach represents a group of economic activities which are relevant to research.

The urban and peri-urban production of horticultural products is regarded in the following study as an agricultural sub-sector. It serves as a basis for the use of the SCP paradigm, whereby the concept of vertical production and marketing systems offers a suitable description of the system for evaluating the performance. This represents an extension of the concept of 'vertical systems', as found in marketing literature, to include production. This appears to be supported, amongst others, by the following list of conditions:

- the influence of social and political factors and those of production technology at producer level on the marketing activities;
- the co-ordinating function of the marketing system for the producers' activities;
- the significance of efficient co-ordination of production and sales with behaviour, rapidly changing marketrelations, etc.;
- the contractual agreements and transfer of property rights between producers and traders;
- the influence of conflicts and co-operation between producers and traders on the system performance;
- the possibility of vertical integration of production and trade (e.g., wholesaler with his own production);
- the possible take-over of production functions by trade (harvesting, sorting, mixing,cleaning, packing, etc.).

The Structure-Conduct-Performance Approach - The SCP Approach

The essential impulses for the SCP approach came from Bain's contribution to industrial organisation. Bain (1968, p.6) defines the term 'industry' in this context as a horizontally grouped collection of firms, which offer products with a high substitutionability on a common market.

The term 'Market Structure' refers, according to Bain (1968, p.7 ff.), to those characteristics of market organisation which have a strategic effect on competition and price formation in the market concerned. He names the following as outstanding aspects of the market structure: the degree of concentration of suppliers and consumers, the degree of product differentiation and the conditions for market entry.

In Bain's opinion the term 'Market Conduct' concerns the behaviour patterns which companies follow when they prepare themselves for the structural conditions of their market. On the seller's side this means, amongst other things, the individual or collective price policy, product policy and product design, and the promotion of sales. It also includes the interactive mechanisms, the adaptation and the co-ordination of the policies of competing suppliers. Similar dimensions of market behaviour can be seen on the demand side.

The term 'Market Performance' is described by Bain as being the results gained in the market by the companies concerned in the form of prices, achievements, production and sales costs, product design etc.

The Bain SCP paradigm has a considerable number of weaknesses. Williamson (1975, p. 7 ff) for example criticises it as follows: 'A goal of profit maximisation is ordinarily imputed to the firm, internal organisation is largely neglected, and the outer environment is described in terms of market structure measures such as concentration, barriers to entry, excess demand, and so forth. The distribution of transactions between firm and market is mainly taken as a datum.' He does, however, see the chance to explain the behaviour and performance better, by combining the criteria of the internal organisational structure with the criteria of the market structure.

Further weaknesses can be found, for example, in various reports in which Bain's SCP concept was used to examine and explain the competitiveness of markets and the level of market integration in the agricultural sector. This mainly concerns comparative studies of product prices at various levels (Fleming, 1986, p.8). The main criticism of these studies, which were carried out in too close relationship to the Bain concept, is that they are orientated to too small a number of economic parameters, and that the chosen parameters are perhaps not the most important ones (Harris, 1979, p.213 ff. and Shaffer, 1980, p. 310 f.).

Whilst Bain dispenses with the examination of vertical relationships of firms for pragmatic reasons, the sub-sector approach discussed above includes for identical products or for a group of related products both the horizontal and the vertical relationships of the production and marketing system at the different levels of this system, paying particular attention to the problems of co-ordination.

The SCP framework was extended considerably for the project study NC 117, 'Organisation and Performance of the US Food System', which the US Department of Agriculture commissioned in the 1980's (Marion, 1986).

In this project comprehensive comparative studies were carried out for different agricultural sub-sectors in the United States. The basic model of the SCP approach thereby used works on the assumption that the external framework conditions and the structure of the sub-sector have a major influence on the behaviour of the participants of the system and thus have a decisive effect on the performance of the sub-sector.

This extended SCP framework takes into account, amongst other things, transaction costs and property rights, and with the latter also the influence of government programmes and regulations on the market structure, the behaviour and the performance; likewise the effects, in connection with these programmes and regulations, on income distribution, employment, inflation, standard of living and the distribution of political and economic power. Some of the criteria of this approach to the evaluation of agricultural sub-sectors were included in the extended SCP approach shown in Fig. 1 for the evaluation of vertical production and marketing systems for urban and peri-urban horticultural products in developing countries.

For Shaffer (1980, p. 310 ff.) this extension of the SCP approach is not sufficient. He rightly criticises, amongst other things, the fact that the firms involved are treated as a black box and are not asked about their behaviour pattern concerning decisions or the behaviour of organisations (including governments, households and business associations), all of which contribute to system performance. He is concerned most of all with decision-taking under risk (e.g. investments and product orientation).

With a view to the connection between the behaviour of the participants and the performance of the system, Shaffer et al. (1985, p. 306 ff.) state:

Co-ordination of economic activity takes place through transactions among participants in a system which is defined as simply as a set of inter-relationships. Transactions take place across markets and within organisations such as firms, households, communities, and government agencies. At any particular time, participants in a system face a set of constraints and opportunities, which we will call their opportunity sets. An opportunity set consists of resources (incl. knowledge) and the formal and informal mechanisms guiding relationships among participants - a bundle of rights, laws, customs, markets etc. Participants respond to their perceived opportunity sets, producing, consuming, and engaging in transactions. The aggregate consequences of the behaviour of the participants in a system we call system performance.

According to Shaffer (1980, p. 311 ff.), the system's environment can be regarded conceptionally as overlapping opportunity sets, resulting from the corresponding existing restrictions and possibilities. The political and economical system structures the relations between the participants in the system and thus also the restrictions and possibilities for individuals or groups by making rules, which should determine, for example, the access to resources, the limitation of externalising costs and the reimbursement from the aggregated opportunity set. Shaffer describes the opportunity sets of individual participants in the system as a function of the location in the political economy, in which the individual participates as a member of organisations (e.g. government, firms, households and other associations). His opportunity set is determined by the external environment and the internal structure of the organisations and their positions. According to Shaffer, the external environment of organisations includes the factor and product markets and any other variables which belong to the structure of the SCP concept, all rights and regulations, the acknowledged social and political pressure, expected market developments and the technical function of transformation.

As far as behaviour is concerned, Shaffer remarks, amongst other things, that this is closely linked to the preferences of the system's participants. These preferences are expressed in the objectives of the corresponding individuals, which they try to realise by means of market transactions, political transactions and social transactions, whereby the latter promote information, influence, advantages and costs.

On the subject of performance Shaffer says, amongst other things: 'In the dynamic framework, performance is a complex concept. Performance is the outcome of the behaviour of the sum of participants acting within the constraints of their perceived individual opportunity sets.' These perceptions concern the actual condition and the alterations of the individual opportunity sets of the system's participants with regard to their physical environment and the political and economic structure. They are relevant to the distribution of costs and benefits among the participants in the system. The distribution results anticipated by the participants act as an incentive or a disincentive for their future behaviour. In other words, the expectations lead to an alteration of the perception and preferences of the system's participants and thus to an alteration in their reactions. The individual reacts to his environment according to his knowledge of the consequence and with a readiness to take risks in an ever-continuing process.

As the behaviour of individuals and organisations represents the link between the political and economic organisations and the performance of the system, Shaffer (1980, p. 213) demands: 'We need to incorporate concepts about behaviour into the conceptual framework to form the basis of realistic assumptions for theory development and for practical policy analyses'. On the basis of these considerations he developed his Environment-Behavioural Response-Performance-Approach (Shaffer, 1980, p. 311), an SCP variant, the system processes of which can be stated, much simplified, as follows:

- The participants in the system live in an environmental situation which represents their specific opportunity set.
- The individual participants react to their respective environmental situation; the aggregate reactions of the system's participants alter the environmental situation.
- The altered environment leads to changes in costs and benefits for the participants of the system.
- These alterations change the views of the participants of the system concerning their environment: they try to adapt their behaviour to the new situation.

The consequences of this process are described by Shaffer as 'Performance'. The system which is developing is driven by the trinominal sequence of 'environment', 'behavioural response' and 'performance' (E-B-P... E-B-P..).

With regard to this behaviour-orientated strengthening of the SCP approach, however, Shaffer well knows that no single conceptual framework can do justice to the total complexity of the object of research. In his opinion the task is to classify strategically important characteristics of the system's environment, the participants in the system and their behaviour, and the results of the system, and to develop clear hypotheses on their inter-relationships.

Seen on a whole, the development of the SCP approach shows a strong socio-economic orientation under the influence of the 'New Political Economy' and the 'Institutional Economy'.

An Extended SCP Approach for the Evaluation of Vertical Production and Marketing Systems for Urban and Peri-Urban Fruits and Vegetables

Figure 1 presents an extended SCP approach, which was adapted for the examination of vertical production and marketing systems for urban and peri-urban production in developing countries. With this approach an attempt was made to take into account to a large extent the above-mentioned criticisms of the use of earlier SCP approaches for sub-sector analysis. It includes a large number of comprehensive criteria on the presentation and evaluation of the framework conditions of the system, its structure, the behaviour of the system's participants and the performance of the system. This does not, however, mean that these criteria must or can be referred to as a whole for a detailed examination of the system. They are meant rather as a frame of references, which can be simplified or extended according to each individual case. This concept is intended not only for intensive investigations or evaluations, but also for short-term examinations, such as Rapid-Appraisal procedures, although it may not seem this way at first sight due to its size.

For the evaluation of performance-determining criteria a procedure according to the principles of a Strength-and-Weakness-Analysis is recommended (cf. Ansoff, 1966, and Aurich and Schröder, 1972). This static procedure has the advantage that it forces concentration on the most important aspects which strengthen or weaken performance.

In order to pay more attention to the future aspect and to provide a suitable basis for decisions concerning an improvement in performance, it would be appropriate to supplement the Strength-and-Weakness analysis with a Chance-Risk-Analysis, with which the dynamic aspect of socio-economic systems could be taken into account (cf. Hörmann and Storck, 1981, p.50). With the chance-risk analysis, changes in the areas to be examined are integrated in the analysis within the given framework of the conditions. The tendencies of such factors of influence and measures, which promote the given vertical production and marketing system and which reduce its weaknesses and help to reduce risks, should be illustrated whenever possible. Here we must bear in mind that the factors which influence performance represent only partially alterable variables and that it is often difficult or impossible to alter them.

As far as the evaluation of performance-determining criteria is concerned, it must be pointed out that the current state of scientific knowledge does not allow any proof of immediate causal relationships between the performance of the system and individual criteria of SCP approaches. Furthermore, there are substitutive relationships between various SCP criteria concerning the evaluation of vertical production and marketing systems, so that particularly favourable conditions in one area, for example, may to a certain extent balance negative effects in another area.

Advantages and Disadvantages of the Extended SCP Approach

The SCP approach extended by Shaffer to include behavioural science has an advantage over earlier SCP models in that it also sees the future development of the market structure in its interdependent relationship to current market behaviour and to the current performance of the system (Fleming, 1986, p. 10), and that it makes it necessary to tackle the question of the behaviour of the participants in the system. This SCP variant, therefore, better illustrates an interdependent process than the usual, simpler SCP models, which are orientated in one direction only.

The fact that this SCP paradigm makes a flexible analysis of marketing problems possible is regarded as a further advantage, as it does not contain any fixed concepts about the desired condition of a marketing system whilst assuming a perfect market (Stevens and Jabara, 1988, p. 338). On the contrary, this model makes the identification of social performance goals necessary, by means of which the evaluation standards are established. In this way weaknesses which reduce the system's performance can be traced, and then methods can be sought to reduce or remove them. This extended approach covers essential new ideas on the 'New Political Economy' and the 'Institutional Economy', which is also advantageous. Furthermore, the grouping of the evaluation criteria is more original and less eclectic than the more simply structured catalogues of criteria (Hörmann and Storck, 1981).

The major disadvantages of this extended SCP approach are in particular its high complexity and the resulting problems of quantification. Another essential point is that the classification of market phenomena concerning the criteria 'structure', 'conduct' and 'performance' is not always clearly defined (Grothe, 1989).

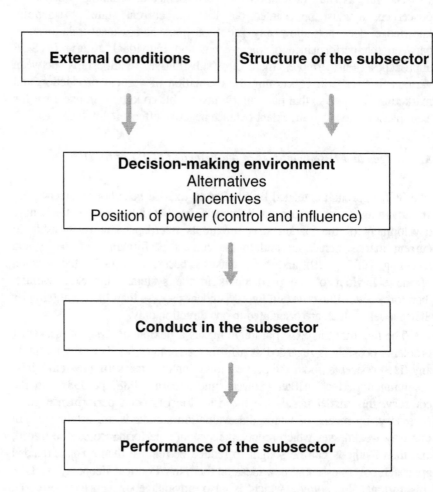

Figure 16.1   Structure-Conduct-Performance (SCP) for the Investigation of Production and Marketing of Vegetables in Urban and Peri-Urban Systems in the Tropics and Subtropics

Sources: Marion, 1996; Hörmann, 1994.

Empirical Observations Concerning Selected Criteria For An Extended SCP Approach

In the following part some empirical observations are discussed concerning selected criteria of the extended SCP approach. Due to the limited scope of this contribution, these observations are mainly limited to the areas of structure, conduct and performance.

The Structure of the Sub-Sector

1   Horizontal dimension: In urban Africa, the **production** of fruit and vegetables can be found in home gardens, along roads, in river valleys (flood plains) and on open spaces (wedges) (Smit, 1995, p.32f). Home garden production, which usually takes place on very small plots, ranges from purely subsistence-level production, which is not dealt with further here, to a mainly market orientated intensive production. In East Africa this statement concerns mainly the production of vegetables, whereas fruit is generally less common and is mainly grown in small quantities in scattered production.

According to an investigation which was conducted by Yachkaschi (1996) in Tanzania, the median household plot size is 220 square metres (sqm) for Dar-es-Salaam, and 330 sqm for Arusha. Here we must bear in mind that often only a small part of the plot is used for the cultivation of fruit and vegetables, whereas the remaining part is often used for other agricultural activities. The market orientation of vegetable production in urban home gardens has probably increased considerably, above all in those developing countries whose economic development has suffered large setbacks in recent years. This market orientated cultivation has also grown in recent years in households which belong to middle-income groups, but which are subject to the danger of marginalisation due to an increasing loss of purchasing power. These households usually have access to land and often regard this supplementary income from the market production of vegetables as an essential part of their household income.

In marginalised households the market orientation of home garden production can be so strong that when market prices are high very few crops are kept for consumption in the producer's own household, because the income from the sale is needed to cover more necessary basic needs. It is difficult to give a generally valid definition of the term peri-urban production. The term peri-urban depends not only on the distance between the place of production and the urban consumer centre, but also on the given infrastructure of the traffic system. If the infrastructure is poor, for example, a distance of just twenty kilometres can be too great to for considering a given locality as peri-urban. On the other hand, if the infrastructure is adequate, the peri-urban zone may extend much farther than twenty kilometres. That means that the definition of peri-urban production depends mainly on the time needed for transport, i.e., on accessibility rather than pure distance.

The peri-urban production of fruit and vegetables takes place either as specialised intensive production for the market, or as part of farming activities. Many producers use their land intensively because of the small size of their farms. For this intensification they often prefer the vegetable production, since in most cases the cultivation of fruit is much more capital intensive and needs a higher level of technical know how. For the agricultural area of peri-urban producers of fruit and vegetables in Tanzania Yachkaschi (1996) names a median value of 6,000 sqm per smallholding in Dar-es-Salaam and 4,000 sqm in Arusha.

Peri-urban production as a rule differs from market production in homegardens in its fulltime farming character and its larger production areas. Also, a different assortment of vegetables is frequently cultivated. For example, in the home gardens of the major cities in Tanzania, leafy vegetables are grown, which are very perishable and have a short cultivation period, whereas in peri-urban production there is often a wider range of types of vegetables which are often less perishable. These perishable leafy vegetables, which cannot survive long transport distances without a cooling system, are very competitive with regard to the factor allocation of urban producers. In Tanzania this is especially true for Amaranthus. This indigenous leafy vegetable needs only a short cultivation period (about twenty to twenty-five days from sowing to harvesting) and is relatively insensitive to pests which reduces production risks and provides fast income generation.

The rapid growth of the cities has a considerable influence on the locations of urban production. When the production does not take place in areas specially reserved for horticultural or agricultural use (e.g. green belts) or in fixed settlement areas, it is moved to the expanding outskirts of the town due to the ever-increasing number and density of buildings in the town centre. Therefore, one has to bear in mind that today's peri-urban locations of production may soon fall prey to urban growth and only continue to exist as urban locations of production, if at all. This consideration is of great importance with regards to the objective of a sustainable development of market gardening.

The conditions of access to production of fruit and vegetables require primarily the availability of land and water, and, in urban areas, toleration of the production by the city council. Von Braun et al (1993, p.38) comment on this:

Urban agriculture has become a permanent feature throughout the cities of the developing world, despite being actively discouraged for reasons ranging from aesthetics (it detracts from the beauty of the cities) to ideological (it is a manifestation of rural habits and does not reflect the principles of modern urban living)'. One must add that many city councils are probably no longer able to implement the laws preventing a market orientated urban agricultural production, due to the enormous social problems and possible shortages of food provisions caused by the rapidly growing number of inhabitants with marginal income.

As a rule the very low income households have no access to irrigable land in and around the cities. But also for existing urban and peri-urban producers the limitation of the availability of irrigable land for an extension of their cultivation of fruit and vegetables is a severe problem, as the investigation of Yachkaschi (1996) shows clearly for Tanzanian cities.

In the production of indigenous vegetables, which have been little improved by breeding and which are primarily required by poor households, the capital input is very low, and may in fact be limited to simple tools to work the land manually. Here the seed predominantly originates from the cultivators` own production, and the input of chemical fertilisers and pesticides is often minimal. The cultivation and marketing risks can partly be reduced without a great deal of effort by spacing out the production dates. The necessary know-how can be learnt relatively easily.

The cultivation of non-indigenous vegetables often makes much higher demands on the capital requirements for investment and on the use of purchased inputs, and also on the producers` know-how of plant production. For various towns in Tanzania, the know-how of the urban and peri-urban vegetable producers can be generally evaluated as follows: The most common examples for the low standard of production technology can be found in the insufficient irrigation practices and uneconomic utilisation of the available water, insufficient manuring methods, irregular sowing, too high density of seedlings, too narrow or too wide spacing of plants, bad practices in transplanting seedlings, use of own vegetable seed with low yield potential and seedborn diseases, severe and dangerous mistakes in plant protection, lack of weed control, poor harvesting methods and post-harvest treatment of the products (Hörmann, 1993, p.5).

The conditions of access to the market must be termed simple, unless great transport distances have to be overcome, and provided the producers can manage to market their products without wholesalers due to the close proximity of the market. This applies in particular to urban production. Peri-urban production, on the other hand, relies partly on wholesale trade. These simple conditions of access can be regarded as an important advantage of location on the part of vegetable production close to the market, in comparison with deliveries from distant domestic or foreign locations.

In many cases where purchased input and hired labour are used, loans are probably necessary for market production, partly because the income from the cultivation of cash crops is often used consumptively. If loans are necessary to finance production, these loans in particular are likely to come from non-institutional credit systems. This concerns loans granted by relatives, friends, self-help groups, traders and private money-lenders.

In theory, co-operatives are in a better position to negotiate on the procurement of production means and on the marketing of the products. However, they are not as important for urban production in developing countries since co-operative functions, such as the collection of larger quantities and the organisation of transport, become less important because of the closeness of the production to the market. Because of this, and due to higher transaction costs in marketing, peri-urban vegetable production partly shows a different situation.

2   *The vertical dimension*: The functional structure concerns the level at which the functions have to be fulfilled within a vertical production and marketing system and the system elements involved. The *supply of production means* causes problems for several reasons if purchased input becomes necessary. One of these problems is the often poor availability of required input. Further problems are caused by high costs for industrial input, which are partly due to inefficient competition between suppliers of production means in the countries concerned. However, one can assume that the procurement problem is often more severe for rural producers than for

urban producers. Frequently, a further shortcoming is the producers' poor knowledge of the characteristics and quality of inputs.

A lack of availability of high-quality seed and planting material often causes considerable bottlenecks in supplying the market with products in terms of both quantity and quality. This does not necessarily mean the supply of high-yielding varieties, which place high demands on the remaining industrial input. It also concerns local varieties which have not been improved or only little improved by breeding, likewise genetic populations with a low seed value due to genetic characteristics and insufficient production and preparation of the seed. A further problem is that non-indigenous types of fruit and vegetables often lack varieties which are suitable for the location.

The fulfilment of *transport functions* between the places of supply and demand are simpler for urban and peri-urban production locations than for outside locations, due to the shorter distances to the markets. For urban production the simplest means of transport are usually sufficient. The producers or the small retailers can carry their products to the market or other sales locations or transport them by bicycle or handcart. Public means of transport (taxis and buses) are also often used because they are relatively easily accessible. Likewise, it is easier for the producers or traders to organise rented transport or their own transport (pick-ups, tractors etc.) than if the production location is further away.

In peri-urban cultivation, some producers organise joint transport to the markets. Often, however, the take-over of the transport function by traders is a major reason for indirect sales via collecting wholesalers or large retailers. These traders collect the fruit and vegetables either from the producers' plot or from collecting points within the corresponding peri-urban areas. This depends above all on the quantities offered and on the access to the producers by means of transport.

Amongst the participants of the system it is partly wholesalers who take over a *credit function*, in that they pre-finance production means in intensive market gardening, or grant the producers credit for consumption to bridge the time until harvest. This pre-financing and granting of credits by traders is usually accompanied by high credit costs, which are reflected by lower prices for the producers.

The *quantity function* is often assumed by traders or co-operatives in that they take over different quantities of products than they sell. As long as this concerns the collecting function, the quantity function is of little importance for urban production. It can, however, be important for peri-urban production. If the quantities are very small, collecting wholesalers often employ agents to purchase these products on their behalf. The extent to which the collecting wholesalers actively assume their functions in the production areas often depends on the market situation. Frequently they visit the producers when supply is short and take over the transport of the products themselves, whereas when supply is abundant they often expect the producers to deliver the crops to their place of sale themselves.

When wholesale trade is involved in the marketing of urban or peri-urban products, semi-wholesalers, who deal in wholesale and retail trade, may be involved in the next stage of distribution of the products. They get their goods from distributing wholesalers and sell them to consumers and to small traders who do not have the necessary financial means to purchase the minimum quantities stipulated by the distributing wholesalers. Small retail traders are generally very important in the marketing of vegetables, and they are to be found in particular at informal markets. Thus in most African towns there are numerous retail markets which are frequented by consumers with a low income and a great number of women and children who only have a few kilos of vegetables to sell   (Hörmann and Shawel, 1985, p.183f; Yachkaschi, 1996).

As far as the degree of of urban or peri-urban production is concerned, one must mention that sometimes wholesalers or retailers may also cultivate fruit and vegetables too. This vertical integration can help to save on marketing costs, amongst other things due to lower transaction costs.

The number and size of the suppliers and customers shows the existing morphology of the market structure, which has to be extended to include the behaviour of the market participants in incomplete, multi-stage markets. Polypolistic relations dominate the supply from urban vegetable production at producer and trade levels. In peri-urban production there is also a price taker situation at producer and retail level, whereas at wholesale level the structures are more likely to be oligopsonic or oligopolistic. The producers' price taker situation generally makes one expect cyclical fluctuations in the supply of crops, especially of vegetables. These fluctuations are probably stronger for types of vegetables requiring more purchased input than for types of vegetables requiring less or no purchased input, particularly as the marginal costs of labour tend towards zero in many developing countries.

In general the marketing channels for fruit and vegetables tend to be long, fragmented and inefficient in developing countries. There are a lot of wholesalers who supply a much larger number of small retailers. The quantities offered are usually small. Deficiencies in weights and measures are common, likewise high rates of spoilage.

As far as urban and peri-urban fruit and vegetable production is concerned, one must adjust this statement as follows: The marketing of *urban* products mainly takes place via retailers or direct sales to the consumers, without wholesalers. As a rule, *peri-urban* production also uses comparatively short marketing channels. If wholesalers are included, they often take over the tasks of both collection and distribution.

It is also common for peri-urban producers to sell to retailers. In this producer group, direct sales to consumers are more limited (e.g. road-side marketing, local markets). This can also be explained by the vast amount of time necessary for direct marketing, due to which the producers prefer to concentrate on a larger production, from which they expect a higher income (Uli, 1991, p.187).

Producers' information about the market for fruit and vegetables is generally distinctly lacking in developing countries, whereas the wholesalers' level of information is much better, but often still insufficient (Hörmann, 1994, p.139). Some of the reasons for this lack of information are the missing standardisation of weights, packaging and quality, a severely fragmented supply which comes unsorted, in small and spatially separated lots, which are available irregularly, and insufficient pre-conditions of the infrastructure (e.g. traffic systems, markets, communications). Moreover, there is usually a lack of efficient public market information systems.

These general statements are only partly true for urban and peri-urban vegetable production. The market information of these producers tends to be considerably better than for those who are distant from the market. This applies particularly for the direct sellers, but also for producers with indirect marketing, who can gain their information about the market situation relatively simply and independently, by visiting the market themselves.

Urban and peri-urban vegetable production places fewer demands on the capacity and infrastructure of the formal municipal wholesale and retail markets, which are mostly hopelessly overburdened, than vegetable deliveries from more distant production locations. This view is very important, because the long marketing channels and formal market institutions, which exist in developing countries and which market-distant production particularly relies upon, are generally under a great deal of pressure due to the rapid growth of the population. They are often less able to cope with the demands of efficient marketing than in former times. Mostly the only reaction to the increase in supply and demand is a growing number of traditional wholesalers and retailers. On most formal markets there is little or no evidence of an increase in performance by economies of scale, modern management, the implementation of technical progress etc.

This inefficiency of formal markets aggravates the high spoilage rate of deliveries of fruit and vegetables from market-distant locations, in addition to the problems already caused by the length and quality of transport, poor handling practices, the length of marketing channels, etc. Apart from the high transport costs, this also leads to high consumer prices for crops produced a long way from the market. This makes it often virtually impossible for low-income households to purchase crops of this origin.

The urban and peri-urban production of fruit and vegetables does not suffer as much from this inefficiency of the formal markets. Among other things, this is due to the direct sales to consumers and institutional buyers, which often does not take place at the market. Furthermore, suppliers offering locally produced vegetables can judge better the quantities they harvest daily, according to the actual market situation. Therefore, they require little or no storage space at the market.

As far as informal markets are concerned, one has to mention that their total lack of infrastructure does not lead to such a high rate of spoilage for locally produced crops as for supplies from distant production locations, because the products arrive at the market freshly harvested.

The Behaviour in the Sub-Sector

1   *The horizontal dimension:* When a product policy is applied for the domestic supply of fruit and vegetables for the domestic market in most developing countries, this is limited to the supply being differentiated according to quality. This differentiation is orientated to the small market segment of high-income households. These customers are supplied in particular by retailers, who are specialised in the supply of higher-quality products and often pick out for them the best products from the quantities they have purchased. The remaining products of poorer quality are than sold to retailers who supply low-income customers (Hörmann, 1993, p.10).

The supply of less known types of vegetables is also orientated to high-income customers. The less known types of vegetables are predominantly non-indigenous. The urban poor can hardly afford to buy more expensive non-traditional vegetables as well as indigenous vegetables during the off-season. For these more expensive items in many of the least developed countries the income elasticity seems to be very low, since their budget is not sufficient to satisfy the daily requirements of staple food. This means that an increase in income would be spent predominantly on basic food including the cheaper types of vegetables. These marginal consumers would also react inelastically to a certain decrease in price for the more expensive crops (Hörmann and Shawel, 1985).

Like other agricultural producers, producers of fruit and vegetables can not actively practise any price policy. Due to their very small share of the market and their poor supplier situation, they have no other choice but to behave as price takers and to decide which products and what quantities they want to produce for the market price they expect. Due to the closeness to the market and different marketing channels for urban and peri-urban produce, price agreements between traders which would reduce the competition on the procurement and marketing side, are less likely than for products from distant production locations, which reach the city markets via much more closely defined structures of marketing channels. For the production close to the market, the economic theory of what constitutes a perfect market is therefore more likely to apply.

Price policy also includes the form of price agreement between the market partners. Essentially, for the urban and peri-urban vegetable supply one can differentiate between the two following types of price agreement, each of which includes a different distribution of the price and sales risks between the market partners: purchase at fixed prices, and business on a commission basis.

Business on a commission basis can take place primarily in the dyads producer - commission agent or collecting wholesaler - commission agent. For the indirect marketing of peri-urban produce, however, one is more likely to have fixed price purchases than for products from distant locations. This can be an advantage for production close to the market because the price risk and the risk of spoilage are lower than for business on a commission basis. Furthermore, business on a commission basis can cause considerable additional transaction costs due to the surveillance of the transactions by the owner of the goods. It can also be responsible for higher transaction costs due to the procurement of market information by the suppliers, if they do not deliver their products to the market themselves. This can be explained by the fact that commission agents are generally not particularly interested in exchanging information with their suppliers because they do not take over the sales risk (Hörmann and Stamer, 1989, p.93f). Furthermore, the purchase of unharvested fruit and vegetables at a fixed price is also common practice.

The granting of periods of payment by producers to traders or by wholesalers to retailers, which is equivalent to sales financing, is of some importance in marketing urban and peri-urban products. This takes into consideration the often poor liquidity of traders.

As far as risk-taking in market gardening is concerned, one must mention that the level of risk in market production is only lower if no large and long-term investments are necessary, if the required purchase costs of production means are not too high, and if the producers know how to apply the production technology and still use a sufficient share of their production capacity to produce other cash crops and/or to provide for their own households. Traders who harvest themselves do so to try to reduce their procurement and sales risks. By harvesting themselves they can decide on the quality on the plot, and adapt the quantity to the demand, thus reducing the rate of spoilage.

Horizontal activities of co-ordination can be found mainly in the joint transport of crops from peri-urban areas to the markets. Co-ordinators can be either producers, who organise common transport, or small collecting wholesalers, who can not procure and market complete shipments just for themselves. This activity reduces the transport costs considerably. A joint procurement of production means is most likely seldom due to the low level of the producers' horizontal organisation.

2   *The vertical dimension:* The vertical dimension of the behaviour of the system participants in the production and marketing system has to be seen in close connection with the internal economic and socio-political processes of the system.

The information behaviour of the system's participants is generally influenced by the given technical means of communication, the closeness to the market, differences in interests, a differentiated understanding of information and the cost of information. For the urban and peri-urban vegetable producers, the procurement of reliable information is easier than for producers who are further away from the market. They can gain their own information about market prices without a great deal of time and expenditure. This is of significance for the formation of producer prices and for production behaviour.

The transfer of price signals from the markets to the producers is known to influence their production decisions with regard to types of fruit and vegetables, varieties, volume, the season and the quality of the production. These should be more reliable for urban and peri-urban producers than for distant producers due to their closeness to the market.

Concerning the vertical co-ordination it can be assumed that traders are less involved in an active co-ordination of urban and peri-urban vegetable production. Besides direct sales and shorter marketing channels, this is mainly due to high transaction costs of a vertical co-ordination of this often rather fragmented production. (A certain influence of traders on production can be recognized when they try to finance it.) Production on contract is likely to remain an exception in production close to the market.

Performance in the Sub-Sector

The following is mainly an attempt to evaluate the performance of production close to the market in comparison with the supply from distant production areas. Here hypothetical assumptions are sometimes referred to due to lack of empirical experience.

First, however, some definitions have to be given concerning the performance criteria technical allocative efficiency. Concerning the *optimal allocation of resources* in marketing systems Marion (1986, p.84) states:

> Resource allocation is optimal when, given property rights as defined, and available knowledge when allocative decision must be made, the allocation is such that no reallocation could be made that would increase the satisfaction of anyone without reducing the satisfaction of another (Pareto optimality). The allocation of resources to information gathering, analysis and distribution must be included. One must recognise time, information and risk. Efficient allocation implies maximisation of the value of resources to their owners.

The Pareto optimality referred to here, however, corresponds to the typical ideal situation, which can only be achieved in a real economy with approximate solutions.

According to Schubert (1972, p.206) a marketing system is, theoretically speaking, *technically efficient* if it reaches a certain achievement at a minimum cost or, in other words, if the relation between output (contribution to the social product) and input (factor input) is maximised. According to Bain (1968, p.24) it is allocatively efficient if *its output rate should be such that its marginal cost of production equals the selling price of its output*. With reference to marketing, Schubert states that practically, technical efficiency concerns an investigation of marketing costs for a given achievement, while the allocative evaluation deals with the marketing profits.

1   Horizontal Dimension: Of the criteria shown in Fig. 1 concerning the horizontal evaluation of the performance of vertical production and marketing systems, the following deals primarily with some aspects of the technical and allocative efficiency at individual levels of the system.

For the input-output or the cost-return relations and for the area productivity as important indicators of technical efficiency of production, no basic statements can be made as to whether distant locations of vegetable production are more efficient than those close to the market, or whether the opposite applies. This depends essentially on whether the ecological conditions and factor prices and the factor availability of the local or distant locations to be compared differ from one another. Furthermore, one must consider whether, and at which location, the knowledge of production technology is better developed. Here one must mention that according to experience the larger vegetable production areas are more likely to profit from advantages of agglomeration according to production technology, such as more frequent assistance by the extension service or a more intensive exchange of experience between the producers.

The technical efficiency of production close to the market may only be so far below the technical efficiency of competing distant suppliers as can be balanced by its advantages of location (especially lower transport costs, lower rate of spoilage, higher producer returns etc.) provided that the factor prices are the same. One can only expect a small improvement at most in the cost-return relation for crops produced locally through higher producer prices, which reflect the freshness of the products, certainly in the least developed countries. This is because the buyer behaviour of the vast majority of the consumers is extremely price-orientated because of their limited household budget.

For most of the countries in East Africa one can assume that the technical efficiency of urban and peri-urban production suffers considerably under the lack of knowledge of production technology. However, this does not automatically mean that producers in rural production areas have better knowledge. Furthermore, the efficiency-reducing shortcomings in the supply of production means are very significant, likewise the generally high lack of capital which greatly limits an optimal factor input.

It is obvious that the lack of suitable *storage space* for a short-term storage of the fruit and vegetables is less of a problem for products grown close to the market than for deliveries from distant production areas, due to the much shorter period between harvest and consumption. In other words, the lack of suitable storage increases the rate of spoilage more for products of distant origin than for those locally cultivated. This applies at all levels of the production and marketing systems.

This aspect of efficiency provides an important argument for local vegetable production, if one considers that in many developing countries neither producers nor traders or city councils are likely to be able to improve the storage situation remarkably in the foreseeable future, in order to reduce significantly the generally very high rate of spoilage. This also corresponds to the comments concerning the considerably lower demands placed by locally grown crops on the infrastructure of wholesale and retail markets, as mentioned earlier.

The advantages of local vegetable production concerning the technical efficiency, however, have also to be considered from a relative point of view. Gutman (1987, p.41) rightly comments on this, with particular regard to the transport costs, as follows: 'Lower costs of transport have in fact maintained the commercial production of fresh products near the cities, but they can not always offset the advantages of more distant rural areas with regard to land prices, greater chances for mechanisation, and more suitable ecosystems'.

In the wholesale and retail trade the low *turnover quantities* make the provision of the consumer with fresh fruit and vegetables considerably more expensive. In the evaluation of this aspect, one can probably recognise certain locational disadvantages on the part of local production. This evaluation, however, causes problems from a socio-economic point of view, as a high rate of hidden unemployment is concealed behind the low turnover quantities. Moreover, one has to consider that a particularly high proportion of small traders marketing urban and peri-urban produce at retail level may be women. This activity at least helps them to gain a marginal income. This aspect is important, because during recent decades the number of marginalised households not headed by a man has increased a great deal in many countries.

2   *Vertical dimension*: Several aspects must be considered when evaluating the correspondence between the supply and the preferences of demand. Among other things, this may concern the types and varieties of fruit and vegetables preferred by consumers, the quality, the degree of ripeness and the availability during the off-season. With regard to this subject, a few general comments can be made, some of which must be considered independent of the differentiation between urban and rural production.

Thus the preferences of demand can vary between ethnic groups or according to the regional origin of the consumers. This applies for example for the consumption of black nightshade, a leafy vegetable, in Tanzania. There are also market segments specialised in the demands of immigrants. The demand for non-indigenous types of vegetables often depends on the level of education and income. A study made in Ethiopia shows that members of low-income households are often unfamiliar with the taste and preparation of such types of vegetables (Hörmann and Shawel, 1985).

In many developing countries, the products from local production are more likely to meet the expectations of traders and consumers concerning the quality aspect freshness than crops from distant production. However, urban vegetables can have a lack of quality which is not visible, but which makes the health value of vegetable consumption very questionable. This happens when water contaminated with pathogenic agents or chemicals (e.g. amœba, heavy metals) is used in the production of vegetables and when the internal quality of the crops is influenced by air pollution.

Some of the time grave errors are made when pesticides are applied, which also has a negative effect on the product quality. This concerns the application of unsuitable types of pesticides, too high concentration of the pesticide and the abuse of waiting periods. One can, however, assume that in homegarden production often no - or less - pesticide is used than in intensive market gardening. Residues of pesticides and the advantages of organically produced fruit and vegetables are usually not noticed by the consumers, because they are not informed accordingly and due to their price-orientated demand.

According to Schubert (1972, p.260) the determination of the gross trade margin is the first step in investigating the technical and allocative efficiency. This margin reflects, in the difference between producer and consumer prices, the costs and profits of the total marketing process of the marketing system. Both the absolute and the relative size of the gross trade margin say little about the performance of the system as such. Its evaluation must take into account the extent of the functions fulfilled at the various levels of trade, the marketing risks and the specific input of capital and labour (Warmbier and Böttcher, 1984, p.127).

The lower marketing costs result (or should result) in higher producer prices for local producers than for producers at distant locations. Provided that the production factor land is not markedly more expensive, that there is sufficient suitable land available and that the opportunity costs of the factor labour are low, then likewise comparatively lower production costs should lead to an expansion and intensification of local production which contributes to lower consumer prices and also to a greater sales volume.

The cost factor spoilage is particularly important for all highly perishable products. It is a further significant argument for local production. The rate of spoilage correlates directly to the length of transport time and the length of the marketing channel, whereby poor road conditions and the use of less suitable means of transport cause additional problems. In comparison, local production makes much lower demands on the standard of transport.

Further important reasons for high spoilage rates are to be seen in disadvantageous post-harvest handling practices. Often products are repackaged and thereby damaged at the various levels of trade. This is because packing material (sacks, boxes, baskets) is frequently scarce and no proper deposit system exists, and therefore participants of the system want to keep their own packaging (Hörmann 1994, p.190). Sometimes products are also repackaged because standardised weights are only customary at a later stage.

When discussing the efficiency of the price formation, one must take into account the high perishability of most types of products, which can result in particularly high price fluctuations due to seasonal and erratic surpluses. Moreover, in many countries it suffers from the lack of standardised qualities and weights.

One can assume that for urban and peri-urban produced products the price at the various levels of the system is more often similar to the theoretical market equilibrium price than for supplies from outside. This is essentially due to the market transparency, which is often better within the local subsystem, and the given market structure and the easier access to the market. Furthermore, this has also to be seen in connection with the lower level of importance of wholesale trade in the marketing of urban and peri-urban products.

The common practice of traders in indirect marketing of passing on immediately to the consumers any price increases due to short supply, although the producers do not benefit from these increases until much later, applies less for local fruit and vegetable production due to some of the structures and patterns of behaviour already described (Lorenzl et al., 1975, p.211). Price agreements, which are detrimental to the efficiency of price formation, occur less often for urban and peri-urban fruits and vegetables than for outside deliveries. From this point of view there is much less danger of excessive prices for locally supplied products. Such price agreements can easily result in lower producer prices and higher consumer prices. The lower producer revenue acts in turn as a disincentive for the producers. On the other hand, on the consumer side excessive prices limit the demand volume and thus the consumption of fruit and vegetables.

When one speaks of system equity, the discussion about the level of the trade margin and the share of the producer prices in the consumer prices is a central theme (Hörmann, 1994, p.205). It depends essentially on the distribution of power within the system. The problems of equity, which occur when market power and information are unequally distributed, should be far fewer for local production, because the producers generally have better chances of getting information. Such problems can occur, however, when there are problems of transport or when a producer depends on the pre-financing of his production by a trader.

The evaluation of the ecological compatibility of urban and peri-urban market gardening must not be neglected, although only a few examples can be mentioned here. It is important, for example, when the limited supply of tap water in the cities is used for crop production, leaving the city households even less drinking water, or when an extensive use of fertilisers and pesticides contributes to the contamination of local resources of drinking water.

On the other hand, local production eases the strain on the environment by reducing transport from distant production locations to centres of consumption and by contributing to the closing of open nutrient cycles and of the carbon cycle (Smit, 1995).

Conclusions

The development of the SCP - approach used for the investigation of agricultural sub-sectors is presented in the first part of this contribution. SCP was given its strongest impetus through Bain's contribution to industrial organisation in the sixties. At the beginning, the close adherence to Bain's concept proved to be unsatisfactory for the investigation of agricultural sub-sectors because of its orientation on too small a number of economic parameters. Therefore the SCP framework was considerably extended for studies conducted later. This extension was brought about as a result of the the New Political Economy and the Institutional Economy, among others. However, as the participating enterprises and organisations were being treated as a black box and not according to their decision-making behavior, Shaffer developed a dynamic SCP concept oriented to behavior science which he calls the 'Environment - Behavioral response - Performance' (EBP) approach. This concept is discussed more comprehensively.

Furthermore, an extended SCP approach for the examination of vertical production and marketing systems for urban and peri-urban horticultural products in developing countries is presented and the advantages and disadvantages of this concept are described.

In the second part, selected criteria of this extended SCP - approach are discussed according to empirical observations related to urban and peri-urban production and marketing systems. In a number of aspects a comparison is made between the supply of fruit and vegetables from local and distant production locations, bearing in mind the strengths and weaknesses of both types of origin.

References

Ansoff, J. (1966), *Management Strategie*, München: Moderne Industrie.

Aurich, W. and Schröder, H.U. (1972), *System der Wachstumsplanung in Unternehmen*. München: Moderne Industrie.

Bain, J.S. (1968), *Industrial Organization.*, New York: Wiley.

Von Braun, J., McComb, J., Fred-Mensah, B.K. and Pandaya-Lorch, R. (1993), *Urban Food Insecurity and Malnutrition in Developing Countries - Trends,*

Policies, and Research Implications, Washington D.C.: International Food Policy Research Institute.

Fleming, E. (1986), *A Study of Agricultural Market Development in the South PacificRregion: Structure, Conduct, Perfrmance,* Occasional Paper No.3, South Pacific Smallholder Project, University of New England, Armidale, N.S.W.

Goldberg, R.A. (1974), *Agribusiness management for developing countries - Latin America.* Cambridge, Mass: Bollinger.

Grothe, B. (1989*), Markt-Struktur-Marktverhalten und Marktergebnis als Analyseansatz in der Industrieökonomik,* WISU: Das Wirtschaftforum, 12/89, 669-670.

Gutman, P. (1987), 'Urban Agriculture: The potential and limitations of an urban self-reliance strategy', *Food and Nutrition Bulletin,* Vol. 9, pp. 37-42.

Harris, B. (1979), 'There is method in my madness: Or is it vice versa? - Measuring agricultural market performance', *Food Research Institute Studies,* Vol.17, pp.197-218.

Heidhues, F. (1985), 'Agricultural credit and agricultural development', *Economics.* Vol. 1:31, pp. 59-70.

Holtzman, J.S. (1982) *A Socio-economic Analysis of Stall-feed Cattle Production and Marketing in the Mandara Mountains Region of Northern Cameroon,* Ph.D. Dissertation, Michigan State University.

Hörmann, D.M. (1993), *Urban production of fruit and vegetables for the poor in urban Tanzania. - A rapid appraisal for selected cities, Institute for Horticultural Economics,* University of Hannover (unpublished).

Hörmann, D.M. (1994), Konzepte zur Beurteilung der Leistungsfähigkeit vertikaler Produktions- und Absatzsysteme für frische Gartenbauerzeugnisse in Entwicklungsländern. Kiel.

Hörmann, D.M. (1995), 'Production and marketing systems for fresh vegetables from urban and peri-urban areas in the tropics and subtropics', in J. Richter, et al (eds), *Vegetable Production in Peri-urban Areas in the Tropics and Subtropics - Food, Income and Quality of Life,* Feldafing: German Foundation for International Development (DSE) and Council for Tropical and Subtropical Agricultural Research (ATSAF).

Hörmann, D.M. and Storck H. (1981), *Exportorientierter Gartenbau in Entwicklungsländern - Kriterien zur Beurteilung von Erfolg, Wettbewerbsposition und Effizienz,* München, Köln, London: Forschungsberichte des Bundesministeriums für Wirtschaftliche Zusammenarbeit, No. 24.

Hörmann, D.M. and Shawel, H. (1985), *The Domestic Market For Fresh and Processed Fruit and Vegetables and Its Supply In Important Urban Centres of Ethiopia,* Eschborn: Sonderpublikation der GTZ, No. 184.

Hörmann, D.M. and Stamer, H. (1989), *The Vertical Production and Marketing System for Fresh Fruit and Vegetables in the Algarve in Portugal,* Working paper No. 62, Institute for Horticultural Economics, University of Hannover.

Lorenzl, G., Gsänger, H. and Heinrich, F. (1975), *Möglichkeiten der Leistungsbeurteilung von Vermarktungssystemen für Agrarprodukte unter den Bedingungen Wirtschaftlicher Entwicklung - Das Beispiel der Vermarktung von Obst und Gemüse in Kenia.* Berlin: Institut für Sozialökonomie der Agrarentwicklung, Technische Universiät Berlin.

Marion, B.W. (1976), *Application of the Structure, Conduct, Performance Paradigm to Sub-Sector Analysis.* N.C. Project 117, Studies of the Organization and Control of the U.S. Food System, WP7, Agricultural Experiment Stations of California, Cornell, Florida etc.

Marion, B.W. (1986), *The Organization and Performance of the U.S. Food System.* Lexington, Massachusetts: Lexicon Books.

Sanyal, B. (1985) 'Urban agriculture: who cultivates and why? A case study of Lusaka ', *Food and Nutrition Bulletin,* Vol. 7, pp. 15-24.

Schubert, B. (1972), 'Die Evaluierung von Vermarktungssystemen für Agrarprodukte in Entwicklungsln Pndern', *Zeitschrift für ausländische Landwirtschaf,* Vol. 11, pp. 259-273.

Shaffer, J.D. (1973), 'On the concept of sub-sector studies', *American Journal of Agricultural Economics.* Vol. 55:, pp. 333-335.

Shaffer, J.D. (1980), 'Food system organization and performance: Toward a conceptual framework', *American Journal of Agricultural Economics,* 62:3, 310-318.

Shaffer, J.D., Weber, M.T., Riley, H.M. and Staatz, J. (1985), 'Designing marketing systems to promote development in the third world countries. Agricultural markets in semi-arid tropics', *Proceedings of the International Workshop, 24 - 28 October 1983,* ICRISAT Center, India.

Shaffer, J.D. (1987), *Influencing the Design of Marketing Systems to Promote Development in Third World Countries,* MSU International Development Paper, Department of Agricultural Economics. Michigan State University.

Smit, J. (1995), 'Peri-urban vegetable production: An upcoming challenge of combinging urban planning and food supplies in cities', in J. Richter, W.A. Schnitzler and S. Gura (eds), *Vegetable Production in Peri-Urban Areas In the Tropics and Subtropics - Food, Income and Quality of Life,* Feldafing: German Foundation for International Development (DSE) and Council for Tropical and Subtropical Agricultural Research (ATSAF).

Stevens, R.D. and C.L. Jabara (1988), *Agricultural Development Principles - Economic Theory and Empirical Evidence,* Baltimore: John Hopkins University Press.

Uli, J. (1991), 'Adoption of vegetable market gardening as cash raising activity among the Bidayuh farmers in Siburan', *Sawarak Museum Journal,* Vol. 42:63, pp.177-192.

Warmbier, W. and Böttcher, D. (1984), *Vermarktung von Agrarprodukten.* Bd.1, Handbuchreihe ländliche Entwicklung, Eschborn, Deutsche Gesellschaft fur Technische Zusammenarbeit (GTZ).

Williamson, O.E. (1975), *Markets and Hierarchies: Analysis and Antitrust Implications,* New York: Free Press.

Yachkaschi, J. (1996), *In-Depth Study on Production, Marketing and Consumption of Fruit and Vegetables in Urban and Peri-Urban Tanzania,* Institute for Horticultural Economics, University of Hannover (unpublished).

17 Urban Agriculture in Southern and Eastern Africa: Policy Questions and Challenges

BEACON MBIBA

Introduction

Despite successes in churning out volumes of information on the activity of urban agriculture in Southern and Eastern Africa since the late 1980s, it appears that there has been no corresponding success in terms of positive pro-active policies for this sector. There is a need on the part of those involved in information gathering exercises to develop appropriate techniques for affecting policy makers. Maybe the information on the activity is not very convincing or the evidence is sometimes contradictory. The challenge for urban agriculture and those with interest in it is to establish a proper place within the broader image and role of the city in national development. On the part of planners and social scientists, we have to boost our understanding of policy processes, and see to it that our research on urban agriculture captures the essential elements of these processes. We lack knowledge, skills and understanding of the policy processes and hence our failure to elevate urban agriculture from its current 'trivial' status to one of a respectable urban economic sector.

The Changing Challenges of Urban Agriculture; From Research to Action

The literature on urban agriculture is replete with complaints on the negative treatment which the sector has received from researchers, urban managers, and policy makers alike (e.g., Rakodi, 1985, p.53; Freeman, 1991, p. 121-22; Maxwell et al., 1992, p.2-3, p.55 - 57; Rogerson, 1993, p.41; Mougeot, 1994, p.11). At present there are passive support frameworks in Malawi, Lesotho, Zambia and Uganda while attitudes have changed for the better in Zimbabwe, Kenya, Tanzania, Botswana and Ethiopia. For example, in Isiolo, a drought area in Kenya, urban farmers are helped to dig irrigation furrows and plant crops (Smith, 1991, p.3). However, it may be fair to claim that with respect to research studies, almost all major cities in Southern Africa have been covered to such an extent that we now know most of the basics on socio-economic, environmental, spatial and legal aspects of the activity.   Most of the questions asked by researchers in the 1980s have already received reasonable answers, including those areas that Rakodi (1985, p.60) had offered as suggestions to be included in future research. Aspects of inputs and outputs, quantities and contributions have been assessed in all East African countries. Table 17.1 gives an overview of the cities where research has been carried out, and the main researchers who conducted it.

With reference to Dar-es-Salaam in 1995, a workshop participant from Tanzania made the following comment: 'Urban agriculture in Dar-es-Salaam supports a large portion of the population; it contributes to the micro and macro economies of the city, it contributes to food security, it adds value to hazard lands, it is illegal and it gives planners a hell of a headache' (Mtani, 1995).

Other than stressing the 'headache', this statement summaries the general mood and status of urban agriculture in the large cities of the region. Although the literature and strategies on urban agriculture cannot be comparable to the volumes witnessed on other sectors of the urban environment such as housing, we now have reasonable materials covering Europe (Smith et. al., 1994; Mbiba, 1995, Greenhow, 1994) covering Asian Cities (Smit 1994; Rogerson 1993; Yeung 1993) and on Sub-Sahara African Cities as given on Table 17.1. Primate cities of these areas have received the greatest attention with limited focus on medium size and small urban settlements.

The Scramble to Score

The period 1991 to 1995 has witnessed increased research activities in Sub-Saharan Africa. Serious efforts were made to establish the research record, the status, and the opportunities for urban agriculture (Egziabher et al., 1994). However, browsing through the literature makes it clear that institutionsare not coordinated; international NGOs, local NGOs, local governments, and research institutions, pursue 'enclave' programmes oblivious of efforts taking place down the road. Urban agriculture is regarded as a new 'eldorado' to be grabbed and exploited by whoever gets there first. This situation may be a contributing factor to the next 'grey area' i.e., the policy impact of these research and workshop activities.

Table 17.1   Researchers and Cities: Urban Agriculture in Southern and Eastern Africa

Major Cities	Major Research Works By
Lusaka	Rakodi, Sanyal, Mulenga
Nairobi (Kenya)	Mazingira Institute, Freeman, Lee Smith
Kampala	Maxwell and Zziwa
Addis Ababa	Egziabher
Lilongwe	Aipira
Harare (Zimbabwe)	Mazambani, Enda-Zim, Mbiba
Maseru	Phororo, Mbiba, Greenhow
Dar-es-Salaam	Mosha, Mvena (et al), Sawio
Johannesburg, Cape Town	Rogerson, UCT
Gaborone	Mosha
Maputo	(Materials not available)
Windhoek	Greenhow
Luanda	(Materials not available)

Despite revelations of the actual and perceived benefits of urban agriculture to the urban economy, most cities in the region do not have policies which vigorously support it. Absence of supportive or accommodative policies is cited as the major constraint inhibiting further benefits from this activity. The view of most commentators on this issue is that certain provisions should be vital components of that policy:

a   provide more land;

b   make use of waste water;

c   provide security for crops and gardens;
d   improve technologies;
e   initiate more demonstration projects;
f   carry out more research;
g   provide credit, loans and extension services.

Such a view, as this presentation would like to urge, is very limited. All the above are already available. The question is why they are not fully utilized? Development scientists may also be part of the problem, as far as this question is concerned.

The Concept and Image of the City

Up to the 1980s development scientists of the present century bequeathed to us a yet unresolved conceptualization problem; that of the African city. What is, and should be the city's role in national development; what is its relationship with the countryside; and what is its internal composition? In dealing with urban agriculture and policies for its growth, this conceptualization problem is fundamental in determining the absence or presence of a policy and the content of any policy that may exist. This presentation will seek to expose 'conceptualization of urban' as the most critical variable that militates against formulation of a coherent urban agriculture policy in Southern Africa. A policy solution to urban agriculture will not be found in urban agriculture as such but by taking the debate outside urban agriculture.

This also requires a good grasp of policy and planning within a clearly developed image and role of the city. For Southern Africa, the image of the city at present underplays economic processes and roles of urban settlements. Yet it is economic collapse and decay of city regions which needs to be addressed if the squalor, squatters, crime, deteriorating infrastructure and other problems are to be resolved. In the research and policy studies carried out so far, there is a glaringly weak blending of spatial approaches to city management with the economic and sociological dimensions of regional dynamics. Once resolved, it is within this framework that urban agriculture would find its proper place. It is also vital to define 'policy' and study how policies are formulated? The next section will outline the ingredients of policy and will discuss the considerations involved in policy formulation. Against this background, we will be able to evaluate the process of policy formulation vis a vis the urban agriculture sector.

What is Policy ? A Basic Sketch

A policy is a statement of intent giving broad guidelines on preferred actions to achieve a desired future. Such a guideline can be a feature of any institution (both private and public); we find policies at individual and family levels. Policy can be informal unwritten or very formal and written/documented. Both scenarios can exist in the public sector for which policy means 'statecraft; course of action adopted by government party, company etc.; a sagacious procedure' Gillingwater 1975, p.9).

According to this definition policy is an indispensable operational tool of organizations demanding the presence of experts to formulate and manage it. In this regard a more succinct view of policy is that by Alexander Hamilton, a lawyer and banker who served as secretary of the Treasury under George Washington (1790). The view is based on a sociological analysis of human beings which concludes that a state is always necessary to manage collective affairs of these beings:

> Matters of state require cool and steadfast minds and the charismatic leadership of the well educated and well bred. Ordinary people might confabulate about the goals and values of polity, but the serious business of devising policies ... must be left to experts. Government ... is a complicated science and requires ability and knowledge of a variety of other subjects to understand it (Friedman, 1987, p.3-4).

This definition is more wholesome because it ascribes to policy two major attributes namely facts and values. The facts and realities are what educated analysts will collect. But the values are the domain of those delegated with the duty to lead society i.e., the politicians. Consequently there are very few policy makers and a plethora of policy analysts - the planners. A fundamental message coming from this view is that policies are not only made to suit existing facts but are made in tandem with values of a given society as perceived by the politicians. Policy formulation thus requires knowledge of the policy environment and the problems at hand plus future expectations. Such knowledge derives from facts (collected by us planners) and values (possessed by a few through living in a given society and gaining wisdom applicable to that society

Activities and studies have only made reference to policy as an obstacle area without thorough attempts to unravel how policies can be adjusted. The question is how do we transmit our research output so that it impacts positively on policy makers? Most of those who seem to make such efforts, equate planners to policy makers and blame land use planners and land use laws for the slow progress in formal promotion of urban agriculture. To an extent planners are to blame especially in as far as they fail to articulate land use laws. These laws, generally derived from British Town and Country Planning laws do not prohibit urban agriculture. Rather they give the planner the room to use his/her discretion - using available technical knowledge and with adequate public consultation, to proceed and provide for use of land resources as optimally as possible. Consequently, in this process, if the planner considers urban agriculture to be a priority, existing legislation in Southern Africa does not prohibit from planning and designating for that activity.

Thus, if policy is law (written statements) then that policy in Southern Africa is in place and can be used positively to promote urban agriculture. But given the history of neglect and government of urban agriculture in the region it is necessary to promulgate new and explicit statements of support to bind all planners and urban managers to do something about urban agriculture. This draws us inevitably into a reflection of planners and policy makers. My submission is that planners generally are not policy makers. Policy making is the domain of politicians. Planners are tools of politicians and if we are to change the fortunes of urban agriculture, attention should now focus on politicians (local and national) to understand how they make policies and to influence that process. Politics and policy making are two sides of the same coin whose character development scientists and planners often neglect resulting in extreme frustration and conflicts. The message here is that as far as new policies on urban agriculture are concerned, politicians and policy makers have a greater role to play than planners. However, they need to be targeted.

From Knowledge to Action

We now have the knowledge on sectoral aspects of Urban Agriculture but not the policy aspect. Knowledge of how policies are made and how to influence that process rather than knowledge on the activity of Urban Agriculture is now the obstacle to sustainable Urban Agriculture in the region. Before putting energies on how strategies can be implemented, we need to invest on 'assessing' and 'influencing the political will and leadership of cities in the region. Sawio alluded to this by stating:

> For urban agriculture to prosper and for urbanites to enjoy the acclaimed benefits, the city government and planners need to demonstrate the will to include Urban Agriculture as an integral part of the built-up environment (Sawio,1993, p.9).

The same theme is considered as critical by Mbiba (1994; 1995) when focusing on institutional responses. An important issue is the extent of public consultation. This has been identified as a an issue which compounds the policy problem. The question is how to ensure that planning and policy processes capture as much as possible the views of the grassroots in the policy development process.

For those who do not have an adequate participatory environment the *governance* theme currently in vogue is an appropriate framework within which to follow up on the issue of bringing/enabling society to fully articulate its vital needs, and influence the urban agriculture policy of the authorities. Such an effort comes up against the question of equity and plurality of urban society. Protagonists will inevitably have to resolve questions such as entry point; the poor and the means of poverty alleviation; general urban food security and employment. Because of the plural nature of urban society, however, it is difficult to reach a consensus as to the value at any given activity. This is why there have been repeated failures to reach a coherent response on this vital issue.

References

Aipira, H. et al. (1993), *Urban Farming in Low Income Cities*, Unpublished Proceedings of The First Workshop on Urban Farming: Strategy for Food and Environmental Health in Low Income Cities, York University, UK.

Bohrt, J.P. (1993), *Urban Agriculture Research in Latin America: Record Capacities and Opportunities*, Ottawa: Cities Feeding People Series, IDRC (The International Development Research Centre, Canada). Report no. 7.

Egziabher, A.G., Lee-Smith, D., Maxwell, D.G., Memon, P.A., Mougeot, L.J.A., and Sawio, C.J. (1994), *Cities Feeding People, An Examination of Urban*

Agriculture in East Africa, Ottawa: IDRC (The International Development Research Centre, Canada).

Fisher, R. and Ury, W. (1987), *Getting to Yes, Negotiating Agreement Without Giving In,* London: Arrow Books.

Forester, J. (1989), *Planning in the Face of Power,* Berkeley: California University Press.

Freeman, B.D. (1991), *A City of Farmers, Informal Urban Agriculture in the Open Spaces of Nairobi, Kenya,* Montreal: McGill-Queen's University Press.

Friedman, J. (1987), *Planning in the Public Domain, From Knowledge to Action,* Princeton: Princeton University Press.

Gillingwater, G. (1975), *Regional Planning and Social Change.* Aldershot: Gower.

Greenhow, T. (1994), *Urban Agriculture, Can Planners Make a Difference? Cities Feeding People Series,* Ottawa: IDRC (The International Development Research Centre, Canada), Report no. 12.

Lamba, D. (1993), *Urban Agriculture in East Africa, Record, Capacities and Opportunities,* Cities Feeding People Series, Ottawa: IDRC (The International Development Research Centre, Canada), Report no. 2.

Lee-Smith, D. (1992), 'Experience in Research and Networking on Urban Issues', Paper presented in the *Rupsea Conference on Urban Management in Eastern and Southern Africa,* Lilongwe.

Maxwell, D. and Zziwa, S. (1992), *Urban Farming in Africa, The Case of Kampala, Uganda.* Nairobi: ACTS Press.

Mbiba, B. (1994), 'Institutional Responses to Uncontrolled Urban Cultivation in Harare, Prohibitive or Accommodative?' *Environment and Urbanisation,* Vol. 6, pp. 188-202.

Mbiba, B. (1995), *Urban Agriculture in Zimbabwe, Implications for Urban Management and Poverty.* Aldershot: Avebury.

Mtani, A.W. (1995), 'Urban Agriculture in Dar-es-Salaam', Paper presented at a Workshop on *Environmental, Social and Economic Impacts of (Illegal) Urban Agriculture in Harare,* University of Zimbabwe, Harare, 30-31 August.

Mougeot, R.J.A. (1994), *Urban Food Production, Evolution, Official Support and Significance,* Cities Feeding People Series, Ottowa: IDRC (The International Development Research Centre, Canada), Report no. 8.

Rakodi, C. (1985), 'Self-Reliance or Survival? Food Production in African Cities with Particular Reference to Zambia', *African Urban Studies,* Vol. 21, 53-63.

Sawio, C.J. (1994), *Urban Agriculture Research in East Central Africa, Record, Capacities and Opportunities,* Cities Feeding People Series, Ottawa: IDRC (The International Development Research Centre, Canada). Report no. 1.

Simme, J.M. (1974), *Citizens in Conflict, The Sociology of Town Planning,* London: Hutchinson (for the Open University).

Smit, J. and Nasr, J. (1992), 'Urban Agriculture for Sustainable Cities, Using Wastes and Idle Land and Water Bodies as Resources', *Environment and Urbanisation*, Vol. 4, 141-152.

Smit, J. and Sommers, P. (1994), *Promoting Urban Agriculture, A Strategy Framework for Planners in North America, Europe and Asia*, Cities Feeding People Series, Ottawa: IDRC (The International Development Research Centre, Canada), Report no. 9.

Yeung, Y. (1993), *Urban Agriculture Research in East and Southeast Asia, Record, Capacities and Opportunities*, Cities Feeding People Series, Ottawa: IDRC (International Development Research Centre, Canada), Report no. 6.

18 The Role of Non-Governmental Organizations in Agricultural Development

OBIORA IKE

Introduction: Born To Die - The Situation of the World's Poor

The facts on the ground show that there are certain unacceptable inadequacies in our world such as the news that:

More than 1 billion people live in absolute poverty and more than half of them go hungry daily;
- More than 2 million children die annually of easily preventable infectious diseases;
- About one and a third million people, roughly a quarter of humanity, lack access to safe drinking water;
- Over 120 million people worldwide are officially unemployed; 80 million children don't even attend primary school (Editorial, EarthAction, 1994).

Meanwhile, global military spending, despite a decline since the end of the Cold War, still equals the combined income of the poorest half of humanity. This is an unjust, unfair and inhuman situation which needs to be challenged and changed.

The Case of Nigeria

With all its resources in human, material, space and otherwise potentials of wealth, Nigeria as many other African nations are agriculturally dependent, import food, are agriculturally under-productive, and lack adequate modern agricultural technology basic services. Most vital needs are often not met and the various global pronouncements on freedom, civilization, or technological progress are but pep-talk.

The citizenry are hungry and many of them die young. The cities are overcrowded. Lagos, Kano and Ibadan have a population of about ten million each. This morbid picture of Nigeria (and this is as a paradigm of many Societies) is the result of a combination of several lacunae. Some of the main ones are:

a   basic education for the majority of people;
b   basic healthcare, clean water and sanitation;
c   basic children's immunization;
d   women and material care ;
e   adult literacy programmes;
f   proper nourishment;
g   decent housing, jobs and a free environment.

The ingredients for agricultural productivity are not absent. Land, labour and even capital are available. However, agricultural output is only about 10 percent of the Nigeria's GNP, while the agricultural population is about 60 percent of the total (FAO, 1994). Explanations to this anomaly are available, but the practical remedies are not forthcoming. How can we feed 120 million mouths by importing food and exporting crude oil as was actually the case in the 1970s and 1980s. Young people are still abandoning the rural villages for the cities, to do nothing! As a result of insufficient job opportunities the crime rate is increasing. Agriculture is still said to be the mainstay of the developing nations, but it fails to provide a solution. This is the setting that activates NGOs into action. An example of the activities of one of them, and its communal impacts is provided below.

The Justice and Peace Farms - A Model

CIDJAP (Catholic Institute for Development, Justice, Peace and Caritas) is a non-governmental, research oriented, and non-profit charitable and religious-humanitarian organization. It is located in Enugu, Nigeria. Its motto is, 'To teach by doing'. In 1986, supported by good people, it established the Justice and Peace Farms in the rural Community of Ugwuomu Nike, approximately 25 kilometers from the city of Enugu (a city has about 2 million people). Most of the approach road leading to the farm is in poor condition. It is untarred and erosion-aggressed. The local and the

State governments have not given a listening ear to the repeated requests to repair the roads. Yet, despite the hard conditions, the farm supplies a large percentage of the food needs of the State. Furthermore, CIDJAP also works in several rural communities in Nigeria in the campaign against hunger, ignorance, disease and injustice. Some of its activities which it promotes are listed below

The size of the Peace Farm land is approximately 190 hectares. It contains two sizeable lakes and several permanent streams. Much of the land is covered by a low evergreen forest, which is used as a source of timber and firewood. The goals of the Farm, as stated by the time of its foundation, included:

to make agriculture more attractive and lessen emphasis on crude oil and other productive areas;
- to encourage young people in the locality to stay at home instead of migrating to the big cities;
- to increase food production by raising a variety of livestock and crops;
- to improve the living conditions of the adjoining rural populations (about 15000 people) by promoting and improving education, sanitation, health, and social services);
- to become self-reliant by adopting strategies of profitable agricultural maximization;
- to create co-operative farming in the original spirit of moshav and kibbutz (i.e., encouraging mutual help and solidarity);
- to promote environmental productivity and alternative, sustainable, farm systems;
- to encourage others to start such projects no matter how small;
- to improve self-help and pave the way for sustainable improvement in the living conditions of the people, especially the poor.

CIDJAP and Linkages to Other NGOs

CIDJAP is recognized by the pontifical Council on Justice and Peace in the Vatican and is a registered Non-Governmental Organization in Nigeria, under the Corporate Affairs Commission. CIDJAP has links and co-operation agreements with various local, regional and international organizations, and has carried out certain agricultural projects together with these organizations for a full decade, i.e., since 1986. A few of the institutions that are relevant to the themes of the workshop are:

a   The Centre for International Agricultural Development Co-operation (CINADCO) of the Ministry of Agriculture, Israel;
b   The Barneveld International College, The Netherlands;
c   The Landesregierung, Vorarlberg, Austria;
d   The Landwitschaftliche Berufschule, Hohenems, Austria;
e   The School of Agriculture, Nieder Osterreich;
f   The International Institute of Tropical Agriculture (IITA) Ibadan, Nigeria;
g   The Catholic Agency For Development And Peace, Montreal, Canada;
h   The German Catholic Bishop's Organization for Development Co-Operation (MISEREOR) Aachen;
i   The Pontifical Missionary Works in Aachen, Germany;
j   The IRED (Innovations et Reseaux Pour Le Development) Niamey, Nigeria Republic;
k   The Theological Faculties of The Universities of Bonn and Frankfurt (Germany), and Tilburg (The Netherlands);
l   The Enugu State University of Science and Technology (Esut), Enugu, and The University Of Nigeria, Nsukka (UNN).

CIDJAP's link with the FAO; UNICEF; UNDP; UN-NGLS, and other UN agencies, has continued to grow in content and extent. Its general purposes can be summarised as follows:

a   CIDJAP promotes human values and its orientation via education and social ethics; Catholic social teaching, training, and leadership Programmes; alternative financing; lobbying for the weakest and the socially marginalized. It is also engaged in teaching management and organization skills and in the development of relevant, adaptable and appropriate technologies in the context of Nigerian socio-economic conditions.

b   CIDJAP acts both as a facilitator and an agent for development in co-ordination with donors and partner agencies, attempting to help the rural and urban populations to respond adequately to the many problems of our society. It believes in the benefit of strengthening the culture of human societies, and also in democratization, the efficient management of goods, and the promotion of advocacy for human rights and dignity, and the sharing of experiences which lead to mutual benefit and partnership.

In carrying out practical projects, we have enriched others and have also been enriched. Only when humanity realizes that 'what affects you affects me', shall there be a better integrated response to the social question worldwide. The Christian Apostle St. Paul realized this fact when in the year 63 he wrote: 'No one lives for himself alone' (Gal. 2:20 or ROM. 14:18).

Sustainable Agriculture and Rural Development (SARD)

The Environment and Development file of the United Nations Non-Governmental Liaison services (NGLS) carried a dossier in the third volume (No. 8) of December 1994. This publication is very rich in its analysis of the development problems, and contains many observations that are especially relevant to our area of discussion.

Theis publication, called SARD (Sustainable Agriculture and Rural Development), was compiled by FAO for NGLS. Its purpose was to suggest 'how to harmonise agricultural Development with nature in order to respond to the growing realisation that modern agricultural practices are simply not sustainable and will not ensure food and fibre needs into the coming century' (FAO, 1994). The various points raised in the document which deal with Agenda 21 and follow-up of the UNEC need serious re-study. The basic point is that development concerns people - agriculture is a fundamental dimension of development. But agriculture without ecological responsibility is dangerous. The *mad cow* disease, which was a public concern in the United Kingdom in 1996, may be an example of this situation. The forces at work are numerous: Soil erosion, depletion of aquifers, pollution of water sources, loss of biodiversity, high vulnerability to crop and animal diseases, waste of resources and the demise of rural communities due to rural depopulation; heavy reliance on chemical pesticides and fertilisers, mechanical energy replacement of human labour, have made the role of NGOs urgent, relevant and highly necessary.

Non-governmental organisations are called and urged to fill a gap between the people and the Government; between the people and the environment; between the north and the south; between the people and their foreign world ever in change and dynamism; between the Government and its lack of orientation, or rather lost identity. Non-Governmental Organisation's in the language of SARD are called to champion the 'battle for recognition of the social and environmental damage being caused by economic growth, terms of exchange on world markets and the increasing divorce between natural processes and agricultural development' (FAO, 1994).

This role can be carried out in manifold ways. The following is an attempt to present, in a brief outline, and not necessarily exhaustively or in order of priority, the various roles of NGOs.

a   To establish a dialogue and provide opportunities for exchange of experiences between governments, international organisations, academic and training institutions, so as to enrich the traditional concepts surrounding development and to encourage the emergence of innovative points of view with regard to the fight against poverty;

b   To create networks and linkages. People in developing countries require partners to participate in their processes of development and liberation. NGOs have a function here: to link up groups and organisations between the developing and industrialised societies, which can offer bold and enduring partnerships.

c   NGOs feature particularly in facilitating and promoting Development Programmes of disadvantaged or oppressed population groups, such as cultural minorities, women, children, agricultural labourers, migrant labourers, refugees and victims of political persecution. These programmes aim to facilitate the organisation of self-help structures and activities by these groups, or may offer protection against human rights violations.

d   Agricultural improvement must be people centred. NGOs move from thought to action, from theory to practice. It is not just saying but doing. The approach of the Justice and Peace Farms is based on asking 'what has one achieved' rather than on 'what has one theorised'.

e   The need and the search for self-reliant options, self-financing, do it yourself methods, 'Help to self-help' is most credible and reliable method of doing development which many NGOs can use, against the dependency and cheap commercialisation antics of traders and some multinationals which believe in manipulation, dependency, and perpetual hegemony. Governments and international bodies are not dependable. Food is traded for a vote at the United Nation lobby. The NGOs role is, therefore, to assist people, so as to strenghten their desire for independence and self-help, and to enable people to shape their own lives, both as individuals and communities, as they themselves wish.

f   Because people develop and liberate themselves, NGOs can only play the role of support through solidarity and development co-operation which involves exerting influence wherever there is a need, especially in cases of injustice and violence. This is called advocacy.

g   It should become clear in the field of agricultural development that the purpose of any development project is to sustainably improve the lives of the people. This is possible if there are long-term processes in which the people clearly recognize their situation, learn to understand how they can change it through their own efforts and with the assistance of others acquire the will and capability to take whatever action is necessary with courage and responsibility. NGOs must measure their success by how far they assist self-confident communities to become agents of self-development.

h   In the areas of basic education, primary health-care, rural development, urban development, human rights issues and democratic participation, NGOs can show how the inter-link creates relevant dynamism which catapults development towards expected heights.   There is need, therefore, for such activities to integrate a number of sectoral approaches. Agriculture and animal husbandry are improved, taking into account both economic and ecological criteria.   Access to natural resources such as water, land and forests is improved and rights are allocated more fairly.   People's long-term security and sense of responsibility towards the natural resource base on which their lives depend increase if and when they also have access to markets, to credit and savings programmes; to basic health services, to basic education, and to extension inputs.   They also increase where people are able to build resources and form capital themselves rather than always losing it as a result of inappropriate agricultural policies,

i   Even in urban development environments, NGOs can help people own a small piece of land to live on, plant on, and trade the goods grown on it. They can organize self help, vocational training structures, relevant to local employment prospects, and even create small business establishments. Especially in the urban centres, there is need for greater decentralization of agricultural programmes geared towards enabling people to participate more actively. With less government interference at each level there should also be less taxes. However, to make such a process work NGOs must form pressure groups with clear and articulate plans.

j   The aim of NGOs must remain to enable people, especially the poorest, to reach to a certain measure of satisfying their basic needs for food, shelter and a healthy environment, through 'educating the spirit and preserving our planet, not ignoring the ancient, traditional wisdoms of humanity' especially of the developing countries.

Conclusions

Permit me to conclude with some observations, for as we draw near to the close of the Twentieth century we owe ourselves a reckoning.

Many people would definitely agree with me that this century was history's bloodiest. It gave us besides several regional and local wars two world wars which claimed in a brutal manner the lives of more than a hundred and fifty million persons. Beyond the war dead, there were also millions of prisoners of war, refugees, destruction of goods and property, and numerous displaced persons and helpless migrants. Psychologically, socially and morally shattered persons still abound in our midst and we are yet to cope with all the consequences. What is however worrisome is that as we approach the Twenty-first century, there is no guarantee that it could not be bloodier. The indices on the ground are too sad to allow laughter or joy. The poor are getting poorer. Hunger is increasing. Africa is impoverished. Jobs are not easy to find. The result is that many people abandon their homes for 'free slavery', i..e., they prefer to die as refugees, or even live in prisons in various countries in Europe or America, rather than live as free persons in their own African homelands.

The achievements mankind was able to make in technology, science, spacecraft medicine, agriculture, education, political information and communication, social and economic achievements reduce our present world to a *global village*. However, we still miss the human achievements which can usher in a new era for peace, progress and prosperity for mankind in the approaching new millennium. The risk is still there that if the lessons of the Twentieth century are not learnt from the ashes we see, we shall repeat the mistakes of this century even in the Twenty-first century (God forbid).

References

Editorial, (1994), EarthAction Parliamentary Alert. EarthAction International Office Newsletter, London: Social Summit Background Information, February issue.

FAO (1994), *SARD (Sustainable Agriculture and Rural Development), Environment and Development File*, Geneva: FAO Newsletter, vol. 3, no. 8.

19 Three Israeli Approaches to Development Projects in Africa (Abstracts)

a Managed Farm Development Enterprise (M.F.D.E.) and Transfer of Technology in Agriculture

MICHAEL ATZMON

In recent years, the Israeli Center for International Agricultural Development (CINADCO), has conceived the development of integrated agricultural projects by linking private or individual enterprise with public incentives.

This implies in many cases the establishment of core farms that not only produce and market selected commodities, but also encourage small-holders in the vicinity to produce the same or similar commodities. In such cases the core farm not only produces but also supports production on other holdings by supplying know-how, inputs, extension and marketing service.

The role of government in such cases is to provide a basic infra-structure and some financial resources for an adequate research and extension delivery system (R&D). The government also has an indicative role to play in assuring an acceptable return paid by the core farm enterprise for produce supplied by small-holders.

This approach is called 'Managed Farm Development Enterprise' (MADE) and operates successfully in a number of projects in different developing countries. The theory behind MFDE, as explained above, is the establishment of a central 'core farm' in a rural area, in the midst of farmers and farming villages. The functions of the 'core farm' can be summarized as follows:

a   to operate under both commercial as well as semi-commercial conditions;
b   to carry out farm experiments and demonstrations;

c   to train manpower at different levels, on theoretical and practical
     agricultural aspects;
d   to act as a centre for input supplies, i.e. seeds, fertilizers, or pesticides;
e   to act as a centre for the marketing of agricultural produce (outputs);
f   as a basis for the establishment of an agro-industry;
g   as a basis for rural organizations (associations or cooperatives).

b   **Agro-Ecological Aspects of the Peri-Urban Process**

     RAANAN KATZIR

The paper discusses the many social, economic and environmental changes
caused by the confrontation between the continuing urbanisation process and
the surrounding rural areas. The recent changes in the urban-rural
relationships have some positive aspects, such as the various ways in which
farms become specialized to meet the growing needs of the city for
agricultural products, agro-industry and agro-tourism. They generated
income from external trade, facilitated the provision of raw material for
handicrafts and local artisans as well as for many other transportation-
related businesses.

    However, the positive impact of the city was accompanied by less
desirable ones. After farm land is taken over by urban expansion, the
remaining farmland tends to be organised in small units, which may not
assure complete survival. Because of this, and for other reasons, part of the
family's income is derived from working in town. Many of those remaining
on the small farms intensify their operations and produce specialised,
perishable crops for the city by taking advantage of the marketing potential
resulting from proximity of the urban centres. Their production process
becomes relatively capital intensive. A further step would be agro-industry:
the processing of agricultural products such as fruits, vegetables, dairy and
poultry. This could go as far as preparing certain delicacies intended for
specialised shops or hotels.

    Farms near a big city also benefit from having easy access to labour and
from proximity to an international airport. A variety of sensitive agricultural
products can thus be taken quickly to markets in the richer countries in the
North. In their spare time, many urban residents will disperse into the
surrounding countryside to enjoy the scenery and panoramic views. They

will be looking for restaurants, recreation areas and campsites where they can spend a good time with their families in a healthy rural environment. Some farmers exploit the recreational market for agro-tourism and eventually they may even build hotels and centres for special events. Others may develop family industries like carpet weaving, woodcarving, and other crafts. Sometimes a whole village specialises in a certain craft or industry.

But intensive urbanisation is also creating extreme ecological disturbances, which are caused by sewage water, city garbage, industrial waste, and other pollutants. A large urban centre that includes industrial areas and nearby intensive agricultural production systems, may cause contamination of the underground aquifer by nitrates, chemical solubles and heavy metals. Also, the intensive use of water has led to water shortages in many areas. This necessitates the planning of large water supply projects. In the process, clean water becomes an increasingly economic commodity. There is need to set its price and to establish mechanisms for controlling and limiting its 'free' use.

Solid waste is another result of urbanisation that may have positive impart on agriculture. In developed countries, the daily average per capita production of refuse is around 3 to 5 kilograms. In developing countries the amounts are about 1 to 1.5 kilograms per day. In big cities this results in 'mountains' of refuse. These large amounts are main sources of contamination and result in many ecological disturbances. However, proper agro-ecological solutions can offer mutual benefits, both to farmers and to the city population. These include recycling sewage water for irrigation or changing refuse into compost and industrial waste into animal feed. If farmers use recycled urban water they should be assured that it has been sufficiently purified to be applied for edible vegetables or fruits, or use it only for irrigating ornamental, industrial, or fuel crops.

Water conservation techniques are increasingly important in urbanising areas. This includes the need to properly maintain water-conveying installations. In certain cases, especially where outdated and inefficient piping systems exist, water losses may reach 30 percent and even 50 percent.

To solve the ecological disturbances caused by garbage dumps, the minimal solution is to assign special areas for them. This should be far away from population centres. Their base must be sealed completely by plastics or other means in order to avoid the penetration of contaminated water into the underground aquifer. The daily amount of refuse should also be covered by soil to avoid flies and bad odours. Other solutions include the burning of biogaz from these dumps, separation of the various components for subsequent recycling and turning the organic component of the waste, which can be as high as 80 percent, into compost, in a form usable by farmers as a substitute for chemical fertilisers. Many industrial wastes could even be separated from other 'garbage' and be used directly as agricultural inputs. Examples are residues from cheese manufacturing, from extracting edible oil, from sugar refineries (molasses), and from the juice extracting industry. Most of these residues can be used directly for feeding animals. Intensive agricultural production around big cities not only produces its own contaminants; it is also very sensitive to diseases and pests. The common pesticides can be very toxic and dangerous to human beings living in their vicinity. The main solution to this form of ecological disturbance is the approach to pest control called the Integrated Pest Management (IPM) system. This involves the integration of agro-technical methods, resistant varieties, and biological controls instead of chemical control. Regular field monitoring to determine the exact biological conditions of pests and disease levels will thereby enable the use of proper amounts and applications of the different control systems and thus reduce the level of toxic residues on the plant products.

In developed countries with adequate economic resources, agro-ecological solutions are being applied, whereas in developing countries with less economic resources the ecological disturbances in the peri-urban areas are not dealt with sufficiently. Quite frequently, they are neglected completely. They create, therefore, hazardous conditions for both population and the environment.

c   Small-holder Centre Pivot Irrigation System in Senegal

SHAUL MANOR

Difficulties in achieving good performance in irrigating small plots are a serious limiting factor in the development of irrigation for small farmers. Although a significant effort has been made to promote a farmer-managed irrigation system, its performance is still far from meeting exceptions. Therefore, sometimes it might be difficult to justify economically investment in improved technology of irrigation for small plots.

An attempt is being made in Senegal to overcome problem's irrigation management in smallholdings. This is done by the introduction of a centre pivot irrigation system, and by strengthening the farmers' associations. In this case farmers need not be concerned about the operation and management of irrigation. Their plots, regardless of size or shape, will be irrigated with high efficiency by a single centre pivot that may cover an area of about 40 hectares. In this case farmers will continue to cultivate and manage their own lands but as an integral part of a program as planned by the farmers association. From the farmer's point of view it will be as if he will continue to practice rain-fed agriculture but with 'rainfall applications' given at given known dates. A special trained team among the farmers assigned by the association will take care of the operation and management of the whole system.

The demonstration of the centre pivot system is done in the Fossil Delta Valley of Senegal, in an area of dry climate and sandy soils, that is currently under development. With the introduction of the centre pivot system it will be possible to irrigate a wide range of field crops. The first step in the introduction of the system consists of establishing the associations, as part of a special programme of training that is expected to reach every single farmer. It is expected that a strong association will be capable of taking up some other tasks, including agricultural marketing.

This project may offer a real breakthrough in terms of agricultural production, and may become a model for similar developments. It is expected to raise the level of performance of the farmer-managed irrigation techniques, and may open new opportunities for smallholder's irrigation programmes. The paper provides detailed information on the model, on the project's organizational and social aspects, and on the characteristics of the technical aspects will be discussed.

20 Summary of the Open Discussions during the Netanya Workshop (June 23-27, 1996) and Concluding Remarks

THE EDITORS

The Netanya Workshop included four sessions at which participants were asked to present their own conclusions. The first session concentrated on the formation of growers' associations to face both access to land and to the consumers. The second session covered the transfer of technology for water management; the third ecological aspects of urban and peri-urban gardening and the fourth merely listed the mission statements that were asked from each participant after having lived through all paper presentations and discussions.

In the following sections we will quote as many of these concluding remarks as possible while answering the four basic questions that were asked in the introductory chapter. These questions were:

1   To what extent is urban and peri-urban farming a strategy among (poorer) urban households for food security?
2   To what extent is urban and peri-urban farming a serious way for households to secure a sustainable income?
3   To what extent is urban and peri-urban agriculture able to turn urban waste into a resource? The conclusions from the thematic discussion on 'ecological aspects of (peri-)urban agriculture' will be incorporated in the answer to this question.
4   And to what extent differ urban and peri-urban agriculture systematically on the above three topics?

As some of the thematic discussions do not really fit under these four headings we will deal with these separately:

5   The formation of growers' associations
6   The issues associated with water use and the transfer of technology.
7   Other, or miscellaneous, points and main conclusion.

1. Food Security

'Farming is a way of life' is what many gardeners interviewed would state, irrespective of where the researcher found her or him cultivating the land. Even commercial farmers would say the same thing when confronted with disheartening figures about the economics of their enterprise. Agriculture is considered a productive, and therefore responsible, way of spending free time in a healthy environment. This attitude towards gardening applies equally to the allotment gardener near the centre of London, Berlin or The Hague as to the woman in Maseru, Harare, Nairobi or Dar es Salaam growing tomatoes or rearing chickens on her residential plot, or maize on vacant land. However subjective, such strong sentiments for working the land explain much of the worldwide motive to practice farming in urban areas. Is it a feeling of self-sufficiency and therefore independence, that makes these people continue an activity that doesn't earn them as high a return on investment, notably labour, as economists would deem fit? Growing your own food, at least part of it, on whatever land you find available for that is indeed a mentally rewarding activity, even if it doesn't seem to make much sense from an economic point of view and in terms of quantities produced. Such activity may be laborious and much may be in vain, but more productive ways of spending one's time are often not available. One participant in the Netanya Workshop put it this way:

> This Workshop dealt on the one hand with urban agriculture (or more specifically urban horticulture) and on the other with feeding the urban population (and the urban poor in particular). These topics are sometimes confused, but they are distinctly different.

In other words, while urban agriculture is an essential source of food for substantial numbers of urban households it only covers a small proportion of the food demands of most of them. Even those households that spend considerable time and effort on urban farming obtain most of the staple foods (such as maize, cassava or yams) from bulk producers in the *rural* areas. This implies that urban and peri-urban agriculture can never provide enough food to completely feed an urban population. But it certainly helps. It also plays a far more important role when it comes to fresh vegetables, chicken and eggs, fruits and flowers.

This book focuses on Africa, but Africa is a varied continent. Hence, its chapters deal with areas having totally different climatic, economic and cultural conditions. The focus is also on urban areas. This implies, that within this variety each case presents a complex, heterogeneous society, with different population groups having different skills, tastes and **income levels.** This creates niches for producers and traders of fresh, perishable commodities that had previously been unknown or unmarketable to the area. Many of these niches have been discovered, developed and exploited by urban and peri-urban farmers. The researchers whose findings are reported here also show, however, the kind of obstacles against the exploitation of these supposed niches. For instance:

> Lesotho exports water to South Africa and has to buy its vegetables in return. More research is needed to find out how local vegetable production can be increased on the small plots available within and around urban areas.

All relevant resources, as well as consumers' market, seem to be there, but local Lesotho producers have so far not been able to outsmart their South-African competitors. The answer learned from other societies is that it is necessary to *specialise* and concentrate on those commodities, which have relative advantage, i.e., those of whose local production would be cheaper or more in line with the local taste than that originated in other areas. This is usually achieved where local conditions are favourable both in terms of knowledge among the producers and because of unique climate and soils conditions. The growers in and around the towns can always have advantage over more remote producers for some of the marketing processes. But, their benefits not solely related to pure accessibility and low transportation costs. They also consist of confidence and advertising. Such niches are found by trial and error, but as the case of Jos has shown, the fame of local quality goods may quickly spread to outside consumer markets.

2. Income

The various authors in the volume could be categorised into on the one hand those analysing a farming system and advising how it could be consolidated or improved, and on the other hand those involved with farmers and actively trying to improve their position. They could also be divided into those who focus on the urban subsistence farmers using vacant land and those who describe the emergent commercial farmers. The latter are less common in the urban areas proper (in and between the residential or industrial neighbourhoods) but numerous in the peri-urban area (just outside the built-up area in general). The following citation is typical for the first in both distinctions: 'Urban farming as an activity is the result of urban poverty rather than a lasting solution to urban problems like food supply and employment generation.' Someone else in the same category put it as follows: 'The urban food system needs to be placed in the context of the urban poor: on illegal sites and in small gardens they aim at production for the market but mostly end up eating the little they grow.' They made the following recommendation: 'In order to escape from the circle of poverty small-scale growers need clear and reliable credit schemes, including the acceptance of the need to repay loans with interest.' But other authors are more involved with the commercial, true market gardeners, at whatever small scale they may operate. These authors do not deny the need for credit, but they are also aware of the fact that the more business-like farmers are able to find credit if and when they need it. For them, it is more a matter of organisation, of effectively and jointly facing the outside world and of finding reliable allies in this outside world of greedy suppliers, middlemen and civil servants. Among these authors optimism is more widespread: 'Despite the many obstacles (e.g. water, pollution, land tenure) small-scale growers near urban areas seem to have advantages over those further away. In exploiting these advantages they should not overlook the tourist industry and the production of flowers and herbs.' To them, the poor performance of many market gardeners is not caused by their own poverty, but: 'The fundamental tragedy of African societies during the present era is the downfall of purchasing power of the middle class, and of the civil service in particular.'

Market gardeners, at least most of those operating in peri-urban rather than in urban areas, are professional, resourceful and inventive people. Their generally low income, as compared with market gardeners in the western world, is not a result of being 'urban farmers', but of the organisational hardships and the socio-economic setting of the societies in which they have to operate. As long as their business surroundings remain unreliable there is little hope for further advancement beyond the level of being relatively well off compared with the urban poor who lack access to peri-urban land.

3. Urban Waste and General Ecological Aspects

The main synergy expected from urban and peri-urban farming is its utilisation of urban waste products in exchange for fresh agricultural produce, in other words: its presumed ability to turn waste into an asset. How seriously are our African farmers doing this and how successful are they? The small-scale growers in and around Jos are using urban waste for sure, both sewage water and solid waste and there is enough historical evidence that gardeners around at least the Sahelian cities have been doing so for centuries. They are, however, far from sure whether this is still an asset to them as they experience daily how tricky this waste has become over the last few decades: with modern components like batteries, plastics and new industrial effluents. None of the case studies presented in this book refer to attempts to systematically treat or at least monitor urban waste flows. Those present at the Workshop in Netanya could learn a lot from the experiences in Israel. We were told and actually saw part of the Israeli schemes of recycling water and using the final effluents of urban sewerage to irrigate non-food crops. The warning from Israel is clear: 'Do not combine waste water treatment with vegetable production, but use treated water for crops like cotton or flowers.' This is the safe way. It specifies the rather vague statement that: 'Sustainable agricultural production means the right crop at the right place at the right time'.

In practice (peri-)urban growers all over the world do not use the safe way. They use a more tricky one instead, growing any profitable crop, most likely food crops, on soils and with water of dubious quality hoping that the pollutants will not reach the products that are taken to the market for human consumption. We couldn't go back and tell those around African cities irrigating their crops from streams that are fed by sewerage effluents to stop vegetable production immediately and turn to pot plants, flowers or ornamental trees. Less radical but still rather ambitious would be to demand for routine chemical and micro-organic analysis of both the inputs like irrigation water and manure and the products sold to the market. But there is definitely an urgent need for reliable, low-cost laboratory facilities, run by neutral institutions like a public health (inspection) department. Only when confronted with convincing test results, that are also available to the general public, individual urban farmers can be made to change their practice, crops or production site. This implies outside support, technical, organisational and financial, for such institutions to become well established.

What applies to irrigation water that is used by both commercial and subsistence growers in and around town, also applies to many growers on vacant land during the rainy season. Vacant land can be heavily polluted land. This can be particularly dangerous to families who consume their total production themselves. It is not only a matter of not knowing about the dangers to human health of certain farming techniques and inputs and suddenly being made aware of these. Equally important is to accept that the situation for urban and peri-urban farming is highly unstable. What has been perfectly safe for the last decades can suddenly become dangerous as a result of any new urban activity or investment:

> The confrontation between urban expansion and the peri-urban rural systems not only leads to continuous adaptations to farming patterns, but also to ecological disturbances and imbalances. Lack of economic resources should not be an excuse for neglecting the latter. Proper agro-ecological solutions need to be sought to combine recycling waste water and garbage with agricultural inputs like irrigation, compost and animal feeds.

One needs a separate Workshop, with experts on environmental hazards, in order to turn this general concern into practical yardsticks and solutions that would really bring about the type of synergy, which policy makers expect nowadays from urban agriculture. This Workshop drew attention to ecologically sensitive gardening practices and inputs: the need to avoid environmental and resource degradation and pollution, but also to encourage sustainability, conservation, high quality production and high environmental quality. It was stressed that these objectives can be achieved by low-cost environmental reclamation and rehabilitation techniques, by organic gardening making use of compost manure in combination with aquaculture, and by avoiding over-use of inorganic fertilisers or of the soil. The harmful effect of leaded petrol used by cars through lead poisoning in roadside vegetables was pointed out. In addition, participants discussed various practices that prevent excessive evaporation, spread of weeds, high salt concentration, hardening of the soil and erosion/gullying, among others. The use and advantages of plastic mulching and solar-sterilisation of the soil were mentioned as useful to contain weeds in gardens. It was agreed that there is need for legislation regarding ecological considerations in farming in general and in urban and peri-urban gardening in particular. This is also in view of the methane gas from urban wastes, the industrial wastes that pollute soil and irrigation water sources or lead from petrol fumes polluting fruits and vegetables. Thus such legislation should try and protect the gardeners, the soil, water and products as well as the environment generally from the activities of both the growers and the urban and industrial activities.

The ecological conclusion from this Workshop can be summarised in the words of one participant: 'We really have to do something about the sustainability of human and natural resources'.

4. Urban and Peri-Urban Agriculture

At the end of the Workshop there was considerable doubt as to whether the distinction between urban and peri-urban farming was made convincingly clear. One participant concluded as follows: 'We have not yet made clear what we mean by Urban and Peri-urban Agriculture and our research efforts on how to use open spaces in and around towns for the production of food and flowers has not yet resulted in information that convinces policy makers'. Another said: 'The term 'peri-urban' remains confusing'.

These are clear warnings, but even so we made some progress. An interesting conclusion to us was, for instance, that the papers from Zimbabwe in particular, which focussed on the very low-input, predominantly rain-fed gardens, were also those referring to the use of vacant, urban land. For them, the peri-urban, intensive and relatively large-scale, commercial market gardening around cities like Harare, which is still dominated by white growers, was not a topic for research. On the other hand, the paper by Dijkstra, which concentrated on Kenyan horticulture in general, warned us not to expect much in terms of food security from the growers in urban areas. Such findings reinforce one another. Farming within an urban agglomeration means relatively little in term of income and quantities produced, but is important in terms of a productive hobby, of subsistence for low-income urban residents, and of maintaining 'green lungs' that produce oxygen for often highly polluted population clusters.

However, there is more to be considered: 'In the process of urban growth productive agricultural fields are turned into residential plots where crops are grown for fun or home consumption instead of for the market'. In Lesotho this runs against the desire to become less dependent on food supplies from neighbouring countries (75% of Maseru's food comes from

South Africa). Urban growth turns comfortable peri-urban farmers into hard-pressed urban farmers. As long is the city is nearby: 'The advantage of proximity to a city and to the markets in general is in itself a good reason to advise peri-urban market gardeners on increasing their productivity, security and prosperity'. But once the town is at their doorstep we need to say: 'Almost by definition, urban farmers will have a hard time. It may sometimes be better to stop urban farming altogether and help those concerned to either find a better place to farm or other means of acquiring incomes'. In other words, in the distinction between peri-urban and urban we are dealing with a highly dynamic situation. We can expect a great deal of inventiveness from those who find themselves in it: 'The overlap between the city as an expanding amoeba and an adjusting rural system is found all over the world. In this adjustment process we should be confident that there is always a way for certain categories of people, such as market gardeners, of organising themselves without confrontation'.

However, without some support from the outside world such organising does not get the sector far enough. There will be too much uncertainty. The process from peri-urban to urban is worth steering diligently:

> In order to achieve sustainability for individual market gardeners in the urban and peri-urban area a relocation may sometimes be necessary. In this process, the farmers affected need and deserve organised assistance as the best way of compensation in kind. Organised assisted relocation is the key to success of small-scale but highly skilled market gardeners.

In other words, not only do urban farmers, whose land is needed for building, deserve a decent compensation for their loss of production capacity. We may also conclude that in many cases the best type of compensation is not in cash but in the form of alternative, properly serviced land. This could be a well laid out complex of allotment gardens in an urban or peri-urban setting. It could also be a modern block of horticultural smallholdings in a peri-urban area with good access to irrigation water, or good farmland further away. Local governments and agriculture ministries have an important role to play in this.

Geographers and cartographers have an important role to play when it comes to giving peri-urban and urban farmers the right type of support. Policy makers tend to refer to one or two specific locations they know about, which represent only one type of farming, while there are many. How widespread is each type and where is it found?

In the absence of up-to-date maps and aerial photographs satellite images can provide a useful tool to identify present and potential areas for market gardening. This tool won't replace fieldwork but makes it easier and more accurate. Provided the necessary hard- and software is available to process satellite imagery, not much effort is required to produce the relevant, regional landuse maps.

The term 'geography' was hardly used during this workshop. Nevertheless, both the papers and our discussions had a strong geographical component. For instance, each time somebody asked whether a certain experience could be transferred to Africa a geographical question was asked. Also the issue of urban farming being different from peri-urban and from rural farming and different for each type of city, is a geographical one. Thirdly, our common concern about the ecological problems of urban farming is a problem of man-land relationships and hence a geographical concern. And fourthly, geography features in assessing the relevance of human, economic and physical infrastructure.

5. The Formation of Growers' Associations

It seems as if we have to accept that in all societies the access to land differs between different population groups. Where land is scarce it is only by teaming up, that those who need to use it would be able to take it over from those who sit on it without putting it to a meaningful use. This puts the persons responsible for allocating land between competing users in a crucial position. Although there are objective ways available to assist them, in Africa the issue is politically that sensitive, that these are rarely applied. In the chapter by FORD one such structured way of making the allocation more objective is mentioned: using GIS he has successfully worked with villagers in Kenya on a Multiple Objectives Land Allocation System.

It was observed that land-tenure problems are most severe where there are migrants without land at the bottom of the social structure. Governments tend to help certain categories of such migrants, but not all. In Tanzania the land tenure system is presently under review in Parliament. One of the outcomes will be that gardeners in urban areas can be given 4-year leases on the land they farm. But there is scepticism whether this would be enough. Experience elsewhere in Africa has taught us that, where towns grow onto communal land, the farmers tend not to be properly compensated for loss of farm business and investment. This is unlike the freehold or leasehold farms around many towns in Southern Africa, where normal market forces operate with regard to land that is under urban pressure. In other words, unlike a proper title deed, the right of occupancy is not enough for farmers in peri-urban areas to invest in their land. Such a farmer would know that the government can make him forego such investment at short notice with meagre financial compensation and (what is probably even more important) without obligation to find him a new site to continue. In addition, the implementation of whatever improved legislation will always be a major stumbling block. The designation of Green Belts around African cities is a case in point.

Should governments be urged to designate agricultural land in urban and peri-urban areas? The answer might be different for each of the three basic types of farming that were distinguished during the Workshop: gardening for home consumption, proper horticultural undertakings (market gardening) and the maize fields or other staple crops one often finds in open land between or within the built-up areas? The question is particularly pressing for the areas within a city that are not suitable for building, or are not zoned to any function yet, but have been put into productive uses by small-scale farmers (either for home consumption or for market production). Companies which are aware that such land is 'free' and only needs some reclamation to become suitable for building, could at any time invade it. What should a government do in such instances: support the developer and allow green areas in the city to become smaller and fewer all the time? Or support the farmers as providers of both food and 'green lungs' to the city dwellers by stopping the developers from invading into this land? Some would argue that this depends on the significance of urban farming, both in terms of food supply and in term of employment generation for urban residents. Others say, that it doesn't matter what planners decide as long as the farmers who want to carry on at a certain location organise themselves, lobby for their joint interests and face the government as a group. There was substantial agreement, for instance, that:

> The four papers from the Jos project team have demonstrated that it is absolutely necessary to enhance smallholders associations in order to arrive at sustainable marketing systems, to facilitate intensive on-farm training and extension work, for the mobilisation of cash to raise the level of independence of the farmers, to benefit from economies of scale, and for improved living conditions (including hours of rest). This requires international effort by researchers, community development workers, NGO's (local and international) and both governmental and multinational organisations.

Smallholders associations are, by definition, non-governmental organisations. However, the above quotation emphasises the need for outside assistance (e.g., advocating and mediating) by NGO's, including that from outside the continent. The odds are so much against local agricultural producers in urban settings in Africa, that outside support is essential for their advancement. In any case: 'Non-Governmental Organisations have an increasing role to play in the promotion of the wellbeing of all people involved in the market gardening system.' But how can this be done? One participant put it as follows in his conclusions from the Workshop:

> It is imperative to take good care of public relations, especially when the goal is formation of smallholders associations. This applies to the farmers on the one hand: build trust among the different ethnic groups and between the leadership and the followers. It also applies to the authorities: advocacy at the highest possible level for the removal of structural problems, such as those regarding land accessibility and stable use rights, urban waste composting, manure and urban and industrial pollution.

It also depends on the socio-economic conditions in an area, what alternatives the various interest groups would be able to choose. For some scientists the challenge is to make these alternatives clear by allocating different weights to the various interests and then use one of the computer models to show what land use would turn out to be the most appropriate at each location. For NGO's the challenge is different. For instance, the justice-oriented NGO's in Nigeria are becoming to have an impact in their advocacy with government departments on behalf of the less privileged groups, including farmers who are threatened by local governments taking their land for urban projects. The situation in Southern Africa seems less severe, as temporary designation (5 years) of agricultural land in urban areas is now an accepted planning instrument. But not all farming or gardening needs to be regulated or organised. Some just happens and is fun to observe:

> As many urban people tend to have a rural background we will always see some who want to farm, like the gatekeeper of a multi-storey office block who plants a couple of maize seeds next to the gate. Such farming just happens and doesn't need to be planned for.

6. Water Use and the Transfer of Technology

The basic concept of modern Israeli irrigated farming, 'You irrigate the plants, not the soil!' was used as a motto for this discussion. But the sophisticated water-saving devices as used in Israel need a completely different context from the ones presently found in most developing countries. This should include the institutional capacity to maintain these systems and enable farmers to leave devices like pumps or tubes for drip irrigation in their fields overnight without fear of theft. One of the Israeli participants stated that the situation is even more complex, as Israel has now started to use recycled sewage water on a large scale for irrigation in the South of Israel. Also brackish water is now increasingly used for new species of crops that thrive on it. Fish farming is increasingly combined with irrigation. In the face of such rapid sequences of innovations the opinions are divided. Some Israeli participants would maintain: 'Those in developing countries cannot learn from Israel's peri-urban and urban farming experiences.'

One reason not to expect much from such systems in Africa is that they operate when people are primarily geared at profit maximisation, whereas rural communities in Africa are mainly involved in risk minimisation. Even if this applies less to peri-urban market gardeners than to rural farmers the point is worth considering. Another reason is that the introduction of these new irrigation packages brings about a dependency by the growers on the services of those who introduced them. After they leave, such projects tend to collapse. 'Taking new production techniques and (hybrid) crop varieties to Africa harbours the danger of a new colonialism. How can this be averted?' Only large-scale farmers can afford to fly in experts whenever there is a problem: 'Do not create dependency when it is not necessary.'

It was, however, observed that for a researcher to state such drawbacks is one thing, but an agent of change has to do something with them. 'Researchers have a lot more work to do before they can ask policy makers to respond on the issues of urban farming.' Many of their recommendations are considered immature and impractical. Also, agents of change cannot wait for their results. Some are inclined to advise their clients to embrace radical innovations and face squarely the consequence: 'Do not improve step by step, but aim at 'Shortcuts to Change'. Accept that you need money for that and money is always available, provided you are willing to pay its price: you have to pay back with interest.' They would, for instance, help the small-scale growers to organise themselves in such a way that together they would be able to secure these services. This sparked a lot of discussion: 'There are no shortcuts to change. You can't just copy what is now practised in Israel and the main stumbling block is credit. It is not so much a problem of availability of money but of the ways in which it is distributed.' This made the agents of change in the Workshop conclude: 'We need to help decision makers in establishing links between available sources of credit and those in need of it.'

It is clear, that in this respect government departments have a crucial role to play as reliable partners, accepting that they are to be held responsible for specified inputs and services. It was also noted, that this is working quite well in a big project of smallholder farms (2 ha each) around the cities of Egypt. As far as water supply is concerned, the central question is: 'Should (market) gardeners like those in the Jos area be advised to adopt irrigation techniques that make themselves more dependent on the outside world, or should they be encouraged to remain self-reliant even if this limits their production?'

The answers are inclined to the latter. Reference was made to a FAO programme on low-cost irrigation that is presently operating on 30 plots in 16 countries in sub-Saharan Africa. The experience there is that small-scale gardeners should be allowed considerable independence regarding water sourcing, using their own pumps and making their own decisions. Referring specifically to situations like the Jos area this led to the following concrete recommendations:

a   use gravity irrigation as much as possible; and
b   form water users associations that have the authority to resolve disputes, to allocate water when there is a shortage, to expel members who disobey the rules or cheat, and to collect fees in order to keep the system up-to-date.

It was concluded that for small-scale gardeners to be successful it is essential, while maintaining a high degree of independence, to pool their resources to develop and manage communal irrigation water sources, that would be more economical and reliable than individual ones. It is important not to overlook the need for these local organisations, however small they may be, to have 'teeth': to be able to collect fees and punish cheating.

Turning specifically to the topic of transfer of knowledge, several participants emphasised the need of working through pilot farmers or projects: 'When trying to improve the operation of farmers, do not work with all of them in an area at the same time, but concentrate on a few farmers for specific crops or activities, who would be the examples for others'. Quoting from his own experience one participant put it as follows: 'For innovations to be successful they have to pass through local, enterprising people (e.g. farmers), who are willing to act as examples. At present this applies to the use of solar energy for disinfecting of water, soil and human waste'. The general mood at the Workshop was not pessimistic:

> When the need for solutions is at its highest there is always something about to come at the rescue. Too often, researchers tend to suggest solutions for problems people are not experiencing (yet). By focusing on problems and solutions as perceived by the people, innovation projects would stay far away from this pitfall.

One of the Nigerian participants confirmed this from a different experience:

> The 'Justice and Piece' Farms I am involved with in Nigeria are good examples of the principle of 'teach by doing'. They are a form of managed farm development that would not have been possible without the backing of an organisation such as the Catholic Church.

Who are the agents of change? Is it true that (peri-)urban farmers haven't encountered enough of them and their fate would greatly improve with the following recommendation?

The established consultancy firms have so far neglected a topic like market gardening. They were involved in programmes and projects of a larger scale. However, large-scale projects are over now and for us consultants advising groups of market gardeners in developing countries and institutions for the marketing of their produce, will soon be a serious business.

7. Other, Miscellaneous, Points and some Conclusions

The first paper in this volume (by Hörmann) outlines a theoretical model. In his statement at the end of the Workshop, the author reiterated that:

> his model should be seen as an attempt to combine quantitative and qualitative elements for the description of the complete system of market gardening in a particular setting, thus including for instance the marketing of horticultural produce. It is meant to be open-ended: if necessary, more criteria could be added to it. It is also meant to be dynamic: open to development processes. Readers are advised to take it

as a tool to help interdisciplinary research work and planning.

Somebody else's concluding statement hopefully encouraged him to carry on with this work: 'There is nothing as practical as a good theory.'

At various points at the Workshop, attention was paid to the controversial role of middlemen in the context of horticultural inputs and marketing:

> Trade is an important component to market gardening. It has many functions and appearances, including the so-called middlemen. You could replace a bad one by a good one but you can't do without them. It is important to establish good links between trade and governments, which need to make appropriate regulations.

The concluding statement by one participant seems to reflect the majority's view after the ensuing debates:

> Do not blame the middlemen for the problems market gardeners experience. They have an important role to play, they may occasionally take too much, but this can be avoided by improving the marketing system: market space, credit, price information, etc.

This is in line with the somewhat moderating concluding remark by another participant:

> Ethical questions should never be overlooked when dealing with the market gardening system. We need to be holistic in our dealing with the human presence and to accept that everywhere there are good people, bad people and 'son-of-a-bitch' people and there will always be some kind of exploitation of one category of people by another.

A few concluding statements remain that do not quite fit under any heading. These are equally worth bearing in mind, when involved with or trying to understand problems of market gardeners or urban farmers elsewhere. One participant cautioned us:

> The processing of agricultural produce has received little attention during this Workshop. In general, too much emphasis tends to be put on large-scale processing, whereas at smaller scales of operation it would be easier to balance the locally produced amounts with the processing capacities.

Although the gender issue of urban farming was mentioned in several of the papers it may have been neglected during the discussions, as one participant concluded that 'this Workshop has not covered sufficiently the gender issue.' She was supported by another who emphasised that, 'the women and the very small among the small-scale gardeners face even greater constraints and should therefore be given extra encouragement.'

The immediate cause for this Workshop was, that a research project in Jos, Nigeria, had produced its first results. Five of the papers in this volume present these. The Nigerian project leader felt very much inspired by both the reactions at the Workshop to the results and the range of knowledge and experience presented by the other participants. His conclusion from the Workshop was a very practical one:

> The Nigerian research group now seeks additional resources to disseminate the findings, including those of the experimental sub-project, and to replicate the trials in other locations and areas, including more women to take to gardening.

This is one of many useful ideas that emerged from the workshop's discussions. The seven themes identified in the chapter contain many issues that deserve serious consideration. They should be seen as a useful pool of ideas from which future proposals for research and development projects can be drawn and formulated. If this materialises, it will have been a worthwhile achievement of our endeavour.